Kinship in the Past

An Anthropology of European Family Life,

1500–1900

Andrejs Plakans

Basil Blackwell

© Andrejs Plakans 1984

First published 1984
First published in paperback 1986

Basil Blackwell Ltd
108 Cowley Road, Oxford OX4 1JF, UK

Basil Blackwell Inc.
432 Park Avenue South, Suite 1503,
New York, NY 10016, USA

British Library Cataloguing in Publication Data

Plakans, Andrejs
Kinship in the past.
1. Kinship
I. Title
306.8'3   GN487

ISBN 0–631–13066–7
ISBN 0-631-15357-8 Pbk

Library of Congress Cataloging in Publication Data

Plakans, Andrejs.
Kinship in the past.

Bibliography: p. 263
Includes index.
1. Kinship—Europe—History. 2. Europe—Social
life and customs. 3. Kinship—History. I. Title.
GN575.P55 1984   306.8'3'094   84–12482
ISBN 0–631–13066–7
ISBN 0-631-15357-8 (pbk.)

Typeset by Freeman Graphic, Tonbridge
Printed in Great Britain by Billing & Sons Ltd, Worcester

Contents

Preface

This book began in 1979 as a set of guest lectures presented at the Free University of Berlin to the participants of a summer workshop (*Sommerkurs*) that dealt with, among many topics, the possibilities of anthropological history. Expanded, these lectures have now become the first part of what I expect to be a short three-part series of studies of kinship in historical Europe. This first part is primarily methodological, juxtaposing certain kinds of documentary historical evidence with the existing methods of kinship study (mostly from social anthropology) that appear to be useful in historical work. The other two parts will be primarily substantive and will deal with, respectively, kinship in the Russian Baltic provinces, where the most readily usable nominal-level sources are cross-sectional (single-year household censuses); and in the Schwalm district of Hesse in West Germany, where the most informative materials come from parish registers and are therefore longitudinal in form. Each of these substantive studies would require a methodological introduction of its own and therefore it seemed logical to integrate the two in a separate volume. The substantive studies are, of course, foreshadowed in the present work, but it has been written to stand by itself because the study of kinship in the European past, when all is said and done, involves more kinds of data and raises more questions than are contained in the Baltic and Schwalm evidence.

The subtitle of the book needs to be explained. The benefits deriving from cross-disciplinary contacts with anthropology have seemed clear to social historians for a long time, so that recent surveys of the connection have been able to point to many examples of how these contacts have worked out in practice (Gaunt, 1982). It is none the less puzzling why the connection between the two disciplines has remained relatively weak in the one research area – kinship – where it could have been expected to be strong. On the one hand, kinship research has been central to anthropology since the beginning of the discipline and the accumulated corpus of methodological procedures and substantive findings is immense; on the other hand, interest among historians in social microstructures in the past has experienced a quantum leap in the past two decades. One would have expected the strongest and most systematic links to have developed precisely at this interface of the two disciplines. After all, anthropologists have always pondered the historical origins of the kinship systems they have encountered in the field and have often felt frustrated over the fact that fieldwork 'cannot provide evidence of unobservable antecedents' (Fortes, 1969: 309). Social historians, by contrast, have frequently had access to evidence – such as genealogies, for example, or successive population lists – in which individuals and groups could be analysed in terms of long historical sequences of connections; but they have not been able to make much headway beyond understanding very short stretches of the long chain. Each discipline had, in no small part, what the other lacked, yet, until very recently, neither saw itself as complementing the other. The progress that has been made has seemed fortuitous and almost serendipitous rather than cumulative, and dependent to a great extent on turns in the research interests of individual scholars rather than on the continuing development of an interdisciplinary field or subfield.

At the level of historical nominal and community data, with which this book is primarily concerned, advances have been understandably slow, to a great extent because substantive information about particular relationships in the past is nearly always embedded in third-party statements. The creators of this evidence, and the historical actors it purports to refer to, cannot be observed and questioned, which means that they all remain beyond the reach of anthropological 'fieldwork' techniques. The uncertainties on which any subsequent descriptions must rest, given this starting-point, can easily be judged to lead to inferior anthropology (from anthropologists using historical materials) or inferior history (from historians using anthropological concepts with historical evidence). If a descriptive statement about kinship in the past is to be credible, it has to have behind it an effort to ascertain that a posited relationship was in some sense 'true'. Sometimes third-party statements in the past are so far removed from the relationships they claim to be summarizing that no way of testing them is present; sometimes there are no records at all about concrete relationships 'on the ground'; and sometimes decisions have to be made many hundreds, if not thousands, of times over in the same data base, creating the need for an immense amount of work to obtain results that are not always unambiguous. The challenge is undoubtedly a difficult one. An earlier generation of anthropologists already dismissed the historical statements of their nineteenth-century predecessors as 'conjectural history' and maintained that the approach most likely to produce scientifically useful results was the synchronic – point-in-time – approach, to be used with people whom the anthropologists could question and observe (Radcliffe-Brown, 1965: 50; original 1941). But because this viewpoint was articulated before *historians* had started to investigate kinship in their own materials in any systematic fashion, the question was still open whether a 'non-conjectural history' of kinship could ever be written.

Now, some decades later, the question is still open and one can read much of the recent work on kinship in the European past as an attempt to lay out the evidence for an answer and to indicate in a preliminary way what the form of an answer should be. The pioneering studies of Alan Macfarlane on the diary of Ralph Josselin (1970) and on community evidence (1977a); the evidentiary collections of household kinship, created and inspired by the work of the Cambridge Group for the History of Population and Social Structure; the recent masterful study by Jack Goody (1983) on the Christian church and kinship patterns in medieval Europe; the studies of Diane Hughes (1975) and F. W. Kent (1977) on lineages in Renaissance Italy; the work of Martine Segalen (1972 and 1979) on marriage alliances in nineteenth-century France – all these and other research cited later in this book can be understood as puzzle pieces slowly being moved into place with the intention of reducing the amount of conjecture in this area of historical understanding. Though the present volume has a different starting-point conceptually than most of these works, and comments on somewhat different matters along the way, it has the same purpose in mind. It is not meant to be a handbook of kinship analysis – for there are good ones already (Keesing, 1975; Pasternak, 1976; Schusky, 1972) – but rather an explication and an assessment of a particular approach, both of which will have to be repeated at some future date if the approach encourages the expansion of the currently narrow data base with which all comparative studies of historical kinship, especially for the European continent, have to work.

In a recent evaluation of the contacts between history and anthropology, the historian Natalie Z. Davis suggested that, when they draw upon anthropological work, historians do not 'need [to] import all the special reservations anthropologists have about each other or all their infighting', although historians do need to be 'aware of the different schools of anthropological interpretation' (Davis, 1982: 273). In the light of this suggestion, two comments are appropriate. First, I have drawn as much attention to anthropological 'infighting' as seemed to me to be necessary to suggest to historians that anthropological ideas about kinship are less fixed than they might think. Whether this is enough is difficult to say. Second, though aware of various 'schools' of kinship interpretation among anthropologists, I have found British structuralism particularly suggestive because of the types of historical kinship evidence that initially presented seemingly formless problems in my own specialized research. Adopting some of the organizing concepts proposed by A. R. Radcliffe-Brown, Meyer Fortes, S. H. Nadel and others helped me to see what the problems were, though not always to find answers to them. Presumably historians who first came to the 'kinship problem' in their own work through other kinds of evidence, or who work in countries with different indigenous anthropological traditions, if any, would write different books. Presumably, also, when such books do appear, historians will be able to benefit from the ensuing debate about historical kinship as much as anthropologists have benefited from their internal controversies (cf. Kuper, 1973).

This book would not have been possible without the already mentioned ground-breaking forays, nor without more direct support from individuals and institutions, which I here acknowledge gratefully. I thank Arthur E. Imhof, of the Friedrich Meinecke Institute of the Free University of Berlin, for inviting me to participate in the 1979 *Sommerkurs* and for sharing with me the computer version of the 'Schwalm file'; and to Gerald L. Soliday, of the University of Texas at Dallas, for allowing me to examine the Marburg *Sippenbuch* and for giving me the benefit of his insights into this valuable document. I am indebted to Joel M. Halpern, of the University of Massachusetts at Amherst, for acquainting me with the problems anthropologists encounter in linking documentary and fieldwork evidence in the European setting. Two grants from the National Endowment for the Humanities (1978–80; Ro–29144–78–648) and the National Science Foundation (1980–84; BNS–7926704) supported the research from which many of the illustrations in the book are drawn; and at the Iowa State University Statistical Laboratory Numerical Analysis and Data Processing Division, Lawrence Kinyon, Kevin Kramer and Sallie Keller McNulty provided the computer programming that transformed raw historical data into usable kinship configurations. To Robert Wheaton, of the *Journal of Family History*, I owe gratitude not only for his permission to use an example from his own kinship research on seventeenth-century Bordeaux, but for may helpful suggestions regarding the manuscript and, above all, for continuous encouragement over the years. Similar encouragement for as long a time came from Peter Laslett. So many of us who continue to ponder the intricacies of historical social structures find ourselves in his debt. Neither he nor anyone else I have mentioned, however, can be held responsible for whatever misconceptions and errors remain.

My thanks also go to Harriet Barry and Margaret Horne at Basil Blackwell for their excellent editorial work on this book.

Andrejs Plakans

Acknowledgements

I am grateful to the Cambridge University Press for permission to reproduce the kin configurations in figure 6; to the Oxford University Press for permission to reproduce the configurations in figures 9 and 13; to the J. G. Herder Institut, Marburg a.d. Lahn, Federal Republic of Germany, for permission to reproduce documents 3 and 4; to the Hessisches Staatsarchiv, Marburg a.d. Lahn, Federal Republic of Germany, for permission to use document 2; and to the Archiv départmental de la Gironde, Bordeaux, France, for permission to reproduce document 1.

1

Historical Sources and the Kinship Domain

Over the past several decades social history has continued to expand its evidentiary base, demonstrating that most aspects of everyday social life in the past received some mention in historical sources. Such documentation ranges from the widespread to the occasional, with evidence about kinship ties – social bonds created through marriage and descent – falling somewhere in the middle of this range. A discussion of what role kinship information should play in descriptions of historical communities therefore could start with any one of a large number of different sources. Regardless of where it starts, however, the discussion must eventually deal with the related questions of retrieval and reliability, both of which grow out of the fact that the historical study of kinship cannot ignore the existing information obtained from contemporary populations, nor the manner in which it has been obtained. These questions are very troublesome. If the most skilled investigators of kinship understand this dimension of social life as emerging for study in all particulars only from close questioning and observation of a small number of representative persons, what is the historian to do with written sources that do not focus on a single individual, or a handful of them, but contain kinship information of some sort about very large numbers of people? If it is direct testimony that is to be taken as a standard, what then is the status of historical evidence which, by definition, consists almost always of reports not created by the historical actors themselves?

In some sources these problems – which are essentially epistemological – appear in a particularly graphic fashion. One of these is a 1797 fiscal census, called a 'revision of souls', from the north-eastern European province of Kurland. Until 1795, when it was incorporated into the Russian Empire, Kurland had been a semi-autonomous duchy ruled by members of the Kettler and Biron dynasties, who were vassals of the Polish kings; after the incorporation, the territory became one of the three Baltic provinces of the Russian Empire (the others were Livland and Estland), and it retained that status until the First World War. Joining the Empire meant, among other things, that for the first time the government of Kurland had to enumerate its population, conforming to a practice initiated in the Empire by Peter the Great in 1720, of periodic counts aimed at determining the number of people subject to the capitation tax.[1] The first soul revision in Kurland was carried out in 1797 and was followed somewhat irregularly by seven others, until the entire series ended everywhere in the Empire in 1859. Each revision in the province resulted in a 'document' containing 40 or more volumes, with an average volume being about 300–400 pages long. Information about taxable people was abstracted from these and used to determine the tax owed by each community. The information on social structure in the revisions, however, was generally ignored by contemporary scholars, and the few subsequent Baltic ethnographers and historians who sought evidence about kinship in the area turned instead to folklore, travellers' accounts and the kinship terminology of the local languages.

The soul revisions thus remained unused for a long time until, in the 1970s, the work of the Cambridge Group for the History of Population and Social Structure demonstrated how historical sources of this type could be used comparatively for the study of social structure in the past.[2] In this undertaking, the revisions emerged as sources of comparative evidence about household size and composition in those parts of historical Europe where, as in Kurland and the other two Baltic provinces of Livland and

---

1 For a description of the soul revisions in Kurland, see Plakans (1975) and (1977). A thorough inventory of these sources does not exist either for the entire Russian Empire (Czap, 1983: 110–11) or for any of its constituent parts, to my knowledge. To be useful for the historian of comparative kinship, such an inventory would have to establish, locality by locality, whether there was internal information in each revision that permitted linkages among households in any single year and across the normal 15-year time period between the revision documents.

2 The classification and measurements appropriate for such comparisons are stated in Hammel and Laslett (1974). It should be noted, however, that in the materials from the Russian Empire that have been analysed in terms of the Hammel–Lazlett categories, local residential patterns sometimes create problems, even within relatively small areas. Thus, for example, Czap (1978, 1982 and 1983) finds that the category of 'household' can be used successfully with materials from Central Russia, and Palli (1983) makes use of it with equal success for the Estonian-speaking regions of the Baltic provinces. In the Latvian-speaking regions of the Baltic area, however, the normal residential unit used by revision documents – the farmstead (*Gesinde*) – remains problematic as far as the 'household' category is concerned (Plakans, 1975) and may perhaps best be analysed as a 'houseful'. The farmstead was clearly a unit of residence, with all of its human population living under one roof, and enumerators quite clearly distinguished between conjugal family units and single people. What is not clear is whether these sub-units were also in any socially relevant sense separated from each other sufficiently for the researcher to designate each as a separate 'household', with the entire collection living in a 'houseful'.

Estland, in Russia proper and in other regions of Eastern Europe, serfdom continued in force into the nineteenth century. In the Baltic serf estates, as elsewhere in the Empire, the officials responsible for preparing the revision documents had been punctilious in their work. They normally listed all persons living in a particular locality, carefully separated each group of co-residents from other groups, and used relatively unambiguous terms to describe the relationship between various members of a group and its head. The Baltic area, in addition, was interesting because of its cultural hetero-geneity. The language of the Baltic landed nobility and urban populations (and therefore of the revisions) was German, the nobles having received from the Crown, along with many other privileges, the right to prepare public documents in their own tongue. The languages of the peasantry, however, were Latvian in Kurland and southern Livland, and Estonian in northern Livland and in the province of Estland. Because of the thorough way these enumerations covered the population 'on the ground', the analysis of household structure in Kurland could look forward to accurate evidence if not for the entire provincial population of 350,000, then certainly for the approximately 23,000 rural farmsteads which contemporary accounts suggested were in the province at the end of the eighteenth century (Plakans, 1983: 174–5).

In due course it became apparent that in a few of the Kurland estates the inquiries connected with the revisions had probed more deeply into the social structures of the peasant population than would have been necessary merely to calculate the head tax. In these estates, each entry in the revision document included a certain amount of genealogical information, suggest-ing that numerous people who were not living together were in fact related to each other. A single-year household list does not have to be modified greatly to be transformed into a substantially different document: an indication of the parentage of each listed person, added to the normal information about marriage, will already be a long step in this direction. The Baltic enumerators had taken this step, as well as a number of others, so that in these few estates the researcher could work from the outset with intergroup connections that otherwise can be identified, if at all, only through the laborious process of linking single-year population lists with other sources (such as, for example, parish registers). In the revision therefore, regardless of where the analysis began, very soon thereafter it found itself having to consider seemingly endless and criss-crossing chains of relationships, and this gave to the 'kinship problem' in these data a complexity that it normally does not have in other similar historical documents. Instead of providing genealogical data for one or two or a handful of select individuals, the revision provided them for virtually the entire population of the estate. Instead of permitting only two or three households to be viewed as connected in some way, the revision clearly connected large clusters of them (Plakans, 1983: 184–5). Instead of presenting to the analyst only named ties, the revision suggested the presence of others that were not named but were strongly implied, as when, for example, two persons were described as the sons of a third person but not as brothers of each other. Instead of using only a single relational terminology, the enumerators had used several simultaneously, so that a relationship based on authority (between a farm head and farmhand, for example) had to be interpreted in the light of the fact that the same individuals were also described as related through kinship (the farm head being the father-in-law of the farmhand, for example). In short, if the estate population were pictured in network terms, with each named individual as a point in the network, the lines representing relationships that could be drawn between these points were of such number and variety that to establish the specific meaning and weight of 'kinship' in this population required finding a way of setting 'kinship' relations apart from all others for further examination.

Such a step would not be unprecedented in the light of various existing methodologies for understanding complex social relationships. The procedure entails the disassociation of some relationships from others and the analysis of those relationships – to use the language of the social anthropologist Meyer Fortes – as a separate *domain*. Fortes holds that the concept of *domain* is useful:

> not as a means of explanation but an aid to systematization. I suggest that the social and cultural elements and processes that make up a given social system fall into determinate sectors of organization. Each such sector – which I call a domain – comprises a range of social relations, customs, norms, statuses, and other analytically discriminable elements linked up in nexuses and unified by the stamp of distinctive functional features that are common to all. (Fortes, 1969: 97)

One such system into which any starting-point in the census – any individual or any domestic group – eventually led the analysis could thus be thought of as the *kinship domain* of this population, with its 'social relations, customs, norms, statuses, and other analytically discriminable elements' having to be worked out by reference to that part of the rich relational terminology of the census that was recognizably of the kinship type. The methodology proposed by the Cambridge Group and other household researchers appeared to be well on its way to ensuring that kinship ties within co-residential groups – clearly a 'discriminable element' of the domain, even in this census – would become well understood in due course. But the Baltic source required that the historian account also in social-structural descriptions for demonstrable connections between large numbers of people who were not in co-residence, but were in the same community.

Beyond helping with initial data organization, the domain concept could be expected to assist in many questions pertaining to particular linkages by lifting the entire body of Baltic data from its specific socio-economic and temporal context into a realm of comparisons with a host of other societies. Such a procedure could help to attribute some meaning to the links established by or implied in the relational terminology of the source, in so far as this terminology itself did not contain much beyond the names of dyadic ties. The dyadic ties implied chains and configurations of various kinds, but were weak on closures, that is, on the question of where to draw boundaries around linked individuals or what social significance to attribute to a set of individuals so bounded. Thus, for example, in the 1797 revision from the estate Spahren, the heads of the 52 residential groups were listed as distinct individuals, with genealogical information attached. Following this information in the directions it pointed revealed that 34 of the 52 heads were kin-linked, a fact that would not emerge if ties beyond the named primary categories (that is, ties not named as such in the source, but implied by named ties) were ignored (Plakans, 1977: 22). It was not at all obvious at this stage, of course, what this interesting feature of the community could be taken to mean, either in the short or the long run, or to what extent this line of inquiry and its attendant time-consuming searches were useful for understanding kinship, either in Spahren or comparatively. The entire experience, however, suggested that it was possible in the source to move a considerable distance beyond the flesh-and-blood individuals listed and to uncover configurations that, at least potentially, could have had social significance.

The same difficulties manifested themselves when the source was investigated via the most obvious social *group* recorded in it: the domestic group, or farmstead (*Gesinde*). In figure 1 I have contrasted the information available when a farmstead is considered as a free-standing unit and the information that needs to be dealt with when all of the genealogical links given for its residents are exploited fully. The revision from which this example is drawn was carried out in 1850 in one of the patrimonial estates of the largest Baltic city of Riga. In 1850, the estate Pinkenhof had a population of 769 male and 800 female residents. Bennusch farmstead (figure 1a), which was no. 24 in the revision listing, was shown to have had a head (*Wirth*) who had in co-residence a second wife, one son from his second marriage and two daughters from the first. The interpretation of the kinship ties within this group (when familial ties are assumed to be a subset

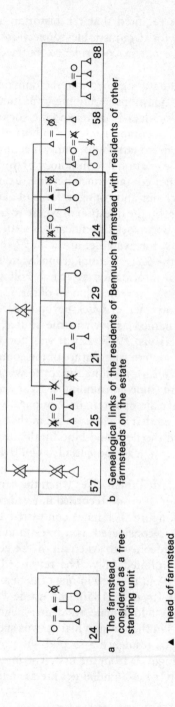

a The farmstead considered as a free-standing unit

b Genealogical links of the residents of Bennusch farmstead with residents of other farmsteads on the estate

▲ head of farmstead
△ male
○ female
✖ deceased male
⊘ deceased female

Figure 1 Genealogical connections in Bennusch farmstead (no. 24), Pinkenhof estate, Livland, 1850

of kinship ties) could be very straightforward: they included the conjugal tie, different forms of the parent–offspring tie and different forms of the sibling tie. When, however, the genealogical information provided by the census for this farmstead was exploited fully, the result was a very problematic configuration (see figure 1b). An interpretation of the kinship ties of the residents of Bennusch farmstead now had to account for connections to people in six other farmsteads (which in the illustration bear the same numbers as in the revision). The universe within which the analysis had to be carried out had enlarged itself considerably. It had ceased to be the closed co-residential group in which a quantitative comparison of particular kinds of ties was possible because a denominator (the total number of ties) was fixed, and had become a relatively open universe in which statistical assessments were difficult to make because the denominator had become uncertain. The very first question likely to occur – whether the two sets of links depicted in figures 1a and 1b denoted relationships that received the same kind of social recognition – had no unambiguous answer, because the boundary so clearly demarcating a field of social interaction (the farmstead boundary) in figure 1a was missing in the case of the large configuration. Were we to pursue this question with care, the inquiry would have to begin to consider the 'relations, customs, norms, statuses and other analytically discriminable elements' that would invest this large configuration with social meaning and allow us to think about it as a kinship configuration. That is, we would need to have a much more thorough understanding of the kinship domain of this population's social life, before we could consider the reconstructed configuration as having rendered some part of the domain capable of being evaluated.

If the source had provided such information for only a single person or a handful of persons, the question raised might not have been as difficult to deal with. But in this case, all, or nearly all, of the more than 1,600 Pinkenhof residents could have had far-reaching configurations constructed around them, consisting of persons whom the source linked to the central actor directly or indirectly. Such persons were connected to each other through their common link to the central person and by other links that did not refer to the common relative. Moreover, such configurations frequently overlapped with each other, requiring that each historical actor be considered 'embedded' in a very complex composite configuration that can be pictured in two-dimensional space only with great difficulty. The source, however, provided only scanty information about which of such 'groups' of people had to be understood as having created kinship roles for the central individual to enact; or about how the fact that individuals A, B and C, who were all in various ways linked to D, may have affected the structural position of D, if they were also linked to each other independently of their links with D. Certainly, one could use the terminology in the source to ascertain that conjugal families were socially recognized units, and the format and place-names to determine that co-residential groups were also accorded this status. But when these 'certified' social groups were factored out of the situation and the membership of the central individual in them was accounted for, the source still left this individual implicated in a substantial number of connections whose social relevance needed to be determined.

To put it another way, the source appeared to be providing a large number of 'facts' (links, connections, configurations, etc.), the value of which for explaining social life in these communities was not immediately apparent. These facts were similar in their ambiguity to another kind of kinship 'fact' frequently encountered in other historical sources: group names (*Sippe,* lineage, *Stamm,* clan, sib, etc.) with no information about their actual composition, rules of membership, and the like. It was very tempting, therefore, in order to reduce the ambiguities, to begin to draw on the detailed analysis of comparative evidence in the vast existing literature about the kinship domain. Perhaps here one could find whether all that the historian could legitimately do with these data was to employ relatively undiscriminating and neutral sorting categories such as 'kin' and 'non-kin'; or, perhaps, with the aid of analogies one could begin to use the organizing concepts provided to kinship study by social anthropologists and deal with the various Baltic configurations as 'descent groups', 'ego-centred networks', 'kindreds' and the like. This step would succeed in transforming inchoate materials into 'discriminable elements' of the kinship domain, and it would also allow the analysis to escape being dominated by the categories used in the historical material. If the analysis consisted of nothing but the tracking down of relations pertinent to the enumerational units – individuals and domestic groups – given in the source, then there would be a good chance, because of this strict definition of the units of inquiry, of losing sight of the ties that could have connected people into units that the source did not mention, such as, for example, local descent groups.

The Baltic file underlines that, for historians, entry into the kinship domain, however helpful potentially, is none the less a strategic choice which may entail loss of empirical evidence. This may be of somewhat less concern to the anthropological fieldworker, who can design a strategy that will not produce evidence extraneous to the objectives at hand; by contrast, the historical source is already prepared, as it were, and the loss of evidence as a result of choice of strategy may well be considerable. The postulation of the kinship domain is a step taken to 'systematize' the data, to place some kind of initial ordering in it, and is therefore by definition an exclusionary procedure:

separation of structure from context, material, and qualitative character implies a move to a higher level of abstraction. For when we are
describing structure we abstract relational features from the totality of
the perceived data, ignoring all that is not 'order' or 'arrangement'.
(Nadel, 1957: 7)

The dilemma posed by the Baltic census is that the clarifying strategy
necessary for making any headway at all may become a limiting strategy, by
forcing the researcher to ignore 'all that is not "order" and "arrangement"'
very early and to decide prematurely in the process of postulating the
domain what the 'discriminable elements' of the kinship domain in a
community may have been. While there can be no expectation that 'the data
will speak for themselves', it would be equally misleading to believe that,
given the present state of understanding of kinship in historical times, we
will make maximum use of historical information by allowing the exploration of a particular locality to be guided entirely by what is already known
about other localities in the past and in the present. The Baltic file is in point
of fact a good example of how a premature decision on 'all that is not
"order" and "arrangement"' could close off potentially rewarding lines of
inquiry. Only some of the relational terms in it can immediately be
understood as being kinship terms, because there is evidence that the ties
they describe have been made use of; other terms remain statements of
genealogical connections, with no evidence of their use whatsoever. Some of
the relational terminology suggests strongly that other ties are present, but
these are not named and thus remain in the realm of inference. Networks of
relationships overlap each other, creating more complicated nets and raising
the question of which subset of relationships had priority over others as far
as social action was concerned. Some reconstructable networks consist of
persons whom the analysis could very well treat under an established rubric,
such as 'descent group', but there is no evidence that such a cluster had the
necessary corporate identity or that its members had to enact roles
appropriate to membership in such a corporate group. The 'hard' evidence
in the source makes immediately obvious what còuld be pursued farther
under the rubrics of 'order' and 'arrangement'; but the 'soft' evidence,
which is equally legitimate historical evidence, is never so unsuggestive that
it would deserve to be ignored. Ignoring it could in fact threaten the
essentially historical nature of the inquiry by pointing the research toward
the kind of extratemporal and extrasocial analysis of kinship that may be of
considerable importance to theory-building, but is of little immediate value
to the effort to understand kinship in communities about which only written
documents have survived.

Fortunately, the resolution of this dilemma can be postponed in favour of a full discussion of the origins of the factual material from which 'discriminable elements' are eventually to be abstracted. This approach, then, constitutes an admission that there is never likely to be a quick answer to the question posed initially: whether there is reliable evidence about kinship in written materials that record relationships among people long since dead. Before an answer becomes available, the data have to be approached, in a manner of speaking, from the other end. Instead of asking what materials in the Baltic census stand out unambiguously as the 'discriminable elements' of the kinship domain, we have to ask instead about the manner in which all the factual materials – the ambiguous as well as the unambiguous – came to be, and whether the intellectual activities in this process may help to sort the former from the latter. This backward step means dealing with the question of kinship classification.

Kinship Classification as a Continuous Social Activity

The historical records from which the stuff of social history comes are expected by social historians to be diverse and to differ in reliability according to where they can be placed on a continuum marked, at one end, by records produced by the historical actors themselves and, at the other one, by second- and third-party reports concerning the historical actors. These records are also expected to be datable, so that information from one set can be assigned precedence or antecedence in relation to another. Sources about kinship in the historical past do not differ with respect to these general characteristics, so that the question of which 'discriminable elements' of a postulated kinship domain historical sources enable the historian to identify also has a variety of answers. The Baltic data are unusual in providing so many different starting-points for kinship analysis and in permitting generalizations to be made about an entire community; by contrast, a diary such as that of Ralph Josselin (Macfarlane, 1970), offers only one starting-point, but provides far deeper insight into how kinship ties are experienced than a single-year population listing ever could. Some sources will provide no more information than the fact that certain kin terms were in currency, whereas others, such as marriage contracts, will take the form of hundreds of recorded instances of the same type of social transaction, with each record of the kin-linked participants being somewhat different than the rest. A typology of this sort could be extended almost indefinitely if we were to include in it, for example, documentation of well-known historical events such as civil wars and political conflicts, in which the kin relations among participants can be identified. Most of these sources are not exclusively about kinship and, indeed, few of them had as their primary goal the recording of kinship ties as such. To the extent that they do contain kinship information, however, they could all become material for a history of the social past written from this particular perspective.

With relational terminology of the kinship type appearing in so many different historical sources, it is somewhat surprising that we have so incomplete an understanding of the one social activity that was logically and experientially antecedent to them all, and ultimately will be responsible for whatever insight into the kinship domain of the past we may obtain. This activity is kinship classification. In the present context, the term 'classification' is not meant to refer to the use of kinship terms alone, but rather to the sum total of mundane activities through which people in the past learned to differentiate among relatives and between relatives and strangers, and to infuse these distinctions with social meaning throughout the rest of their own lives and in the social life of the community. Because the term is meant to be used in this sense of a continuous activity, it may be best to refer to 'classificatory activity', rather than to 'classification' as such. It is this activity that we need to know a great deal more about in order to make proper use of the relational terminology of historical sources. Before we can invest this terminology with social meaning, we have to know what its immediate purpose was, whether it was the product of some idiosyncratic code of the individual record-keeper or reflected a shared system of meanings, and whether its forms inevitably hid certain relationships from view. Ideally, to answer such questions, the source and the particular terms it uses would have to be related back to its point of origin – the mind of the record-keeper – which, in turn, has to be understood in the context of its own individual history and in the history of the larger community. These are, of course, demands which in most cases will be impossible for the historian to meet, but they are set out here to explain the matters about which assumptions may have to be made before a historical source is used for further analysis. It may very well be that the record-keeper's language reflected the accepted terms of kinship reference of the community, but this fact has to be established or assumed.

Classificatory activity in the European past must have begun in the minds of the people who carried it out, in some ways analogous to that described by social anthropologists among the living populations they have observed. Thus, for example, Raymond Firth, in writing about the Tikopia of Polynesia, suggests that:

the child of Tikopia, as elsewhere, does not start off life with a full set of kinship names and attitudes ready made: these have gradually to be imposed upon it by tuition, and not without difficulty does it fit itself into the framework which its elders seek to provide for it. In its earliest years the infant has of course no conception of the nature and scope of

its kinship ties, and behaves to its kin on the basis of personal selection
according to their association with it. (Firth, 1957: 251)

Later in the child's life,

as the child's circle of acquaintance widens, its response to tuition
becomes more conscious and its understanding of relationship
deepens, it certainly extends the little budget of terms it possesses to
novel individuals who come within cognizance and are presented to it
in known categories. But there is another process at work. With more
appreciation of personalities and their status comes an increasing
definition, a narrowing down of the parental terms to certain persons
only within the kinship range and an application of new terms to the
others thus eliminated. (Firth, 1957: 254)

Firth's use of the phrase 'as elsewhere' in the first extract may or may not
apply to the European past: we simply do not know and may never have a
clear view how these mental processes worked in the deceased population
with which we are dealing. But some such process must have taken place in
the minds of the people who eventually came to employ the relational
terminology of the sources. What is more, however, this classifying activity
very probably was continuous, as for various social reasons the kin universe
of the individual expanded and contracted over the life-cycle, and as the
community sought to ensure that all of its members, early in life and
throughout the rest of their lives, divided up relatives in a similar manner.
   Another way of putting this is to say that for interpreting the kinship
terminology of historical documents we cannot conceive of classification as
a one-time action, producing an individual or collective result that remained
unchanged in all particulars and in that final form found its way into a
historical document. That may be the image which the fixed format of a
historical document creates, but some consideration will reveal that the
image is misleading. The distinctions among relatives and between relatives
and strangers that were learned early in life were very likely later reaffirmed
continuously in action and more infrequently by mnemonic devices of
various sorts. Just as likely, long and short-term processes of socio-
economic and demographic change, operating on individuals, familial
groups and entire communities required alteration, adjustment, clarification
and revisions of the terminology and its meaning. Remarriages, adoptions
and similar 'repairs' of the social group would have necessitated withdrawal
and transfer of initial and later classifications. At this point in historical
kinship research, all that is possible is an outline of the phenomenology of
classificatory activities, of the situations that required them and of the
settings in which they took place – a phenomenology that is not based on a

deep knowledge of any historical population, but on the experiences of kinship researchers with living populations. Yet it does not stretch the imagination too far to believe that this should be the proper context in which the ultimate meaning of the relational terminology of the sources is to be sought. Whatever else the record-keepers were doing when they created a record with relational terminology, they were engaging in classificatory activity which may or may not have been identical in its results to the activities of the historical actors, but has to be understood as an activity of the same type, recognizing relationships and using terms that might seem anachronistic earlier and later in the history of the same community.

Certain consequences flow from this contextual approach to the relational terminology in the source. We assume that when a population has existed in a permanent enough form to be recognized and inventoried as a community in a source, its members, prior to the inventory, had spent a long time in the activity of classifying each other, until they emerged, in a phase of this unending process, for the historian's consideration, 'locked' into particular positions by the relational terminology of the enumerator. This means that when a data source makes no mention of even a single relational term of the kinship sort, we are still in most cases safe in assuming that the activity had been taking place and that the absence of any empirical evidence about it is more a function of the record-keeper's interests than evidence about the community's social life. This assumption does not have to lead to a particular kind of imagery about the society in question, other than that it was the locus of classifying activity which, for some reason, we continue to know nothing about. We cannot deduce that kinship relations were either sparse or dense, or deep or shallow, but we can certainly wonder in such a record, or one in which only some few relational terms appear, why the record-keeper chose not to make a more extensive use of them.

The absence of systematic exploration of classificatory activity is even more surprising in view of the many different everyday matters with which social historians have been lately concerned. The history of sexual activity would be a prime example, as would be studies of the history of how people worked, provided themselves with food, imposed social controls, resolved everyday conflicts and arranged their living spaces. None of these activities would appear to have involved any more sociability (continued contact with other persons in the community) than the activity that resulted in a community's residents sorting themselves into various kin-based groups, and keeping themselves sorted in this way; or an individual's populating his or her personal social universe with certain persons with whom ancestors or other relatives were shared. The creation of historical records in which kin ties are mentioned would constitute, of course, classificatory activity of a somewhat different kind, but would not necessarily be so different as to be unrecognizable as analogous to what the historical actors were themselves doing. Admittedly, in most records, the terminology employed would be that of reference rather than address, and the researcher would be relying on a third party for information about specific ties.[3] Yet it cannot be assumed that those ties were being used inaccurately or incompletely or without any contact with the historical actors themselves. The experience is that they had these characteristics frequently, but also that the quality of records varied greatly from locality to locality. In the Pinkenhof revisions of 1850, an extreme example, there is a segment of relational terminology which would not have been used at all had the record-keeper not questioned the historical actors to make sure that people in different households, who sometimes even had different surnames, could be assigned the same family number (*Familiennummer*). Or, to put it another way, these relationships, which were lineal, could not have been calculated from the preceding revision alone. The point here is that in the 1850 record the use of certain kinds of terms were the result of face-to-face contact with the people whose marriage, descent and other familial ties were being set down, which made the occasion a recording of social activity. What remains in this record is the task of establishing where in the typology of classificatory activities this particular kind belongs, and whether its product – the positional picture – differs essentially from that which the historical actors themselves would have produced, had they been called upon to write one down.

To what extent the relational terminology in a historical record must be seen as entirely different from what was being used in the community is not a question that can be answered in like fashion for every source, though it must be asked about all of them. The Baltic sources certainly are an extreme example of discontinuity, for in all of them relationships were recorded in a language (German) which most of the people listed in the record (Latvians, Estonians) learned imperfectly, if at all, and did not use to refer to or address their relatives. This was not an unusual circumstance as far as the history of the smaller peoples of Eastern Europe goes; in the West, by contrast, the similarity between the language of the people and the source language in most cases was far greater. The question, however, concerns more than the

---

3 'In constructing kinship nomenclature systems, anthropologists normally gather information about the terms that people use when *referring* to particular kinds of relatives, or kin types, in the presence of a third party. ... There is an important difference between such terms and terms of address, the term that EGO employs when *addressing* a particular relative. Terms of reference are more consistent from context to context than those used in address and the latter are often metaphorically extended to nonkinsmen. ... Possibly confusion is avoided if we elicit terms of reference, and it is for this reason that anthropologists prefer to analyze nomenclature systems that have been established on the basis of such terms' (Pasternak, 1976: 130; italics in original).

fit between language codes, because we also have to know what terms could be expected to be used, given the particular assignment of the record-keeper and the reference point of a set of terms. In some cases, the ostensible purpose for which the record was kept would exclude from mention an entire range of relationships to which the society itself attached importance; in some instances, the use of the same person (such as household head) in a series of documents as the reference point of all relationships would have the same outcome. Thus any move in the analysis beyond the fields of social interaction which were clearly demarcated in the source, immediately raises the problem of how much of the results of continuous classificatory activity is being excluded by the 'frozen' positional pictures in the sources.

A discussion of the kinship domain and classificatory activity in the light of the Baltic evidence leads to one conclusion: as we surround a historical source with the kinship concepts developed in other disciplines and seek in this way to extract from it substantive information, we must insert between the source and the concepts an evaluative step. To simply declare that in using a historical source we are already dealing with the 'analytically discriminable elements' of the kinship domain may be appropriate in some instances, but in most cases such a declaration clearly would be un-warranted. With such sources, the historical researcher finds himself in a position similar to that of an anthropological fieldworker who is forced to make sense of someone else's field notes about kinship. The human terrain may be unknown; the 'notes' are systematic, but inexpertly prepared; the relational terms in them are recognizable, but imprecise; and the intent of and assumptions behind the use of the kinship terms are frequently hidden from view. It is perhaps this situation that Claude Lévi-Strauss had in mind in suggesting that historical sources be seen as having been produced by 'amateur ethnographers' (Lévi-Strauss, 1963: 17), though in these sources it is not always easy to tell whether the 'ethnographer' was not at the same time an 'actor' or an 'informant' in the historical situation being recorded. To make headway, the researcher would most likely test the strengths and shortcomings of this received evidence by directing to it several series of questions, with each series pertaining to their value for different areas of kinship research. It is to a prospectus of such an evaluation that we now turn.

Entering the Kinship Domain

Anyone who has followed the rapidly expanding literature of quantitative social history will recognize in the Baltic file the problem of 'too much data' (Floud, 1979: 165–82). There are literally thousands of dyadic relationships to be investigated, if kinship were pursued in terms of the smallest units; and numerous different ways in which these units can be aggregated and measured. Very clearly, then, the first steps into the kinship domain should involve the reduction of the amount of evidence by sampling and the setting up of limited hypotheses, or by the segregation of subpopulations that can be dealt with independently. But which of these steps should be taken first is not at all obvious. A good argument could be made for the use of the individual as the focus of analysis, because, after all, it is individuals who experience kinship ties. This decision would raise the question, among others, of whether the kinship involvement of individuals should be measured in terms of the number of *persons* an individual was related to, or in terms of the number of different indetifiable kin *roles* that individual enacted toward those persons. At the other extreme, one could make the case that the most fruitful way of using the kinship information in the Pinkenhof estate would be to think of the entire community as the analytical unit and devise some way of stating its kinship features at a high level of abstraction, by analogy with the characterizations of entire societies in the *Ethnographic Atlas* of G. P. Murdock (Murdock, 1967; Barnes, 1971). Both approaches would seem equally valid in terms of the data collection at hand, but at the outset neither recommends itself as the *via regia* for understanding kinship in this particular historical community.

Fortunately we do not need to make a decision on this point at this stage, because we are not testing hypotheses, but rather trying to understand the kinds of substantive information various types of historical sources can yield when conceived of as different entries into the kinship domain. The Baltic sources are particularly well suited for this task, not because they illustrate all the problems (being single-year enumerations, they could not possibly do so), but because they do allow us to identify a substantial number of the major areas of concern. To recapitulate, the sources suggest that the best way to systematize the variable evidence in them is to think of this evidence as leading into a kinship domain; they also give a warning, however, that this domain was continuously being restocked with evidence about 'analytically discriminable elements' by the continuous classificatory activities of the historical actors. Whether the source itself can be thought of as being part of those activities, or as being very much removed from them, has to be determined and cannot be assumed at the outset. It may take the form of an external report, or it may be in the nature of a confirming document drawn up by a person intimately familiar with the recorded ties. The next steps consist of identifying, exploring and evaluating the many different combinations of individual ties (combinations of 'nexuses', to use Fortes's language again) in order to bring research closer to the substance of kinship relations. The expectation is not that at this stage the 'analytically discriminable elements' of the kinship domain will have put themselves forward in some pure form for immediate analysis. Rather, what is hoped is that the available historical evidence will be sufficiently multidimensional for the researcher to distinguish in it data subsets appropriate for answering the pressing questions of reliability. These questions can be organized around a set of central concerns that for a long time have preoccupied kinship research in other disciplines, but have only gradually begun to move to the forefront of recent historical work.

The first of these concerns involves the relationship between genealogical links and kinship ties. The temptation in historical work is to go directly from the former to the latter, on the assumption that terminology of the kinship type would not appear in the source at all unless the ties that were being recorded were those of kinship. In discussing the Baltic data so far we have been using the two almost interchangeably, without giving due recognition to the problem. As will be seen later, there are indeed a number of historical sources in which the question is not bothersome, and the assumption is safe that the person producing the record had kinship ties in mind when using relational terminology of the kinship type. In the Baltic file and analogous materials, however, this assumption can hold only up to a point (which has to be established), because the source presents for scrutiny a great many genealogical links without corresponding proof of a termino-logical sort (or of any kind, for that matter) that they were recognized and used as the basis for kinship relations. It would be useful if we could assume that all classificatory activities, including the preparation of single-year populations listings, always and everywhere made constant reference to a common genealogical grid of which both the historical actors and the enumerators were aware; or, more generally, that genealogy and kinship were two sides of the same coin. Unfortunately, this assumption cannot be made and there is no consensus in the writings of anthropologists about the exact connection between the two. As a consequence, we have to approach the relational terminology in the historical source as containing two distinguishable types of evidence – one about genealogical links and the other about kinship ties – and to make an attempt to see what the one has to do with the other. If it is true, as R. A. Barnes has observed, that 'the genealogy is an analytical tool used by those who study kinship' (Barnes, 1979: 103), then the historian faces the task of establishing under what conditions a historical document, which does not clearly separate the two, has to be dealt with as containing either the one or the other exclusively, or as containing some combination of both. In a source that makes available relational information for all members of a historical community, there are likely to be far fewer ties precisely described with kin terms than there are demonstrable genealogical connections. The research problem consists in laying out the rules, in a community about which relatively little is known, under which it becomes possible to move freely between the two types of connections, so that no potential kin ties are overlooked and no genealogical links are designated as kin ties when they do not deserve such recognition.

The second area of concern pertains to the concept of kinship role and involves a number of related problems that arise when the concept is used with a source in which evidence about behaviour is either non-existent or has to be inferred from the way people are positioned *vis-à-vis* each other by the relational terminology. Social anthropologists work with the idea that 'roles ... materialize only in an interaction setting' (Nadel, 1957: 23) and therefore consider the best evidence about roles as being that which emerges from the observation of people acting in social contexts or reporting that they had acted in certain ways. By definition, people in the past cannot be observed at all, but historical records can be read as if they were reports of observations. Social historians have not hesitated in moving from the world of flesh-and-blood individuals to the more abstract world of social roles in their descriptions. Many aspects of this shift need to be understood better. To begin with, it is necessary to make clear under what circumstances in sources such as the Baltic revision it is valid to reconceptualize relational terminology as a set of role labels, and these in turn as a set of indicators of actual role enactment by historical actors whom we encounter only as names on a list. The problem, in historical sources, is not solved by maintaining that what is needed is direct evidence about enactment, because the source may contain a mixture of direct evidence about norms implied in enactment and evidence which is no more than role labels, signalling potentially enactable roles. The question must then be answered about how strict a definition of valid evidence about roles should be used, because clearly one that is too strict will result in the loss of evidence of some kind about roles and thus diminish further what is already relatively meagre information. The problem of roles is made even more formidable in a source such as the Baltic revision, when the record-keeper systematically employed several different relational terminologies simultaneously, so that the position of a given individual in the source is in reality a combination of positions, each of which can most certainly be explicated by reference to a different framework of meaning (kinship system, estate economy, household arrangement, etc.). But to understand the significance of kinship roles in the total social setting, there has to be an attempt to describe the consequences of an individual's involvement in several different role systems, which is a problem that has already manifested itself in household research in connection with people who are described in the source both as 'kin' and as 'servants' of the household head. Similar investigations have to be carried out entirely within the kinship domain, because it is not difficult to demonstrate that an individual may have had to enact in his or her lifetime several dozens of different kinship roles.

As has already been suggested, the immense number of linkages of various kinds presented by certain historical sources creates the need for sampling, and through that, raises a host of related questions pertaining to the quantitative analysis of the data at hand, which then becomes the third of our areas of concern. In both history and social anthropology, the methodological turn toward measurement is of recent origin, so that in at least this one area anthropological fieldworkers cannot be pictured as being light years ahead of historians (Floud, 1979; Johnson, 1978). The overall problems are similar for the two types of evidence on which kinship research is possible. The historical as well as the fieldwork researcher must be concerned with the question of representativeness: that is, under what conditions is it legitimate to understand the kinship experiences and involvements of an individual as 'standing for' those of a community of individuals, the aggregate experiences of a community for those of a region, and these in turn for the experiences of some even larger geographical entity. When only meagre historical data have survived, the questions answer themselves; but, as has been suggested, historical kinship data are given in some sources for more than a single individual and therefore make this series of questions inescapable. There is, moreover, one other area of particular interest to the historian, who is more likely to be blocked off from evidence about behaviour than is the fieldworker: namely, what kind of evidence and how much of it is required to demonstrate that the ties (or clusters of them) identified in a source registered their presence in the ways people behaved toward each other. Given the great variety of social structures that can be identified in a source such as the Baltic revision, it is surely pertinent to ask how to assess their differential impact on the people who were their 'members'. Anthropologists themselves have not dealt with this question systematically, as we learn from the recent observation that 'very few of the groups that occupy anthropological analysis have had their existence demonstrated with quantitative behavioral data' (Johnson, 1978: 102–3), apparently because researchers have preferred to use evidence of other kinds to 'prove' their existence. When this charge is taken seriously then it follows immediately, as far as the historical study of kinship is concerned, that the researcher has to begin to deal with the operational problems of quantitative method: choice of units of analysis, variables, values, tests of association and tests of significance.

The fourth area of concern has to do with the evidentiary status of the kinship terminology found in the historical sources of a particular locality, and the extent to which the researcher can assume it to contain clues about the structure of kinship relationships. This is, of course, one of the oldest problems of kinship research; its introduction derived from Lewis Henry Morgan's momentous discovery in the nineteenth century that, to use the description of Leslie White, 'customs of designating relatives have scientific significance' (White, 1957: 257; cited in Fortes, 1969: 9). Although in the work of fieldwork anthropologists kinship terminologies are seldom used as the sole source of structural information, in the investigation of historical kinship they may emerge as precisely that. For historians therefore terminological data may turn out to be much more than suggestive complementary evidence: they may be the only shreds of information to have survived about a particular locality, with the only possible testing of their meanings being contained in the very same documents which contain the terms. The essential question is therefore likely to be whether such terms, or any combination of terms, are informative at all about the locality under investigation. In answering the question, the researcher has to remember that the format of the source may have had the effect of excluding the use of entire sectors of terminology used in everyday discourse by the historical actors, so that the list of terms that show up may be far less than a complete listing. Correspondingly, the search for a complete listing that is not dependent on any particular source would raise the problem of how suitable a terminology extracted from a 'national' source (such as a dictionary of, say, eighteenth-century French) would be for identification of socially significant kin ties in a given locality. There is also the continuous problem of cultural layers of traditional Europe, which is well illustrated by the Baltic source in which the terminology is German, but the everyday language of reference and address Latvian and Estonian. Finally, there is also the disquieting fact that in recent anthropological writings on kinship the book seems to be opening again (if it was ever closed) on the nature of the entire relationship. As one recent writer has observed:

> Despite a century of effort, no anthropologist has succeeded in producing a satisfactory general theory of the systematic relationship between kinship classification and social organization ... [the] most recent work seems if anything to erode the expectation that kin terms systematically reflect forms of kin grouping or systems of marriage. (Keesing, 1975: 102)

The fact that the mechanics of record-keeping often kept important segments of a local kinship vocabulary from being used at all creates the fifth area of concern, which has to do with the existence of kin-based social groups that are not mentioned by name in any of the available historical sources. There are several components to this problem. First, anthropologists normally draw the distinction between personal kinship and kin-based aggregates, treating the existence of each not as an argument against the existence of the other, but rather as complementary ways of examining the kinship domain (Fortes, 1969: 196). This means, second, that the decidedly ego-oriented kinship terminology of most sources may turn out to be a true reflection of the relative importance of these two types of kinship experience, or it may just as well be the result of the fact that the nature of the assignment required of the record-keeper is the documentation of only one sector of the kinship domain. Now ego-oriented relational terminology does, in fact, permit the reconstruction of various kin-based groups of people, and some of these (such as the conjugal family and the household) may also be mentioned by name in the source that is providing the information. But if the same source (or a collection of them) permits more inclusive reconstructions (of local descent groups, for example), the question very soon becomes one of the degree of social reality that can be attributed to them if these groups are not designated by name in the sources. To put it another way, in sources that present the researcher with a plenitude of genealogical information, it may well be possible to allocate each named person to one or another group by using criteria of inclusion and exclusion abstracted from societies where such groups are known to have been socially significant. But this process of allocation would remain a simulation exercise unless some grounds were found, perhaps by reference to other sources or through the close study of one exemplar of the group, for making the judgement that all groups of the same type had social reality. Measurements of reconstructions would be possible in either case, of course, because the personnel of the reconstructed units would remain the same, and measuring a reconstruction *as if* it possessed social reality may be instructive in a number of respects (Morgan, 1973). Yet if the final concern has to do with kinship dimension in social history, then the *as if* trait of such reconstructions must be reduced to some acceptable level.

The fact that historical kinship sources (or a combination of them) may as easily involve a single year of the past as several generations makes historical time the sixth area of concern. The adoption by historians of synchronic ('point in past time') analysis does not need much further comment: this way of looking at the data has now become fully a part of the methodological corpus of social historians, and there is a thorough awareness, for the most part deriving from analyses of household listings, of the strengths and weaknesses of the approach. On their side, anthropologists have also devoted much more time than earlier to working out the methodological difficulties of 'long-term research', that is, the problems that obtain when a particular community or population is under the anthropologist's observation for periods of 20–30 years (Foster et al., 1979). But the historian working with sources of certain kinds may at times be confronted, at the level of empirical data, with information that spans not one or two adjoining generations, but several hundreds of years, a period of time, that is, which stands somewhere between the current anthropological under-standing of the 'long term' (20–30 years) and the evolutionary perspective in anthropology, which may include (or imply) historical time, thousands of years in length. There is not, of course, any possibility of obtaining continuous empirical evidence from historical sources to support statements meant to cover thousands of years of existence of a population, but it is not at all impossible, as it now appears, for historical data to form a continuity of some sort for perhaps eight or nine adjacent generations, within the same population. These data may take the form of repeated single-year listings of a regional or national population; and, less often, they may in fact be linked generations of, say, a partriline. They may be in exceptional cases, as will be seen later, evidence about continuous, inter-linked, patrilines in a given region, offering the possibility of measurement of a particular patriline at many points in its eight or nine generations' 'history', and also, over the same span of historical time, of such processes as segmentation, intermarriage and extinction. With such data, the historian is required to add to the 'point-in-the-past-time' and evolutionary approaches one that requires an understanding of how kinship 'works out' in a time period that exceeds in length one human lifetime, but is not long enough for the society in question to have concluded a major shift in its overall patterns (for example, from patrilineality to bilaterialism). If it is possible to accept the idea that an entire culture area in the past can be adequately described with a short descriptive phrase refering to its basic kinship rules, the question that remains is how in the passage of historical time such general rules worked out among the dozens of different societies and subsocieties comprising the cultural area, and whether there existed variations of the general rule.

The seventh area of concern has to do with the kind of uses to which historical kinship data can still be put when the relational terminology of a source (or a set of sources) is very rich, but supplementary or corroborative information is sparse and a full-scale, in-depth description of kinship proves not to be possible. When such a seemingly unpromising situation obtains, it has to be remembered that the available relational terminology carries a double meaning: in its specific references it concerns roles and configur-ations of roles, but in its general significance it is concerned with social connectedness and may be useful for describing the properties of systems or networks of individuals. While it may remain impossible in a particular historical population to describe precisely what the role of MoBr entailed in a dyadic relationship, we might still be able to extract a certain amount of social-structural information from the available source on the basis of the minimal assumption that the relational terminology in the source meant something rather than nothing and that it was evidence of a kind about macrostructure. Variations in connectedness among subpopulations (or among populations in different communities) invite the use of the network concept and the measurements of networks that have recently come into use in a large number of the social sciences (Burt, 1982). In this line of inquiry the objective is not so much the explication of what particular ties meant for the people connected by them (though this aim need not be abandoned), but the description of attributes of entire populations or subpopulations: how tightly or loosely their members are connected, how important certain classes of ties are in creating these characteristics, how central or peripheral some components of the population are in comparison to others, and so forth. One advantage for historians in this approach is that it permits various kinds of measurements on the basis of categorical connections – that is, a tie is assumed to exist when two individuals occupy structural categories ('father-in-law' – 'son-in-law') that are connected by definition – as well as on the basis of connections established by virtue of demonstrated interactions of transactions between the individuals – i.e., the tie is understood to exist only when there is evidence that the two persons did something with or to each other.

To summarize, entry into the kinship domain from the starting-point of a documented historical population may require a thorough review of the data in terms of the areas of concern we have outlined. Only such a review can determine whether the substance of the kinship domain – its 'analytically discriminable elements' – can be reached at all; to what extent the analysis has to rely on indicators; and if quantitative analysis, when used, will produce measurements of kinship phenomena *per se* or of patterns of association from which kinship phenomena have to be inferred. In the discussion of these matters, we have continued to refer to the Baltic evidence not because historical kinship in the Baltic region was comparatively more intriguing than elsewhere, but because, due to various decisions by local record-keepers, the Baltic revision documents have turned out to be very useful for understanding what it means to postulate the existence of a kinship domain and to try to gain access to it on the basis of historical evidence. In anthropological fieldwork, postulation of such a domain is done with justifiable expectations that the empirical evidence will lead directly to substantive matters, so that, for example, a research strategy can be expected to lead to the confirmation or rejection of a hypothesized phenomenon of a certain kind. In historical research, however, the postulation of a kinship domain will help to 'systematize' the available information and to some extent suggest the phenomena about which hypotheses have to be constructed. But before these can be tested – before, that is, the substantive matters can be reached – the researcher will be forced to wonder what frames of reference provided to the record-keeper the meaning of the words that were set on paper (the relational terminology attached to names of individuals), and what meaning was being conveyed by the way the words were set down. These are, as was said earlier, epistemological problems, and they may prove to be intractable. Yet a fuller discussion of them, as will now be carried out in the following chapters, may suggest to archival historians some uses for their data which may not have been considered, and thus result in a better understanding of a dimension of social history which is still largely *terra incognita,* both in terms of widely applicable descriptions and in terms of verified hypotheses (Anderson, 1980; Mitterauer and Sieder, 1982).

2

Genealogical Reconstructions in Recent Social History

Social historians who work with nominal-level sources are all too familiar with how exasperating such evidence can be. The record-keeper may have gone so far as to use the full name of each person and may even have separated blocks of names from each other to indicate which people were living together. But often there will be only sparse information about the social ties the people had with each other – who was master and who was servant, who was father and who was daughter or stepdaughter – with the consequence that most of the specific connections that transform a mere collection of persons into a social group are entirely hidden from view. Sometimes the evidence will be suggestive, as when in a block of names presumed to be a household all persons have the same surname, indicating the possibility that they were related to each other. Sometimes several co-residential groups, appearing next to each other on a list, will also be composed of people of like surnames, inviting the hypothesis that they too may have been related. But in the final analysis there will be little that can be done about verifying these hypotheses. Without clear statements that like-surnamed co-residents of a household, or like-surnamed inhabitants of adjacent households were relatives, the analysis cannot move away from the information that is given. There is no social evidence of any other kind – such as status terms' denoting subordination or superordination, for example – from which the researcher can infer specific generalogical or kinship linkages. These links must be given or they must be capable of being inferred from other links of the same kind. The population of an entire region may be listed at the nominal level, and the characteristics of the region at some point in the past may be such as to allow us to believe that population turnover was very low. And though it may be tempting to assume that among the inhabitants of such localities kinship relations may have been dense indeed, the absence in the evidence of relational terminology of the proper kind will prevent the inquiry from proceeding any farther. This frustrating situation can be generalized: even though the social past of Europeans undoubtedly had a kinship dimension to it, very rarely have the sources permitted the historian to obtain a clear view of the inner architecture and workings of that dimension. It is as if historians were forced to watch a play through a closed curtain which had enough holes in it to indicate that a play was being performed, but no hole large enough to allow us to see the stage and actors in their entirety.

Genealogical Links and Kinship Ties

In the localities where the necessary relational terminology is present, however, historians have become accustomed to the idea that this evidence will be as ambiguous as it is incomplete. The only 'facts' that are not likely to be disputed are those which posit a relationship between two individuals (a dyadic tie) in the form of 'X is the brother of Y', or sometimes three individuals (a triadic tie) in the form of 'X and A had a daughter who was named Z'. In this form, such statements of relationship will be genealogical in nature. In order to transform handfuls or even hundreds of such basic relational facts into information about kinship, the researcher will have to use inferences, identification strategies and clues about social practices in the locality implied in the relational units themselves. Thus, in the two relational statements cited above, the datum that Z was the niece of Y (a relation not named in the source) has to be inferred from the given relation between Y and X and X and Z. Before this inference can be made, however, the researcher will have to establish that the person X in the first statement, which is found in one place in the source, is the same person X as in the second statement, which may be located several pages later in the source. Moreover, if these two steps are taken successfully, the researcher will have to ascertain whether in the locality in question the relationship between a father's brother and brother's daughter was in fact recognized as a kinship relationship, that is, assigned a meaning which created for the older man rights and obligations toward the younger woman that he did not have toward any other younger woman, and vice versa. Only after these steps are taken can the researcher assume that the generalizations that are made about this particular relationship will be in the domain of kinship, rather than simply in the domain of genealogy. If we now consider that a good nominal-level population source which contains the requisite relational terminology will consist of hundreds, perhaps thousands, of simple relational statements, we can begin to appreicate what is involved in approaching kinship through any kind of reconstruction based on state-ments of this nature.

These problems are commonplace to anyone acquainted with the litera-ture on historical demography and historical social structure, but they have to be reiterated in order to underline the distinction between genealogical links and kinship ties. Analysis of the two involves different technical operations, and in the present and subsequent chapters I shall be dealing only with the former, that is, the types of historical evidence in which genealogical data can be found, the differences between the information in each of the types, and the problems that are created when in each type the data are extended or complemented by inferences. In much historical research on kinship questions, of course, the two kind of operations have usually been dealt with more or less simultaneously. Taking cues from the sources, the researcher will have used individual bits of evidence to reconstruct genealogical configurations, while simultaneously conferring upon such configurations meanings in the domain of kinship. As will be seen later, in many sources this is a perfectly sound procedure, because the social situations which produced the sources can be assumed to have been of the kind that required the record-keeper to be recording kinship ties rather than only genealogical links. In other kinds of sources, however, the question to which of these two categories – genealogical or kinship – the relational terms belong is not so easy to answer. The analysis would certainly be aided if the language used in the sources always contained two distinct sets of terms, one for ties that were merely genealogical and the other for ties that fixed relations of kinship, but unfortunately this is not the case. Consequently, for the purpose of clarifying the problems involved, we shall have to posit a more radical disjunction between these two realms of connectedness than may be warranted in most cases, and discuss the shift from the genealogical to the kinship realm in a later chapter.

To bring the genealogy–kinship problem to the forefront in this way means establishing a connection with one particular method in anthropological kinship research – namely, the genealogical method – which now appears to exist among several contending ones.[1] Recognizing that among anthropologists there is now less consensus than there used to be about the connection between genealogy and kinship, I would still argue that the

---

1 For a survey of the literature pertaining to the genealogical method see Hackenberg (1974). To an outsider's eye, the anthropological arguments in this matter concern not so much whether genealogies should or should not be gathered in fieldwork, but the extent to which the specification of genealogical positions of individuals must enter explanatory schemes of the social universe. As summarized by Keesing (1975: 119), the dispute affects, for the most part, interpretations of unilineal societies and focuses on the question of whether individuals orient themselves toward each other primarily by reference to the genealogical positions they occupy *vis-à-vis* each other, or by reference to more inclusive categories (such as 'wife-givers', 'potential spouses', etc.) that include various genealogical positions and, in a sense, make the specification of positions within these larger categories irrelevant. Keesing notes, by way of a conclusion, that 'the controversy rages and resolution does not seem imminent'.

genealogical method seems to me to be of immediate interest to historians precisely because in historical sources it is genealogical connections – stated as 'facts' – that press themselves upon the researcher for consideration. Viewed as a collection of labels, the relational terminology of the sources invites interpretation, of course, and this line of inquiry may operate as a search for meaning that is independent of the historical persons (however anonymous) to whom the terms refer in the source. Viewed as clues about connectedness, however, this terminology leads to a variety of very active reconstruction procedures in which individuals are linked to each other, in a stepwise fashion, until the linking possibilities in the terminology are exhausted. This linking step is held to be important on the assumption that meanings will not emerge until each person is located in precise genealogical positions *vis-à-vis* all others and until there has been produced a kind of genealogical 'map' to which the search for meanings can be referred. The question is whether, given all of the problems historical sources contain, this reconstruction step is as useful as it has traditionally been held to be. Here I would argue that until a systematic effort is made to adapt the genealogical method of the anthropological kinship researchers to the genealogical evidence given or implied in historical sources, we shall not be able to answer this question in any satisfactory way.

I mentioned earlier that simple relational statements tend always to be precise enough not to require additional assumptions, and therefore they have come to be used widely in one kind of kinship analysis, namely, of the kinship content of households. In the set of standard tables that are now widely used in household analysis, one requires a listing of all the relational terms used in the source and a count of the frequency with which such terms appear (Laslett and Wall, 1972: 81). Thus, for example, the list might contain such terms as 'father', 'mother', 'brother', 'sister', 'son-in-law', etc. and the frequency with which they appear is made the basis for generalizations about the importance of certain kinds of dyadic ties and the macrostructure of the group. Two things about this procedure have to be noted, however. First, when they are used in the source, terms of this sort always have a single reference point – the head of the group – and therefore do not include in their number the terms describing relationships or persons who are not heads. Second, the kin terms for which such an inventory is prepared do not include those designating a relationship between the head, his or her spouse, and his or her offspring, In both cases, the number of relationships in the group is, in effect, reduced through the technique itself, in order for the researcher not to have to infer relationships and in order to set the 'family' (of the head) in contradistinction to 'kin'. This measure of 'co-resident kin in the household' has been used widely, particularly for comparative purposes, though in other, similar, classificatory schemes, the rules of inclusion have been modified toward great inclusiveness (e.g. Halpern and Halpern, 1972: 29).

By any measure, analysis of kin within the household has been a very successful line of inquiry, not only because of the yield of comparative substantive information, but also because it has enabled researchers to bring under control heretofore under-utilized historical sources. It is a type of minimal reconstruction, proceeding on the basis of simple relational terms which link a list of names to the head of the group. At times the procedure has had to involve inferences, not only because some household lists do not provide all the terms which would enable the cluster of people to be thought of as a unit, but also because some lists provide several reference points for the reconstruction of sub-units within a reconstructed household. Thus, for example, in the Baltic listings, very large co-residential groups often contained several subsidiary conjugal families whose heads were linked to the group head by a specific term. The spouses and children of these subsidiary families, however, were not referenced to the group head at all, but rather to the family-unit head. In both cases, the researcher has to infer relationships from those which are given: to supplement ties when these are insufficiently described or to probe for the full meaning of ties when all are not stated. It is in this sense that one has to think of households as being reconstructed: working from the specific connections that are given, the researcher draws out their full implications and from that point assumes the unit to have been described fully.

We can state the steps and results of this procedure in a general way, thus understanding it as applicable to a wide variety of sources in which genealogical information exists in the form of small clusters. When minimal reconstruction is carried out systematically for all the entries of a data source suited for the operation, the result is many dozens, perhaps hundreds, of self-enclosed information units that are of the form depicted in figure 2.

In such a reconstruction, there is likely to be a principal person (or persons) in terms of whom the stated relationships are given. These relationships will not be the only ones in the social situation, however. At this point, the researcher will have to decide whether the reconstruction can legitimately involve inferred ties, so that when A is described as the father of B, and C as the wife of A, B can be dealt with also as the son of C. That these inferential relationships are used in dealing with such sources all the time can be documented without any difficulty. What is most important about this kind of reconstruction, however, is that the researcher does not expect to have to deal with relationships that the named persons might have had with people elsewhere. The information about genealogical links is sharply cut off at whatever border or boundary the enumerator has chosen to use;

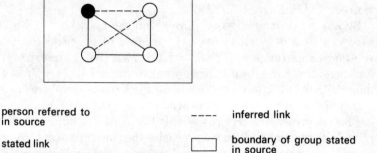

● person referred to   ---- inferred link
  in source

—— stated link   ▭ boundary of group stated
                                 in source

Figure 2 Minimal reconstruction

whatever kinship information the cluster delivers is determined by the nature of the activity the cluster of people is pursuing. The addition of more enclosed clusters to the data file normally will not add additional information about other dimensions of the kinship domain, though the additional clusters may reveal other types of kin who were involved in the activity that the entire set documents. If each of a thousand small clusters of this type represent a household, the entire set of a thousand will no doubt provide thorough evidence about household kinship. But as long as each of the thousand clusters is separated from the rest by the enumerator's recording conventions, the analysis cannot move into other areas of genealogical and kinship relations. Generalizations about kinship in a community for which only a source of this type is available have to be restricted to the workings of kinship as they affect co-residence. In view of this, the claim that household kinship is a significant aspect of kinship generally has to be made – as indeed it can be made – on grounds other than what this kind of source reveals, because the way in which the information in the source is arranged does not bring the researcher into touch with ties other than those among co-residents.

Standing in contrast with minimal reconstruction is the kind to which the adjective *maximal* can be applied, since it makes use of sources which in themselves do not provide borders or boundaries to genealogical configurations. The most productive sources for this procedure are registers of vital events, from which historical demographers have extracted rich information on family demography through the use of the technique of 'family reconstitution'.[2] This type of source, however, does not require that reconstruction

2 The two types of 'reconstruction' discussed in this chapter are not to be understood as techniques in the sense that 'family reconstitution' is a technique with a specific goal, specific time-tried methods, and even specific tools such as 'family reconstitution forms'

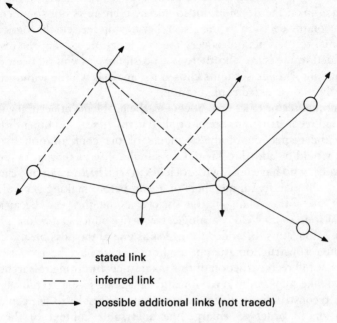

stated link

----- inferred link

→ possible additional links (not traced)

Figure 3 Maximal reconstruction

stop at any particular unit; the conjugal family, in family reconstitution, has been found to be the most useful for the questions demographers wish to ask. Yet these documents can be such that any reconstructed unit which is chosen for analysis remains open-ended, as suggested in figure 3, which presents the form maximal reconstruction should be understood to have. As far as genealogical links are concerned, this form stands in sharp contrast with the form for minimal reconstruction. There are again stated links (for example, between a man and his wife in the entry of a marriage register, a mother and her child in the entry in a birth register) and implied links; but the source itself does not prescribe either the unit which is to be isolated for analysis or an important person to whom all ties should be referenced. In

---

(e.g. Wrigley, 1966a). 'Reconstruction' may very well include 'family reconstitution' as the first step and is likely to include it when the source being used is a parish register. But it does not aim to piece together only nuclear families; its ultimate goal is to bring into genealogical connection with each other all persons in a single source (or a set of sources) to the extent that internal evidence permits. All of the difficulties of identification continue to exist (Wrigley, 1973) and, in fact, become more crucial, because maximal reconstruction links between individuals frequently serve as links between groups as well.

principle, any point (individual) in a maximal reconstruction always has additional links; the decision not to pursue them rests not so much on the source as on the decision by the researcher to stop the search. Measurement in maximal reconstructions is very much a function of what the researcher has decided to measure, and there is a possibility, as will be demonstrated later, that all of the lesser units chosen for analysis will be within the same maximally reconstructed configuration.

In maximal reconstructions, of course, the problems of accuracy inherent in minimal reconstructions are multiplied many times, and other difficulties, such as the dispersion of the members of the configuration over large regions, would be added to them. One should observe that anthropological fieldworkers who have dealt with societies in which, for example, clans were active do not identify all members of a clan before making generalizations about it and other clans in the society. None the less, because some historical sources do yield genealogical evidence which can be used for such a purpose, they must be added to the list as one of the possible directions in which the reconstruction attempt might go. There have been relatively few attempts at full reconstruction of this magnitude, but some researchers have sought to take steps in this direction and have done so successfully.[3]

These reconstruction efforts are aimed at one result: to use genealogical information in order to enlarge the analysable context of the ties of particular individuals and thus to provide empirical evidence for the discussion of kinship groups. At this juncture, however, it is necessary to repeat the observations made earlier about these exercises, namely, that they are being carried out without the assumption that in the same process we have demonstrated that the reconstructed configurations had social reality. Rather, at this point, the reconstructions have the purpose of bringing together the people who may be analytically relevant for an understanding of various kin-based units. All we ask for from the historical data at this point is what the results are if the relational terminology in the data is exploited fully, using certain known rules of group formation or group assembly. Whether the configurations we reconstruct had social relevance to the society in question is a matter that remains to be demonstrated. In some cases, as I pointed out, the demonstration is not likely to be difficult, because the record-keepers, when using relational terminology, were themselves using the same principles of group identity as those which we used for the reconstruction. But in other cases, especially in maximal reconstructions, the gap between what we determine to be analytically relevant and what was socially relevant may be very great, and the job of determining

3 Among the projects that explicitly include maximal reconstruction are those reported in Macfarlane (1977a and 1977b), Halpern and Halpern (1977) and Sabean (1976a and 1976b).

whether the two categories were identical very demanding.

Historical research on kinship questions has demonstrated that many sources come at least part of the way to meet the historian's need for accurate relational terminology, sometimes inadvertently. The principal sources of this kind can be discussed under three headings: interaction documents, certain kinds of household listings, and registers of vital events. They all, to a greater or lesser extent, present to the researcher people from the past as clusters of individuals related in some fashion, rather than as individuals with no demonstrable connection to each other, and they do so for a large enough number of people to permit the reconstruction of a sufficiently large number of configurations to allow some control of the problem of random variations. An interaction document will provide information about at least two, and normally a handful, of persons who are participating in an activity of social importance; a household list, by definition, will provide information at least about the co-residents, and will sometimes link information about others as well; registers of vital events will provide information to link together at least the conjugal family unit, and sometimes even more individuals. While there is no assurance that these sources will in fact allow the analyst to identify ties *between* clusters, the sources at least permit the techniques of reconstruction to be used within a large number of such clusters. Understandably, it is to sources like these that social historians have moved in order to explore the question of whether kinship in the past was only a matter of an Ego and his relatives or involved more than such simple configurations.

Interaction Documents: A French Example

Keeping genealogical clusters as the main concern, we can begin this survey of evidence with a type of document that recorded and sometimes ratified important exchanges. These events were as varied as social life itself, and they generated documents that frequently had long-term consequences for the participants. In a new marriage, for example, there might take place negotiations between the families of the principals involving transfer of property; a multiple family household might decide to divide itself, its land and its movables because it had grown too large numerically; or, at the approach of death a household head might wish to create a testament so as to assure his offspring the rightful share of the family property. Whatever they said about the decisions made or ratified on the occasion, these documents frequently also contained the full names of the participants, witnesses, beneficiaries and benefactors, and specified the genealogical ties among them. In such documents therefore the analytically and socially relevant evidence was nearly identical: the named persons were present

Document 1 Marriage contract, Bordeaux, 1641
Source: Archiv departmental de la Gironde, Bordeaux, no. 3E5201, fos. 285–7

In translation, the above document reads as follows:

In the name of God, Amen. Know all present and future that today, on the date of this document, before me, notary and royal scrivener in Bordeaux and Guyenne subscribed, in the presence of the witnesses named below, there appeared personally Andre Boileau, Bourgeois and Master Saddlemaker of the present city, living there in the Parish of St. Mexant, natural and legitimate son of the late Noël Boileau, in his lifetime also a Bourgeois and Master Blacksmith of the present city, and Philipe Delagarde, his father and mother, for the one part. And Olive Gernays, also natural and legitimate daughter of Martin Gernays, Master Shoemaker of the present city, and Martialle Bethoure, also her father and mother, living in said Bordeaux in the parish of St. Christoly, for the other part. Between which parties, acting with the advice and counsel, to wit, said Boileau of Andre Besse, Lord of Moteplaine, his godfather and uncle by marriage; Peyronne Delagarde, his aunt; Anne Boileau, his sister; Jeanne Gallet, widow, his sister-in-law; Jean Delagarde, also Master Saddlemaker; and said Gernays [with the advice and counsel] of said Gernays and Bethoure, her father and mother; Pierre Bethoure, Master Sworn Tavernkeeper of Bordeaux, her uncle; Olive Bethoure, her aunt and godmother; Alix Gernays, her paternal aunt; Jacques Denallade, Bourgeois and

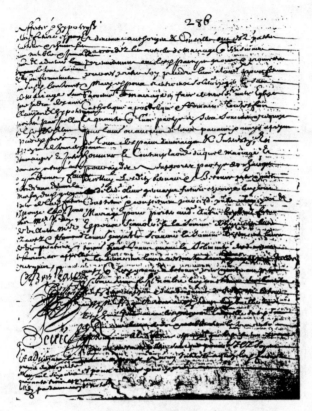

Document 1 continued

Master Arquebussier of said Bordeaux, her godfather; François Rapaneau, Master Pastry-cook, Jean Gernays, her brother; and their other relatives and friends here present, who have well and duly authorized and advised them to do this. The articles of marriage which follow have been passed and agreed on. First, said parties have promised and promise by this present document to take one another as wedded wife and husband, and to solemnize their mutual vows with the holy sacrament of marriage before our holy mother, the Catholic and Apostolic Church, whenever one party is called and required to by the other or any of their relatives and friends, on pain of all expenses, damages, and interests. In honor and contemplation of which marriage, and to aid in supporting part of its costs, said Gernays and Bethoure, father and mother of said Olive Gernays, future bride, have constituted and constitute for her by this present document as a marital dot to bring to said André Boileau, future groom, the sum of eight hundred livres tournois, payable as follows: The sum of six hundred livres turnois eight days before the solemnization of said nuptuals and the remaining two hundred livres in the two years following. Said Gernays and Bethoure, father and mother, have promised and will be obliged to do this by this present document without thereby being obliged to pay any interest, which latter said future groom expressly renounces. Moreover, they constitute to her six new sheets, two tablecloths, two dozen napkins, all also new, which they will be obliged to give him in the said six days before said nuptuals, and this is agreed to

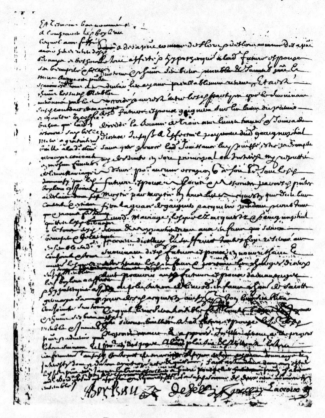

Document 1 continued

without obliging the future bride to renounce her share of the estate of her father and mother, provided she return said dot to the estate, if this seems best to her. The abovementioned sum of eight hundred livres of dot and movables will all be reckoned patrimonial property of the future bride, and for it the future groom has both now and henceforth attached and mortgaged all his property, movable and immovable, present and future, having reserved it for this purpose. And said parties have agreed and decreed that the survivor of the spouses will have a claim to the sum of three hundred livres tournois against the property of the first to die, and will enjoy the property until the actual payment of said nuptual claim, without said enjoyment being deducted as principal or interest and without its being considered usury, under any circumstances. Said future spouses share and will share half and half in all the acquisitions which God gives them the grace to gain and acquire during their said marriage, which acquisitions and nuptual gain will belong to the children who are born of the marriage; with the income from it reserved, however to the survivor of said future spouses, to be used in nourishing and raising said children and in bearing the expenses resulting from the marriage; with the power being granted to said future spouses to favor one or several children with his or her share of said acquired property as seems best; which will be regarded as legal for them to do. Said father and mother of said future bride will be obliged to clothe her on the day of the engagement, and said future groom will also be obliged to clothe her on the day of the

Document 1 continued

nuptuals with necessary garments suitable to her social status. All rings and jewelry given to said future bride on the day of said nuptuals, or before or afterwards, will be her own property, all of which she can dispose of according to her pleasure and will, according to the courts and customs of said Bordeaux and the Bordelais. And to assure the observation and accomplishment of all the above, the said parties pledge all their property, movable and immovable, present and future, which they have for this purpose submitted to the courts and jurisdiction etc. renouncing etc. Thus they have promised and sworn. Drawn up and approved in Bordeaux in the house of said Gernays and Bethoure father and mother of said future bride on the afternoon of the first day of December, 1641, in the presence of said Rapaneau, Raimond Brin, legal clerk, Armand Dugadoneys, scholar, and Master Pierre Peres, Usher in the Bureau of Finance of Guyenne, witnesses duly summoned and required. Said father and mother of said future bride and the other assistants have declared that they did not know how to sign when requested to.

/s/ Beysses
/s/ Olive Gervais
/s/ Anne Boileau
/s/ Dugadonneys notaire royal

/s/ Betoure present
/s/ Bernays present
/s/ Peres present
/s/ Davic present

(Transcribed and translated by Robert Wheaton and Héléne Avisseau)

because the occasion demanded it, and the genealogical links they had with each other were therefore demonstrably kinship ties. Although it is quite true that frequently on such occasions there were non-kin present – friends or sometimes strangers – we are at this moment interested only in the cluster that is kin-linked and with the information the document provides for generalizations about genealogical facts of the situation.

Of the many different types of interaction evidence that exists, only a few have been submitted to thorough structural analysis. In his study of the social structure of seventeenth-century Bordeaux, Robert Wheaton has used a large collection of marriage contracts and the persons named in them to examine a broad range of structural questions, including the relationships among the persons which the document groups around each of the contracting parties (Wheaton, 1980). These contracts (one of which is reproduced and transcribed; see document 1) were extremely rich in detail about the material side of the transaction, but they also contained much information on the clusters of persons who were present at the signing of such a document. These, Wheaton has observed, were 'persons intimately connected, whether as friends or relatives, to the principals, and the marriage can be taken to create a social link between the two groups . . . the contracts therefore provide us with a series of vignettes of small social groups built up by family alliances; and . . . when these vignettes are treated in the aggregate, we have one view of the system functioning on an important occasion in the life of the family' (Wheaton, 1973: 471).

Analysis of these documents can proceed in a number of different directions. For instance, some of these contracts contain clauses relating to the ultimate residence of the elderly parents, which would have given rise to a household containing the married couple (and possibly their children), the groom's parents and the bride's father. A large number of such contracts in which future residential arrangements are mentioned could provide a strong clue to the kinds of kinsfolk who were conceived as *not* outside the range of candidates for cohabitation. The contracting individuals, the bride and groom, were each 'assisted' in the agreement by a cluster of persons which sometimes included friends, sometimes relatives and sometimes both. By analysing these 'assistants' with respect to links of kinship, links of friendship and occupational similarity to the contracting parties, Wheaton has been able to use this particular kind of documental social transaction as an entry into a wide range of structural relationships.

Another kind of source which identifies clusters of people by name are the testaments that have been used for historical studies of inheritance (e.g. Goody, 1976). These, however, are more likely to be informative about the propertied than about those who had no property to transmit to the next generation. None the less, it is surprising what small amounts of property were sometimes regulated through testamentary disposition: and, if property was lacking, dispositions would sometimes be made of an 'office' such as the headship of a farm. A testament at times contained the names of the persons whom the testator wanted to disinherit as well as those of his beneficiaries; it specified the length of time that had to pass before certain property could be made use of; and indeed it often specified what treatment the testator expected from his heirs, and how he expected his spouse to be treated, if the testament were to be implemented. In the course of setting down such provisions, the testament would make reference to specific persons still alive at the time of its creation, as well as persons who might not yet have been born. Thus a testament could be a mixture of names (and genealogical links) of great variety, comprising a special kind of empirical evidence that distinguished between valued persons and those who were not valued. In a testament, an individual expressed, in terms of bequests, his evaluation of the meaning certain relationships had had for him during his life; in other words, his wishes as expressed in this document can be viewed as one part of a transaction (or a series of them), the other part being the behaviour of the cited individuals toward him (Wrightson and Levine, 1979: 91–4).

The expanding administrative apparatuses of European national and regional government had the long-run effect of vastly increasing the documentary legacy about the social life of the common people. Adding to this were several other trends: more accurate record-keeping by intermediary institutions such as churches, whose officials were close to vital events; the expansion of rational agriculture, which in many parts of Europe meant that landowners needed accurate statistics about their properties, including, sometimes incidentally, information about the labour force under their control; and the increasing use of notarial documents. When such records were produced, they stood a good chance of containing usable genealogical information, or at least information which could be made useful when linked to other sources. These documents took the form of:

1 household inventories, which frequently carried not only descriptions of property, but also of the persons who shared in the ownership and use (e.g., Rebel, 1983: 53–6);
2 court records, which noted who assisted whom by witnessing or pledging in court cases (e.g., Smith, 1979);
3 godparent lists, which included the names and sometimes the relationship of persons chosen by parents as 'fictive kin' for their newborn child (Hammel, 1968; cf. Pitt-Rivers, 1976);
4 guardianship documents, in which a family agreed to provide for an orphan and which frequently contained a statement of the guardians' relation to their new charges (Plakans, 1978; Goody, 1976: 66–85).

This is, needless to say, only a partial listing of the kinds of historical interaction evidence that could be put to use. Each of the types of documents we have referred to had its own unique format, depending upon the cultural area from which they came, and their quality varied with the punctiliousness of the record-keepers.

Interaction documents have a number of strengths which have to be noted. First, they are a record of precisely the kind of event at which fieldwork anthropologists have looked for information about 'structure':

> Structure is not immediately visible in the 'concrete reality.' It is discovered by comparison, induction, and analysis based on a sample of actual social happenings in which the institution, organization, usage, etc. with which we are concerned appears in a variety of contexts. (Fortes, 1970: 3)

> Social relations are abstractions since they are not directly visible or tangible, as individuals and activities are, but have to be established by inference. This does not mean that social relations are not real. It is only that they are implicit and general, wrapped up, as it were, in the particular occasions in which they emerge. (Fortes, 1969: 60)

Second, they also satisfy, better perhaps than other sources, what in recent anthropological work is a felt preference for an accurate record of an activity over an elegant explanation of a structure: 'a distinct trend in a substantial corpus of contemporary anthropological writings on kin groups is a growing preoccupation *with what people actually do and with whom they do it* rather than with the formulation of jural norms and formal structures' (my italics) (Holy, 1976: 128; see also Cordell and Beckermann, 1980). Third, they are the one type of historical source in which the link between genealogy and kinship is very close. The genealogical information they contain is immediately translatable into kinship information, on the assumption that no person said to be linked to the principals of the activity was made part of the record only because of the genealogical tie, but precisely because the principals, or someone else who organized the activity, believed it was necessary for certain kinsfolk to be present. The record of their participation is therefore direct proof that the genealogical connections they did have were being recognized as kinship connections, so that any analysis using the relational terminology becomes *ipso facto* an analysis of both genealogy and kinship. If the historical researcher has access to many documents of the same type, these can be viewed, in this sense, as the equivalent of many fieldwork observations, each having a different cast of actors, but each also supplementing the total information about what kinds of people regularly participated with the principals in a certain kind of social activity.

This comparison with anthropological fieldwork, however, points out what is a decided weakness of interaction records. The fieldworker, having collected genealogies, will be able to observe and record social activities with full knowledge of the people who were connected to the principals *but who did not participate in the observed activity*. There will exist, in other words, an independent genealogical record in the light of which the ties that show up in the activity can be clarified and interpreted.

Consider, for example, the problems that arise if no such independent genealogical record is present. In the parish register from the Lutheran parish of Nerft, in the Russian Baltic province of Kurland, baptisms were recorded very neatly starting with the year 1834, and each record had attached to it a list of godparents, as follows:

> Ninth of September, 1834, baptised: *Mahre,* from Bihlan farmstead, the legitimate daughter of the Bihlan farmstead's head's Lutheran brother Martin and his Lutheran wife Dahrte: baptism performed in the Nerft church by Pastor Wagner. Godparents: Mahre and Matsch, the head's children; Bihlan Jahn, the head; Saukajahn Dahrte, the head's daughter.

The record of baptism containing the names of godparents is a good example of an interaction document, though of a somewhat different kind than a marriage contract or a will. The exchange here would be of the 'honour' bestowed by parents upon those who are asked to stand as godparents, in return for the security that these godparents would provide for the child, if anything happened to the parents. In the cited example, we have a record of godparenthood in which the parents had relied rather heavily on their own kin; the two godfathers *apparently* were the nephew and brother of the baptised child's father, and one of the godmothers the niece of the child's father. The link between the child's parents and the second godmother, however, remains obscured. She might be Bihlan Jahn's daughter, or she might be the daughter of the head of Saukajahn farmstead. If there existed an independent record for the Bihlan lineage, however, she could be identified precisely, but as the record stands her exact link to the baptised child cannot be determined. Nor is it possible to tell from this entry which relatives were not chosen, or whether the chosen ones represent a choice or the only surviving relatives. In the case of the anthropological fieldworker, however, the remedy for this problem would be close at hand.

Interaction documents thus tend to be self-enclosed and inward-pointing, as far as genealogical evidence is concerned. The documents might comprise a collection describing the same activity throughout segments of a large population and over a long period of time, but the analysis of them will not in any given instance be able to surmount the questions that arise when the participants cannot be tested as a subset. Though it is very likely that the actors in them did in fact participate in other activities together with other people, we are not able to examine these other contexts and will be forced to limit our interpretations of important kin to one kind of activity alone.

Robert Wheaton's characterization of the Bordeaux marriage contracts – that they offer 'one view of the system of social relations' of the city – can be used for this class of documents as a whole. The fact that the relational terminology in them is always referenced to a few principal actors, that no larger genealogical context is available for any of the actors, that the number of cases available for analysis depends on the accidents of documentary survival, and that a set of such documents is never likely to be complete for a delimited population such as a community or a social class – all these facts ensure that by means of these documents a complete description of the kinship domain remains impossible. From the information in them we can reconstruct a genealogical configuration of limited size with greater or lesser certainty and deal with these genealogical links as kinship links because of the nature of the events the documents record. The description we obtain will be, however, of activity and not of inclusive structures, or more precisely, of the limited structures that appeared in a particular kind of activity. To use Meyer Fortes's words, the signing of the marriage contract, or the creation of a testament, or the baptismal ceremony in which godparents are named will be 'the particular occasions' in which social relations are 'wrapped up'. But by analysing any one kind of occasion we will not be able to tell whether the structures we identify in it were the only kin-based structures present in the entire community. The interaction documents are therefore one of the holes in the curtain which permit us to see something of the play but not all of it. In this, of course, they are no different from other kinds of sources, as will become clear presently.

Records of Vital Events: A German Example

We next come to a class of documents whose potential for maximal genealogical reconstruction has yet to be fully demonstrated, namely, records of vital events in parish registers. The starting-point in these is an individual or a small cluster, depending very much on the practices followed by the clergymen who kept these records. Thus an entry for a baptism, as we have seen, may contain the names of the newborn's father and mother and godparents, but in many places the clusters are smaller than this. The record of a marriage in a parish register will no doubt contain the name of the groom and the bride, but it may not always provide the names of the parents of the new couple. The record of a death or burial may in fact contain only one name. Whatever reconstruction can be achieved with records of this type, of course, will depend on the population history of the locality, and if there was no core population that persisted over time, the reconstruction effort will not get very far. Even when there is a core of persisting persons, the job is very difficult. Normally, the entire record pertaining to no larger a kin-based unit than a conjugal family will be scattered through a register over many pages covering as many as 60 or 70 years, and at no point during the existence of this family would we encounter it listed as a unit in the register. The accumulated experience with these records suggest that all the imaginable problems that can prevent successful linkages – departures of persons from the community, entry into the community of new people, discontinuities in the spelling of names, changes in names, and so forth – should be considered as inescapable (Wrigley, 1973).

There are two reasons why these sources, with all their problems, should be taken very seriously, however. The first is concerned with the variability of recording practices and the demographic histories of particular localities; it cannot be claimed at this time that all continuous records are poor nor that all communities always had so rapid a turnover as to render all facts about birth, death and marriage merely fragments.[4] The second reason is related to the immense advantage of having a record of a genealogical nature that shows, at the individual level, both the discontinuities and continuities in the population history of a particular region. A complex genealogical grid which extends in both space and time would be of undoubted utility for the study and understanding of lesser configurations, and would permit us to provide empirical content to such time-based generalizations about kinship as that 'kinship is a structure of long-duration' (Braudel, 1972: 18). Using the distinctions we have employed so far, such a record would be almost purely genealogical, and would provide much evidence that is analytically relevant, but not demonstrably socially relevant. But, at the same time, it would have embedded in it precisely the kinds of genealogical information which anthropological fieldworkers ask informants to recite, and it might also contain the internal histories of kinship groups spelt out in terms of the individuals which comprised them. Furthermore, because a maximal reconstruction of this sort would be based not on human memory but on thousands of events which were recorded as

4 Population turnover at the local level, as it affects the continuity in family lines, is as yet poorly understood for most of the European continent. To the pioneering studies of Clayworth and Cogenhoe by Peter Laslett (1977: 50–101) and of the French localities cited in the expanded form of the original 1963 version of this piece, there must now be added Robert Netting's work (1981) concerning a Swiss mountain village, where change over a long period of time still left within the population reconstructable 'patrilines' – a kind of core population – having an 'age of some 250 years' (see chapter 9 below).

they took place, it might also be more reliable than the individually recited genealogical information anthropoligical fieldworkers make use of.

Whether there exists a sufficiently large number of localities in which such an undertaking will yield usable results is still an open question. The yield in areas such as England, where rapid turnover of local populations has been a long-term demographic characteristic, is not promising. But on the continent of Europe the situation seems somewhat better; not only because of apparently greater continuity in local populations, but also because of the apparently greater importance assigned to genealogical information in popular culture. Thus in the Balkan region, the recitation of lines of descent has become something like an art form: 'the prosodic characteristics of the recitation (the south Slav epic decasyllable), in consonance with the socio-cultural values of the society in which it occurs, make possible the preservation and oral transmission of detailed and complicated genealogy in Serbian peasant society' (Halpern, 1977: 141). In some areas of Germany local historians–genealogists sometimes turned to the creation of community genealogies (*Ortssippenbücher*) which, as evaluated by contemporary demographers, demonstrate very clearly the potential of the ecclesiastical sources:

> An *Ortssippenbuch* is simply a collection of family histories of the residents of a given place (*Ort*). But unlike most genealogies which confine themselves to a single family tree, an *Ortssippenbuch* includes the ancestries of *every* family to have lived in the community so far as they can be reconstituted from the parish or community records. Although some published *Ortssippenbücher* come from the 1930s, when they were intended as aids to establishing the racial purity of individuals, most have been prepared after the [Second World] War, and serve merely to gratify the genealogical curiousity of the residents of obscure villages. . . . In order to let present-day residents trace back their ancestries, *Ortssippenbuch* compilers have linked together the churchbook entries of baptism, marriages, and burial for every couple in the village from whenever the churchbooks begin to the present, ordered these 'reconstituted' families alphabetically, and then published the results. The *Ortssippenbücher* are sold to local inhabitants, distributed to visitors by the communal administration on ceremonial occasions, and then ... forgotten. (Knodel and Shorter, 1977b: 115–16)

In genealogies prepared on the basis of human memory, the elements of suppression and forgetfulness always play a very large role. In the cases of genealogies which use a particular kind of presentation as a mnemonic device, the latter problem can be reduced somewhat. In the *Ortssippen-bücher*, however, we are confronted with genealogical documents of a very special kind: a set of genealogies with the constituent elements of each genealogy, and the elements of each set, linked lineally and laterally to each other over long periods of time; and, with the entire set of linkages established not on the basis of any individual's memory of them, but on the basis of the outward-pointing information contained in the written record of each small unit of this vast system. While the factors of suppression and misrepresentation are never absent entirely from such a record, the *Ortssippenbücher* appear to be the best example yet discovered of how successive entries of births, deaths and marriages in historical records can be converted not only into genealogical histories of individuals and families, but also of segments of entire communities.

It should be noted that with a genealogical record of such elaborateness, the question of the accuracy of particular links will never be solved in any ultimate way. The question is none the less important if we are to make use of such genealogical records for the purposes of historical kinship analysis. As I have noted before, in the fieldwork setting the genealogical information which is gathered can be verified in a number of ways: through comparison of the different genealogies presented by a number of related informants, through observation of activities pertaining to kinsfolk and, when they are available, through the use of actual records of births and marriages. For the genealogical records of people from the distant past, however, there are no readily available means of verification. The *Ortssippenbücher* have been evaluated as possible sources of demographic information and the con-clusion has been reached that 'in comparative terms the German parish registers on which the *Ortssippenbücher* rest are probably superior to the French, on which so much work has been done to date ... [and] that in absolute terms the standards of accuracy of these local genealogists meet the generally established standards of scientific research. Indeed the genealogists appear to have been conscientious in the extreme, and industrious beyond what most professional historical demographers can manage' (Knodel and Shorter, 1976: 152–3). Still, with the *Ortssippenbücher* we are dealing with records that magnify errors. In calculations of long-term fertility patterns, an error introduced into aggregated data by a missing link between a woman and *one* of her offspring is not likely to be very large. But in calculating the dimensions of the ego-centred kinship universes of these offspring, a missing sister would be of major significance not only because she herself would be excluded, but also, by extension, the person whom she married (an in-law of her siblings) and the offspring of that marriage (the nephews and nieces of the siblings) would also be excluded.

When a local genealogist sat down to prepare an *Ortssippenbuch,* he began by transferring on to separate cards each bit of information from the parish register. Very likely, each person had at least three separate cards: one for his birth, one for his marriage and one for his death. Each of these contained information (names of parents, etc.) that pointed to several other persons; each also contained the relevant dates, the location where the recorded event took place, information about the occupation of the persons or his parents, information on titles and offices, and so forth. All persons whose entry in the records was found had such cards prepared for them; but those whose residence in a particular community was short or those who were not members of the local congregations may not have made their way into the records. The *Ortssippenbücher* therefore are not listings of inhabitants, and there will always have been subpopulations which will not show up anywhere in them. An *Ortssippenbuch* compiled on this basis will resemble page after page the example to be found in document 2, which comes from the *Sippenbuch* of the city of Marburg in the German state of Hesse (Soliday, 1977). Here the links between individual families are implicit as well as explicit, that is, they are established through placing a particular individual and his family of marriage in a certain section containing all families that bore a particular surname, as well as by a system of numeration which links an individual's families of birth and marriage. The size of the Marburg *Sippenbuch* suggests the elaborateness of these genealogical enterprises: it consists of 24 volumes, each about 300 pages in length.

Occasionally these maximal reconstructions led not to the creation of an *Ortssippenbuch* but of *Stammtafeln,* lineage tables which were another way of presenting the information of an *Ortssippenbuch* (Imhof, 1977: 20–9). In form, these sources would be recognized immediately by fieldwork anthropologists, because they consisted of hundreds of genealogical symbols linked to each other on the basis of a recognizable principle, mostly that of partilineage. But they differ from the genealogies that fieldworkers would collect in that, instead of starting with a living Ego and working backward in time, they began with the first individual bearing a particular surname in the register and worked forward in time, linking the offspring of an individual to him, the children of the offspring to their parents, and so forth. The marriages of all male offspring and the offspring of those marriages would be shown on the same *Stammtafel*; the marriages of the female offspring would be keyed to the *Stammtafel* of her husband and the offspring reported in the husband's table. The *Stammtafel* therefore carried the reconstruction effort into what we have called maximal reconstruction, and thus presented to the analyst linked sets of entire partilineages in terms of their constituent members.

A set of documents of this sort enables the researcher immediately to

(R a u t e n h a u s, Johann Christoph, ref.)
weitere Kinder:
  5. Maria Christine, geb. 4.1.1820.
  6. Wigand, geb. 6.1.1823, gest. 9.9.1834.
  7. Heinrich, geb. 3.9.1825, gest. 25.7.1878.
  8. Peter Gottfried, geb. 1.4.1828, gest. 18.1.1860.

R a u t e n h a u s e n, Johann Martin, ref. Weißbinder, | Fam. Blatt Nr.
1839: erhält 2 R. 24 Alb. 11 Hlr. für Weißbinderarbeit | 25 333
  von der Stadt.
er heiratete in 2.Ehe 27.6.1819 Margarethe Arens | 25 337
S.d.Joh.Henr.R.u.d.Anna Cath.Ochlbaum, | 25 330
  geb. 4.5.1787, konf.1800, gest. 8.7.1838.
  verh.1. 7.7.1811 mit Maria Catharina Fittich, luth.
    geb. etwa 1779, gest. 17.3.1814, 35 J. bei der Geburt.
  Kinder: 1. Johann Heinrich, siehe: | 25 341
  2. Anna Katharina, geb. 12.3.1814, gest. 14.3.1814.

R a u t e n h a u s e n, Johann Wiegand, ref. Weißbinder- | Fam. Blatt Nr.
meister in Mbg. Aetzerbach 460. | 334
  S.d.Joh.Martin R.u.d.Anna Marg.Silber, | 25 329
  geb. 15.8.1786, konf.1800, gest. 10.1.1835,
  verh. 27.6.1813 mit Anna Catharina Schw, luth. T.d.Jo-
    seph Fried.Sch.u.d.Elis.Bodenbender; sie hatte 1840
    eine illeg.Verbdg. | 25 342
    geb. 17.5.1893, konf.1810.
  Kinder: 1. totgeb.Kind 6.9.1815.
  2. Christoph, geb. 7.1.1825.
  3. Joseph Friedrich, geb. 19.10.1826.

R a u t e n h a u s, Georg, ref. Weißbinder, Kugelgasse, | Fam. Blatt Nr.
die Frau erwarb 9.12.1817 Bürgerrecht. | 335
  er heiratete in 2.Ehe 1.10.1828 Marg.Dockendorf, | 25 338
  S.d.Martin R.u.d.Anna Marg.Silber, | 25 329
  geb. 13.11.1788, konf.1803, gest. 3.3.1831,
  verh.1. 11.4.1814 mit Philippine Sybille Dockendorf,
    katk katk kath. T.d.Andreas D.in Kreuznach u.d.Margarethe
    Closius, | 11794 a
    geb. etwa 1789(?)Kreuznach, gest. 5.12.1825, 36 J.

R a u t e n h a u s e n, Henrich, ref. Steindecker in | Fam. Blatt Nr.
Mbg. Zwischenhausen 459, | 336
  S.d.Chph.R.u.d.Marg.Elis.Heß, | 25 328
  geb. 12.11.1791, gest. 26.6.1836,
  verh. 6.8.1815 mit Eva Katharina Ammenhäuser, luth. T.d.
    Hafnermstr.Gg.A.u.d.Marie Elis.Rehn; sie hatte 1837
    eine illeg.Verbdg. | 3 45 | 25 339
    geb. 21.11.1796, konf.1810, gest. 28.8.1851 an "as-
    sersucht, Ketzerbach 427,
  Kinder: 1. Martha Elisabetha, geb. 29.1.1816, konf.1830,
    gest. 22.12.1881 ledig.
  2. Christine, geb. 21.3.1817, konf.1830, gest.26.9.71.
  3. Barbara Katharina, geb. 2.4.1319.
  4. Georg, siehe: | 25 343
  5. Sophie Magdalene Wilhelmine, geb. 7.2.1823, gest.
    25.11.1826.
  6. Peter, geb. 9.7.1825, gest. 23.6.1826.
  7. Johannes, geb. 8.4.1827, gest. 18.10.1876.
  8. Hermann, geb. 9.9.1829.
  9. Elisabeth, geb. 14.10.1831, gest. 9.12.1897.
  10. Benedikt, geb. 29.10.1834, gest. 1.3.1836.

Document 2 Page from the Marburg *Sippenbuch,* compiled by the genealogist Kurt Stahr (volume 16, p. 218). The numbers to the right of the vertical marginal line are identification numbers of the family on the left; those to the left are cross-references to the families of birth of spouses.
Source: Hessisches Staatsarchiv, Marburg

place a given individual (or a group) into a genealogical context which extends both spatially and chronologically. Consider, for example, the *Stammtafel* collection from the Schwalm area in the German state of Hesse, where parish registers involving the population of eleven villages have yielded some 800 interlinked lineage tables, some extending from the mid-sixteenth century into the mid-twentieth century. In table 1 I have presented the results of one kind of analysis of these records, stressing their use as genealogical contexts.[5] Quite arbitrarily, I chose to look at the lineage contexts of all the 30 children shown to have been born in the village of Merzhausen in the year 1858. The lineages into which the genealogists had linked these 30 newborns were all of more than passing interest to any structural study of this village, since the numbers of local births over time in these lineages ranged from a minimum of 32 to a maximum of 432. Considered as time-based contexts, these lineages had been supplying children to the Schwalm area for an average of 238 years and to the village of Merzhausen for an average of 161 years. Considered as spatial contexts in the year 1858, most of these Merzhausen 'lineages' were in fact 'lineage segments', because nearly all of them strongly represented in the other villages of the area. This exercise, of course, did not provide a complete record of all the lineages that had ever been represented in Merzhausen, nor did members of these 20 lineages in Merzhausen account for the entire 1858 population. But the available ecclesiastical record, reconstructed maximally, does suggest that beyond the conjugal family, the household and the descent groups identifiable in the year 1858, there existed time-based configurations which also have to be evaluated as structural contexts in the lives of these children.

I have said that these records have to be evaluated because, to repeat, the genealogical record is not a kinship record. Naturally, because the raw data for these maximal reconstructions come from a bounded set of localities, we cannot dismiss the reconstructions as saying nothing at all about kinship in the area. We might take this negative attitude toward genealogical reconstructions which have no locational specificity, in which, that is, each individual is entered regardless of where he or she was born, married or died, or in which the only link between individuals is the human memory. But in the Schwalm case – and other similar cases – the reconstruction has elements of serendipity in it, in so far as the genealogists could not predict

---

5 This analysis is part of a larger project on the Schwalm *Stammtafeln* currently being conducted by the author with support from the US National Science Foundation Grant BNS 7925704. The *Stammtafeln* from the Schwalm area have been shown to be a valuable source for family demography by the work of Arthur Imhof (Imhof, 1977); viewed from a different vantage point, however, they are expected to be as valuable for the study of long-term kinship patterns in this locality.

Table 1 Lineage context at birth, Merzhausen (for the 30 persons born in 1858)

Lineage number	Lineage name	A Merzhausen births in 1858	B Total births in entire lineage	C First birth in Schwalm	D Latest birth in Schwalm	E Years of lineage in Schwalm	F First birth in Merzhausen	G Latest birth in Merzhausen	H Years of lineage in Merzhausen	I Years of lineage in Merzhausen by 1858	J Location of major lineage segments
60	Heimbacher	3	117	1612	1903	291	1787	1870	83	71	Merzhausen, Hauptschwenda, Willingshausen
90	Dorr	1	206	1605	1911	306	1656	1902	246	202	Merzhausen, Holzburg, Wasenberg, Willingshausen
143	Heimbacher	1	47	1773	1894	121	1773	1894	121	85	Merzhausen
187	Jackel	1	123	1596	1912	316	1641	1912	271	217	Merzhausen
192	Jahn	1	32	1791	1907	116	1791	1907	116	67	Merzhausen
198	Gimpel	3	229	1574	1909	335	1764	1874	110	94	Merzhausen, Loshausen, Wasenberg, Zella
200	George	1	149	1613	1908	295	1815	1891	76	43	Merzhausen, Christerode, Loshausen, Wasenberg
225	Grob	1	180	1591	1904	313	1730	1904	174	128	Merzhausen, Wasenberg
229	Grein	3	379	1616	1913	297	1675	1913	238	183	Merzhausen, Wasenberg, Holzburg
255	Keller	3	146	1729	1901	172	1757	1897	140	101	Merzhausen, Wasenberg
263	Hooss	1	144	1694	1906	212	1694	1906	212	164	Merzhausen, Holzburg
280	Knauff	2	432	1575	1908	333	1815	1904	89	43	Merzhausen, Loshausen, Wasenberg, Zella
282	Lanz	1	58	1680	1897	217	1680	1897	217	178	Merzhausen
284	Lorenz	1	215	1637	1888	251	1660	1888	228	198	Merzhausen, Loshausen, Zella
295	Lipphart	2	46	1747	1905	158	1747	1905	158	111	Merzhausen
355	Sprinz	1	101	1729	1906	177	1845	1900	55	13	Merzhausen, Wasenberg
356	Peter	1	162	1716	1912	196	1743	1904	161	115	Merzhausen, Wasenberg
398	Reitz	1	139	1664	1916	252	1664	1916	252	194	Merzhausen
405	Spanknebel	1	62	1650	1917	267	1728	1917	189	130	Merzhausen
536	Will	1	65	1766	1893	127	1819	1893	74	39	Merzhausen, Zella
Means		—	152	—	—	238	—	—	161	119	—

what the outcome of it would be. As it turned out, one set of sources, in which each entry was separated from the rest but contained within itself usable linking information, yielded a record of at least the personnel of certain kinds of kinship groups – patrilineages extending in time – and, by implication, the personnel of all other groups which are embedded in such a record. It is therefore evidence that is analytically very relevant. The social relevance of these purported kin-based groups as well as of any subpopulation which we might choose to use as a context for analysing individual lives remains to be demonstrated in a more convicing way. In the case of these genealogical reconstructions, we do not have, in the same record, even the assistance of the single-year residential census, so as to provide some assurance that the demonstrated links were ties of kinship. If we use these data for more than information about conjugal family units – in reconstructing which we could have recourse to the relational terminology of such units (husband, wife, son, daughter, 'married', etc.) – we must either make so many assumptions about linkages as to make the entire interpretation lack credibility, or establish the minimal set of assumptions that will permit the questionable links to be used.

I have to this point discussed reconstructions as if in a particular historical area no more than a single type of historical source were available at any point in the past. This is actually not an unhelpful assumption to make, because experience has shown that that could very well be the case more often than not. This situation is the root, of course, of many of the problems of historical writing in general, and there is no reason to believe that a historical account of social structure will ever be exempt from it. Yet it will have occurred to the reader that the value of each type of historical record would be enhanced were it possible somehow to link them. What happens to genealogical evidence when record linkage is attempted must therefore be examined next.

3

Record Linkage and Domain Linkage

Record Linkage

Research using historical population sources has shown that totally different sets of data from the same historical community can at times be linked
to each other by matching the names of individuals in them. This is really
the historian's counterpart of the anthropologist's interviews with living
informants, which have the goal of eliciting from each informant as great an
amount of information as possible about involvements in as many different
aspects of community life as possible. The notable difference between these
two methods is that for the anthropologist a set of responses by one
individual are already a package, so to speak, by virtue of their origin;
moreover, the interviewer can always expand lines of questioning at will,
and inquire about matters which may not have seemed important initially.
By contrast, the historian must make do with only those social involvements
about which documentation has survived; and, as far as linkage is concerned, with an informed decision, rather than unambiguous proof, that
various proper names in the different record sets that *seem* to be referring to
the same individual do so *in fact*. This decision has to be surrounded by all
manner of safeguards and frequently has to be made on the basis of internal
evidence that is just a shade more than circumstantial (Pouyez et al., 1983).
But if such linking of sources becomes possible for a sufficiently large
number of persons, then the variety of questions that can be asked about
individuals and the population which they comprise is increased immensely.
Then the researcher is able to pursue a strategy of 'individual reconstitution'
(Macfarlane, 1977a: 37), in which group membership can become a
variable in the study of individual lives. Attempts at record linkage have
been carried out for a substantial number of small historical populations;
each individual effort seeks to link somewhat different documents and has
to solve somewhat different problems. It is difficult to exaggerate the
recalcitrance of historical data in these ventures, and consequently the
number of studies based on a total linkage of all documents available and
intended for linkage operation is at the moment relatively small. Because of

the problems, the number of completed studies is unlikely ever to be very large, but their completion is bound to throw instructive light on localities widely dispersed throughout the European continent in space and time. A list of these localities would have to include Earls Colne, Kirkby Lonsdale and Terling in England (Macfarlane, 1977a and 1977b; Wrightson and Levine, 1979), the village of Orašac in Serbia (Halpern and Halpern 1972), the village of Neckarshausen in Germany (Sabean, 1976a and 1976b) and the Gagarin family estates in nineteenth-century Russia (Czap, 1978, 1982 and 1983).

It is important to recognize, however, that record linkage can be practised successfully entirely within a particular structural sector, or domain, as we have been referring to these subsections of the social system. The point is that not all successful record linkage is domain linkage, when the latter is understood to require the appearance, in sources that document one domain, of the same people that appear in sources that document another. We are here interested of course in the problems of domain linkage when one of the elements to be linked to others is the kinship domain, and from this viewpoint the outcome of linkage is not as predictable as one would like. It is conceivable, for example, that all members of an entire population may appear in a number of different fiscal documents, each of which concerns the collection of a different kind of tax, and in this case linkage of documents would operate only within the domain of economic relationships. It could also happen that these same people show up in marriage contracts, and thus information about their economic position could be complemented by whatever genealogical information the marriage contracts could provide. Experience has shown, however, that while in traditional European communities there may be a core population which appears and reappears in all manner of documented activities, this core is likely to be relatively small and that most people will simply not be examinable in more than a single domain at a time, or at best, in one well-documented domain and one or several subsections of a different domain. Thus, for example, a series of household censuses could enable the researcher to follow a collection of individuals over time, and fully document the changes in household status they experience. These changes may even involve relational terminology of the kinship type, so that a male might appear as 'son of head' in one census, 'head' in the next and 'father of head' in yet another. The inquiry in this case will have linked documents separated by varying lengths of historical time and will have gained from the study of changes of household structure information about the operation of kinship ties within the household. But kin ties among the people in particular households even over time were only a *subsection* of the kinship domain of the community, if this is understood to include kinship configurations linking members of different households. At no point would the link between the domain of household arrangements and the domain of kinship be complete, because the sources would not have permitted the linkage of household members to anyone in the community other than their co-residents.

The problem is one of equity of evidence. The source may permit the placing of all individuals of a historical community in, for example, one or another economic category by reference to taxes paid, size of land owned, household status such as 'head' and 'servant', or various occupational categories. The use of evidence of this kind, from a number of different sources, could well provide a very thorough understanding of how economic factors created structure in a community's population. To be fair to the complexity of past communities, however, we should be enabled, by evidence of other kinds, to explore as readily the working of social factors such as descent and marriage (kinship) in the same collectivity which has been reviewed from the economic standpoint. We should be enabled, that is, to reconstruct, individual by individual, the configurations that existed as a result of the working of marriage and descent, and to examine an individual in a location in the economic structure (hierarchy) and in kinship structures simultaneously. What the sources should enable us to do, in particular, is to overcome the situation in which internal arrangements of one domain (in this case, the economic), as worked out by the researcher, permit the positioning in them of all members of a population, while the positioning of these same members in another domain is made impossible or is restricted by the pre-selected relational terminology of the record-keeper. In such a case, the record-keeper will have been given too much of a voice in pointing to the 'analytically discriminable elements' of the kinship domain. Ideally, each of several linked domains should have a 'map' of its own which, as far as the kinship domain is concerned, would consist of a maximal genealogical reconstruction from which we could 'read' not only the relatives who are directly related to a given individual, but also the connections among these relatives that were independent of their connection to the individual in question. Since, by definition, the evidence cannot include interviews, the only way we can work toward a precise identification of such configurations in the kinship domain is to exploit the genealogical evidence at hand, in the expectation that this evidence, at the very least, will provide us with usable materials for reaching conclusions about kinship ties.

Pre-reconstruction Domain Linkage: An East European Example

The contrast between the desirable and the achievable in domain linkage is, however, considerable. The best way to illustrate what could be done in a nearly ideal situation is to use as an example a historical document – the Baltic household census mentioned in chapter 1 – in which there is what

Document 3 Revision list of one farmstead on the Pinkenhof estate, Livland, 1850
Source: J. G. Herder Institut, Marburg

	Revision List			
	for 9 September, 1850, of Pinkenhof, a patrimonial estate of the city of Riga, located in the province of Livland and in the Riga district			
Family No.	Male Gender	Present at or added since	Removed from last revision	Current list
	Male peasants	Age		Age
	XVI *Farmstead of Remmes Jann*			
53	Jann, Jann's son, Remmes	43	Died 1850	
	Jann Remmes' sons: 1. Jann	17	Died 1848	
	2. Andres	13	In no.XXI[1]	
	3. Jurr	10	In no.VI	
	4. Mikkel	6	To recruits 1849	
	5. Jacob	½	In no.XV	
	his brother Mikkel Remmes	30		46½
	Mikkel Remmes' son Mahrtin	newborn		10½
47	Andres, Indrik's son, Blodneck	30	In no.III	
55	Jann, Indrik's son, Perkohn, *Wirth*[2]	From no.XIX		31½
	Jann Perkohn's son Jann	newborn		9
	his brother Andres Perkohn	From no. CXIV		25¼
161	the *Wirthin's* brothers:[3]			
	1. Jacob	From no.CXIII		16¾
	2. Jann Jacob's sons, Kagge	newborn		11⁷/₁₂
25	Peter, Peter's son, Wiesmann	newborn		13¹¹/₁₂
60	Andres, Jann's son, Kaupe	From no.VII		55¾
53	Indrik, Jann's son, Remmes	See list B[4]		
	Indrik Remmes sons:			
	Georg Gottfried			14⁷/₁₂
	Peter Georg Philipp	newborn		12¾
	Johann Christian			19¹¹/₁₂

[1] He is now living in farmstead no. XXI of the Pinkenhof estate.
[2] Head of farmstead.
[3] The brothers of the head's wife (*Wirthin*).
[4] List B is a separate list of estate residents who were exempted from the head tax.

(Translated version of Document 3)

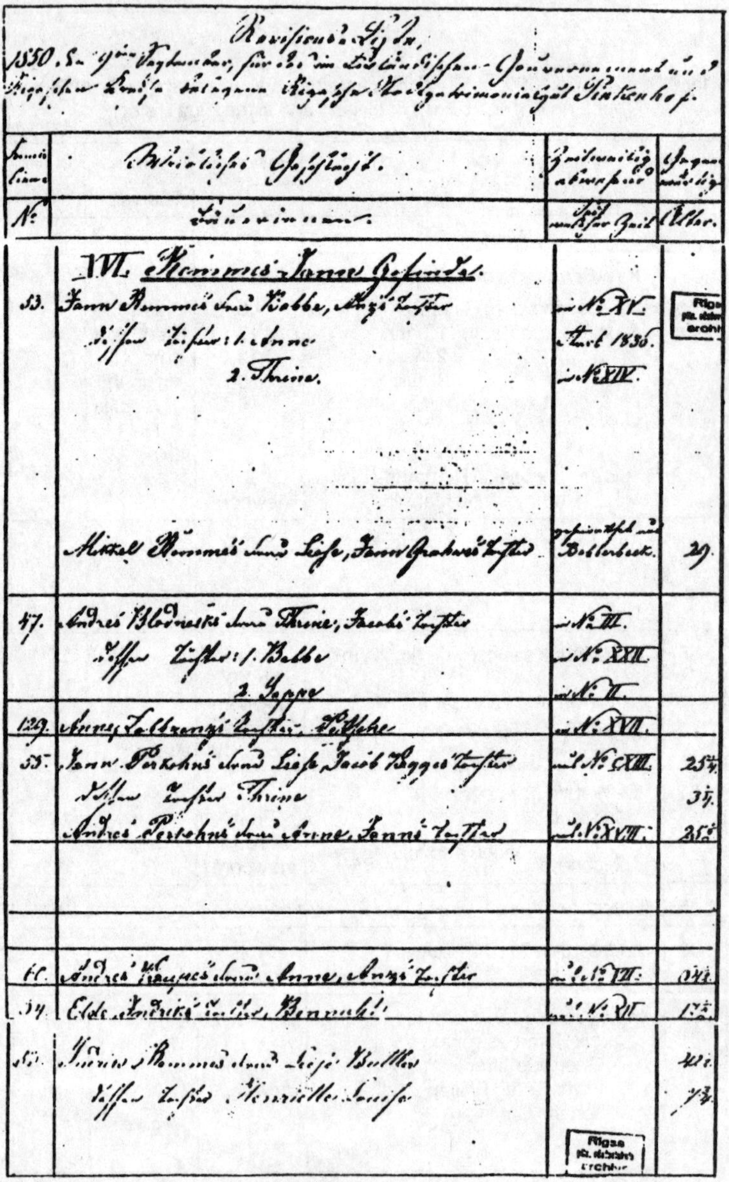

Document 3 continued

Revision List for 9 September, 1850, of Pinkenhof, a patrimonial estate of the city of Riga, located in the province of Livland and in the Riga district			
Family No.	Female gender	Origin or present location	Current
	Female peasants		Age
	XVI *Farmstead of Remmes Jann*		
53	Jann Remmes' wife, Babbe, Anz's daughter his daughters: 1. Anne 2. Thriene	In no.XV Died 1835 In no.XIV	
	Mikkel Remmes' wife Liese, Jann Grahwe's daughter	married in from Bebberbeck[5]	29
47	Andres Blodeck's wife Thrine, Jacob's daughter his daughters: 1. Babbe 2. Sappe	In no.III In no.XXII In no.II	
129	Jann Perkohn's wife Liese, Jacob Kagge's daughter his daughter, Thrine Andres Perkohn's wife Anne, Jann's daughter	From no.CXIII[6] From No.XVIII	25¼ 3¼ 25½
60	Andres Kaupe's wife Anne, Anz's daughter	From no.VII	64½
64	Edde, Intrik's daughter, Bennusch	From no.XII	17½
53	Indrik Remmes' wife Liese Buttler his daughter Henriette Louise		42½ 7¼

[5] Another estate in the patrimonial properties of the city of Riga.
[6] She was listed in no. CXIII in the last revision.

(*Translated version of Document 3* continued)

might be called 'pre-reconstruction domain linkage'. That is, in this source, in each individual entry the record-keeper introduced the sort of information – including genealogical facts – that normally would become available, for the mentioned individuals, only if and when the internal relationships in other documented domains were worked out and the data then linked back to the 'normal' census. To my knowledge, there are relatively few documents of this sort that have been recovered from the European past, and the one we will look at closely is something of a rarity even in the historical records of the area from which it comes.

This source is especially useful for our present purposes, because each of the many hundreds of individuals mentioned in it is recorded as if the enumerator, in making each entry, had tapped five distinct bodies of structuring information. As can be seen in document 3, which is a transcribed sample page from the 1850 census in the Pinkenhof estate, these bodies of information contain data about (a) age, (b) the conjugal family unit, (c) the co-residential unit, (d) a more inclusive kin-based group designated as a *Familie* and identified by a *Familiennummer* in the first column and (e) geographical mobility since the last census. Genealogical information about women is enhanced by the addition to their names of their fathers' names, and of information showing from which co-residential group the woman in question has come. Thus, for example, the wife of the head (at mid-page) – Jann Perkohn's wife Liese – is here listed as a 'member' of *Familie* no. 55, her husband's group; but she can also be analysed in her former position as the daughter of Jacob Kagge, who was still alive in farmstead no. CXIII and a member of *Familie* no. 161. For Liese, therefore, there is information about her structural relationships resulting from both marriage and descent. What the enumerator has accomplished in instance after instance is the kind of linkage of domains that in normal research would require the linking of entirely separate historical records. The basic purpose of the census was to create an inventory of the people who in each community's population were subject to the head tax; but the process of creating such an inventory had always involved, and involved as well in 1850, the preparation of a 'household' list of the entire estate population. In the Pinkenhof estate, however, for reasons that are not at all clear, the complete list was such that a later researcher who wanted to have an identical listing for another estate would have had to turn to residential information, parish registers and migration records to compile it.

In the Pinkenhof census we are dealing with a genealogically enhanced version of the now-familiar 'listing of inhabitants' which, in its 'normal' variants, has already introduced into discussions of historical kinship more empirical content than most other kinds of sources (Laslett and Wall, 1972). It is only residential listings that in the pre-modern period of European history have provided information about some of the kinship ties of all members of village communities, thus permitting the start of more complete domain linkage. In later periods, after the introduction of modern censuses, the original forms on which genealogical information appeared were often destroyed after aggregated figures of various kinds were abstracted from them, and the aggregate figures seldom preserved the original information about all genealogical links at the individual level. Though this situation varied from country to country, it is generally true that the residential censuses from pre-modern times are more immediately useful for the purposes we have in mind, even though they always present the problem of representativeness.

The common form of pre-modern residential censuses places them in the category of interaction documents, even though the genealogical configurations they contain may represent the results of a collection of activities and decisions rather than a single activity such as the signing of a marriage contract. Thus a married couple decided where to live, the people living with them may have entered the household over a period of time after the marriage, and some of these co-residents may have departed shortly after the enumeration was made. None the less, at the moment of past time when the names of the people living together were transferred to a listing, the genealogical ties among them were in all probability important to the enumerator and to the actors themselves. In fact, in an analysis of such groups we can assume that all connections were in one way or another socially significant, because co-residing individuals who were not genealogically linked to the head were in all likelihood linked to him or her through the use of some socio-economic category such as 'servant' or 'lodger'.

The normal residential censuses were also like interaction documents in that genealogical reconstruction in them cannot be carried very far. Even when the information that is present is precise, the units are still self-enclosed and inward-pointing, with the relational terminology referring almost always to the head of the group and never to the links that the inhabitants may have had to people living elsewhere. None the less, residential censuses tend to be more informative than other sources because they were far more likely to contain information on all the people within a recognized population unit such as a village, and thus to provide a sounder basis for generalizations. If a testament, for example, always leaves open the question of representativeness, a listing of a single household's members in a list of all households in a community can be easily evaluated in this respect. If the record-keeper has then decided to enhance the list somewhat by the addition of more genealogical information than it would normally contain, as in the Baltic example, then there is a very good chance of linking structural domains over the entire data set, for individuals as well as for the entire community. Rather than having to work with a select few individuals and having to solve all the problems of name-matching entailed by entirely different documents, we can investigate every individual as a participant of action-sets of various kinds and as an occupant of positions in inclusive genealogical configurations. This is the ideal of domain linkage; but, in the absence of a successful example of how such a linkage would affect all members of a community, we must investigate these consequences in a document in which the linkage has been accomplished by the enumerator before any further manipulation of the data has been begun by an analyst.

The Transformatory Consequences of Domain Linkage

When domain linkage is possible for an entire community, and when one of the linked domains involves genealogical data, the consequences for reconstruction are major. In each instance of an individual or group, reconstruction must now proceed with the expectation that the connections the source identifies directly may not have been the only ones defining the structural position of whatever unit of analysis is chosen. Thus whatever unit is looked at in the non-genealogical sector of the data is immediately referenced to a network of connections in the genealogical sector, with the consequence being that the internal organization of the entire collection of information is transformed. The genealogical information reveals the existence of connections between individuals and groups which heretofore were not visible, making it imperative that the heretofore visible connections be re-evaluated in the light of the discovered ones. The form which this evidence now assumes is shown in figure 4, in which, as in figures 2 and 3, the form is depicted without regard to any concrete content. The circles and solid and dotted lines in the figure stand for the individuals and connections between them that would obtain if these individuals were being tracked down in vital-events sources; in the present example, the individuals and connections would have been abstracted from a single-year list and therefore they would have much less depth in time than if a vital-events source were used. Still, they are connections of the same genealogical type and, unlike in a vital-events source, in the example we are using we do have information (from another domain) to enable us to draw boundaries around some clusters of linked people, from the co-residential information in the Baltic list.

Although the boundaries drawn around some clusters of symbols in the figure would represent, in this example, the co-residence of those individuals, generally speaking, they could stand for any other documented group identified in an interaction source, or for that matter, a mixture of several types of groups, if the community had been documented thoroughly enough

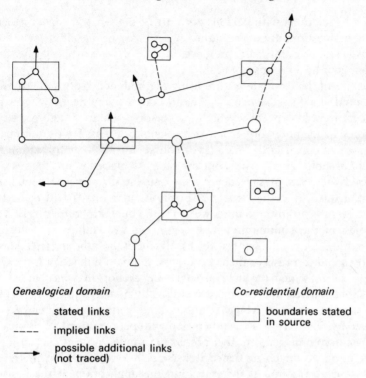

Genealogical domain

——— stated links

- - - - implied links

——▶ possible additional links
(not traced)

Co-residential domain

☐ boundaries stated
in source

Figure 4 Domain linkage

to provide us with interaction data from several different domains of social experience, to be superimposed upon the reconstructed genealogical grid. Thus all of the bounded sets could be of the same kind, including, for example, all the persons mentioned in each of a collection of marriage contracts. Or they could be a mixture, in the sense that some sets could be of co-residence, some of marriage contracts and some of people who assisted each other in court cases. The importance of the genealogical reconstruction and the new light it throws on the interactions of the people in each bounded set would of course have to come from an understanding of the general significance of particular types of activities. But whatever importance we attribute to an activity, we could now interpret it in a way that would not be possible if all we had was information about the ties within each bounded set. The contact the persons involved in each bounded activity have with a network of genealogical ties standing behind, so to speak, all activities, means that it is possible to release the persons within each bounded set from having to be considered only with respect to their relation to the most important person of that set and to examine them with

respect to relations with persons not part of the set. It means, further, the
raising of questions about the nature of kin-based groups, if the genealogical
reconstruction reveals the presence, in the community, of the correct
personnel of such groups.

Because in the example we are using the bounded groups are in fact co-
residential units (or households), we can examine very clearly what happens
to the household concept when all the persons who are heretofore examinable only as members of particular households are assigned positions on a
larger genealogical grid. There is, of course, no loss of information about
their household membership. But the file now places before the researcher
hundreds of cases of self-enclosed co-residential units and demonstrates
simultaneously that the structural positions individuals had by virtue of
their membership in these units were not the only structural positions they
occupied in the community. In a sense, the availability of genealogical
information allows the analyst to dissolve household boundaries for some
purposes and to preserve them for others. Domain linkage in this example
permits us to widen the field of social interaction in which members of
households moved and to begin to track down, as the first step in further
analysis, the ways in which relations among household members were
affected by relations these members had with people outside the household.
This is accomplished, in the present example, not by declaring that
information about co-residence is useless, but by engaging in the same
process of abstraction that lies behind the application of the household
concept to a group of names in a historical source. The relational terminology which heretofore was put to use to understand the structure and infer
the inner workings of a bounded group is now examined for its total
implications.

In linking domains in the example we are using, therefore, there is in
reality no radical break with the intellectual processes that operate in the
realm of household analysis. For clustered names in a population list to be
changed into an analysable entity, the cluster has to be conceptualized in a
particular manner. Without the concept of the household, all we have is a
group of names: with it, the cluster becomes a social group with a corporate
character; a specific identifiable structure; phases of formation, expansion
and dissolution; and functions within the community of which it was a part.
By making use of the household concept, we place the group of names into a
frame of reference which has already been created by analysis of similar
groups elsewhere and assume that our group is in some ways comparable to
others. Henceforth, we no longer think of the cluster as providing empirical
information only about the individuals involved in it, but also as embodying
significant information about a certain kind of group life in the area. It
needs to be underlined that this intellectual operation is not a self-evident

step. For years, such listings were not made use of at all by social historians of European society; or they were used only for information they contained about individuals, particularly if the individuals could be assigned to one or another inclusive socio-economic 'class' by use of evidence about their standing in the community. The introduction of the 'household' concept constituted a revision, in that it implied that structural involvement in 'households' by individuals and the attributes of 'households' themselves were potentially as important data about social structure as the membership of the same individuals in broad inclusive classes or social orders. The use of the concept also linked the analysis performed on these historical groups to certain concerns which anthropologists had had about domestic groups in the communities they worked with, namely, the 'developmental cycle' of the group, which brought into focus variations of the same household in the course of time; and also 'rules of residence', which are used as clues about overall kinship preferences (Goodenough, 1956; Berkner, 1972; Goody, 1958).

By linking domains in the Baltic source we do not supply the co-residents of households with new identities, of course. An individual remains 'wife of head' or 'brother of head', regardless of how many other links we can identify that individual as having had beyond the household. By following the genealogical clues offered by the source, however, we do bring into the analysis the fact that individuals who were related to the household head (and thus to each other) were also related to people who were not directly identified as relatives by the source. We therefore suplement the 'social personality' of the people at the starting-point and obligate further analysis to take into consideration the fact that while an individual was a 'brother', he may have also been a 'brother-in-law' and a 'husband'. By linking the domain of household relationships to a larger kinship domain, we have, as it were, dissolved the residential group boundaries and identified a larger number of potential connections with people beyond the boundaries. The fact that in the Baltic source it is household boundaries that are dissolved is immaterial to the issue at stake: the same dissolution would take place if we were to place any other set of interaction groups on to a genealogical grid. One thing that has to be remembered, though, is that in this initial phase of the procedure we cannot simply shift into the language of kinship, because it is not at all clear that this new, more inclusive context contains nothing but kin. But we can assume that it does contain most, if not all, of the persons an individual will have recognized as kin. The sorting procedure, in other words, requires several additional steps.

Whether domain linkage is accomplished within the same sources, as in our Baltic example, or by means of linking several sources such as an interactional document and a vital-events source, one consequence stands

out clearly: the analyst henceforth must be concerned with many configurations which are not those that stand out in the historical record. Those
which do stand out are not, of course, abandoned or put aside in any sense,
because in them one obtains crucial information about demographic
patterns, residence patterns and such matters as inheritance practices and
social support systems (such as godparenthood). These are all important
matters and they enter whatever final description of kinship the researcher is
seeking to achieve. But the path to an understanding of their importance
now includes accounting for relations of more people than are directly
involved in any of these lesser configurations, until the analyst is prepared to
conclude that they are not affected by ties to persons who are not directly
involved in them. In order to come to such a conclusion it is not sufficient to
be guided simply by the choice made by the record-keeper to highlight one
or another lesser group, or by the fact that a particular source makes a lesser
group easier to reconstruct than a more inclusive group. Nor is it sufficient
to continue to focus on the lesser group and to pull from the total set of
genealogically related persons several individuals who are then examined as
interesting appendages to the identifiable lesser group. All of these procedures continue to permit the original source to set the terms of the
discussion, and therefore go a long way toward foreclosing possible lines of
investigation. If the sources have permitted us to reconstruct very inclusive
genealogical contexts – by positioning as many people as we can and as
accurately as we can in relation to each other – then the subsequent analyses
have to pursue the meaning of these lines of connectedness, even while
recognizing the obligation to conclude that these lines may not be kinship
ties at all. The alternative approach – the analysis of only those configurations which stand out in the sources, with a few limited additional ties
examined as interesting side issues – means having to make very early on the
decision that demonstrable genealogical connections have no social significance, which decision, in the context of historical Europe, would have to be
made on the basis of very scanty evidence indeed.

Assembling and Disassembling Genealogical Configurations

Having complete genealogical information about every person in a historical community is, of course, an ideal which is unlikely ever to be realized on
the basis of historical sources. Even documents as promising as the Baltic
listings will yield reconstructions that fall short for a host of reasons,
including, in this case, the relative shallowness of genealogical information
characteristic of single-year censuses. None the less, the question of where
domain linkage should proceed beyond the initial reconstructions is important, and therefore an exploration of the range of possibilities and problems

has to be made. We can start this exploration by looking at what happens in the analysis of the most obvious units of the record – the individual, the co-residential group, the community as a whole – about which generalizations would need to be made even if the Baltic source were not genealogically enhanced. In the centre square of figure 5c we have extracted one household (farmstead) from the previously used 1850 census of Pinkenhof, and reviewed the individuals in it in the light of the full complement of information which the 1850 enumerator provided. The listing from which this residential group was taken had all the characteristics of a 'normal' household list: a cluster of names separated clearly from other clusters, each designated as a co-residential unit in the community; all persons identified with respect to age and sex; one person in each group designated as the head of that group and all others described with various relational terms. According to the most prominent system of structural classification now in use with material of this type, the dominant family in the farmstead we have chosen to look at – the Remmes farmstead (no. 16) – can be classified as a multiple-family household with one married and one unmarried 'servant'. By noting the structural attributes of this group and by comparing it with others we can develop a series of generalizations about household structure in this community, the developmental cycle of households, generational composition, and so forth. In the course of these analyses we would make use of the relational terminology to distinguish the family of the head from those of his co-resident relatives, and these in turn from the families of farmhands.

As long as Remmes farmstead is thought of as a household or co-residential domestic group, we can be assured that all of the relationships we use in the analysis were socially relevant. The persons listed for 1850 lived together; the enumerator, as it were, drew a boundary around them to separate them from other groups; and even if we know nothing at all concretely about the existence of these people before and after the listing, and the rural economy of the region, we do know that for a time these people, who were connected, had something to do with each other. Households in a single-year list can be classified in terms of degrees of complexity, and a comparison can be made of the changing proportions of households in such categories in a succession of lists from the same locality over a period of time. Assuming that the procedures used to create the listings in each year remained roughly the same, this strategy provides concrete evidence concerning changes in structural contexts in which individuals lived. Another way of introducing the element of time employs a single-year list as cross-sectional data for a given year, and cross-tabulates households of different structure with the ages of the household head. This is a type of simulation procedure, in which it is assumed that the structure of

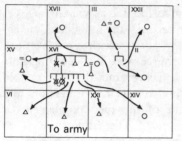

a   Movement out of Remmes farmstead, 1833–50

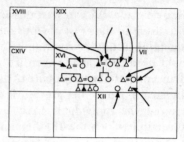

b   Movement into Remmes farmstead, 1833–50

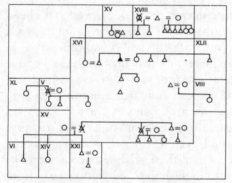

c   Residents of Remmes farmstead and their relatives in other farmsteads, 1850

▲   head of household

△   male

○   female

✖   deceased male

⊗   deceased female

Figure 5   Remmes farmstead (no. XVI), Pinkenhof estate, 1833–50

the 'youngest' households in due course will be that which is reflected in the 'oldest' ones, and vice versa. In both of these procedures, the focus of analysis can be on households as such, or on households as contexts; in the latter case, the statistic aimed for would be the changing proportion of individuals living in households of different structures. A third approach relies on specific individuals, and consists of the identification of their presence in or departure from several successive listings. What one obtains in this case is a precise account of the 'turnover' of the population of localities, in terms of individual lives as well as in terms of how individuals affected particular households, that is, rendering them simple in structure by leaving, or more complex by arriving, or forming new structures entirely. In all of these strategies, the 'household' is taken as the universe of analysis and structural change is described in its terms. These methods of handling listings have now become standard and they will continue to be employed in the areas where listing evidence will surface.

It is more than clear, however, that if the Pinkenhof list were thought about only in terms of delineated co-residential groups, we would neglect much of the evidence that is present. The fact is that the household concept, however useful for analysing the core information, does not permit us to use all of the information in this list. First, all males and females in the list were identified with a 'family number' and the names of many persons, married or unmarried, involved patronymics. Furthermore, the revision format required that the listing of a particular year contain information present in the previous census, so that the cluster of names in Remmes farmstead in 1850 included not only those living there in 1850, but also persons *who had been there* in the last revision, which was carried out in 1833. The entries for persons present in 1833 and not in 1850 carried a notation about where they had gone; those present in 1850 and not in 1833 were annotated as to their origins. Second, many names appeared in the revision twice: first in their original residence in 1833 and then in their 1850 residence, if they had moved. All of this additional evidence is outward-pointing, that is, it suggests that if we enlarge the field of social interaction we would be able to incorporate in the analysis all the information provided by the censuses, rather than only that extracted with the help of the household concept. In other words, the evidence forces us to consider seriously, on a community-wide basis, the same genealogical relationships we have been using to determine the structure of the Remmes group, so that we can locate the individuals who were connected to the Remmes residents, and produce from both sets of individuals a much larger configuration than is presented in the Remmes farmstead.

We can do this in a number of different but complementary ways by following each indicated outward-pointing tie and by using the information about movement which the format of the document presents. Thus, the 1850 list includes the names of people who were residents of the farmstead both in 1850 and in 1833, the year of the preceding revision. We do not know the exact structure of the farmstead in 1833, but during the next 17 years, judging by the given evidence, the structure underwent changes because of the movement of persons in and out of the farmstead (see figures 5a and 5b). The main family of the farmstead lost the headship through the death of the father, and the wife and children left to take up residence in other farmsteads (figure 5a). Their movements did not, however, carry them beyond the boundaries of the estate, and as a consequence structural analysis of the 1850 population would require that these ties be taken seriously as regards those members of the old head's family who remained in the farmstead from 1833. In those same 17 years other people moved in, including the new head and his family (figure 5b). These people, in turn, left relatives behind in the farmsteads from which they moved, so that in 1850 they also had in the estate kinsfolk who were not co-resident with them. In the *1850* listing, therefore, the people who were actually co-residents in that year had genealogical connections not only within the farmstead but also elsewhere in the estate (figure 5c). These ties can be identified by following the movement of persons on the basis of names and also by using the 'family' numbers provided by the enumerators. In 1850, the farmstead would still be classified as a complex family farmstead, and its population size would not have changed much since 1833. But, in 1850, the analyst is also in possession of very concrete data about several dozens of people in other farmsteads who were linked to the persons in the Remmes farmstead through a variety of ties. As a residential unit, the Remmes farmstead in 1850 was connected in this way to ten other farmsteads in the estate; as individuals, the 1850 Remmes residents were implicated not only in the cluster of persons co-resident with them, but also tied to clusters and individuals elsewhere. A complete record of the structural involvement of the 1850 Remmes residents would have to include an account of what it meant for them to be in co-residence with some of their relatives, but also – this being the point at which the argument is aiming – what it meant for them to be sons and daughters, aunts and uncles, nephews and nieces, parents and in-laws to persons residing elsewhere. If these ties are con-- sidered significant within the household, and are used for determining the structure of the co-residential group, then they also have to be considered important, in the initial phases of analysis, when they reach across household boundaries. We cannot assume at this point that co-residence had no special meaning when it came to kin ties; or that non-co-resident kin had ultimately the same significance in individual lives as co-resident kin. But what we do argue is that the existence of identifiable inter-household ties requires us to add to the analysis the clusters that are reconstructable on the basis of the given and implied links.

What is possible for one co-residential group is possible also for an entire community consisting of such groups. Following genealogical clues, the reconstruction can proceed to link all the persons in one household with all their relatives elsewhere in the community until all of the clues for all persons in all households are exhausted and the result resembles figure 6,[1]

1 A full discussion of the meaning of this reconstruction and its various uses is to be found in Plakans (1983). It is difficult to believe that any reconstruction of this type will ever be able to make a claim to completeness. In the Kalitzen source, for example, relational terms attached to married women were far more haphazard than those attached to married males, creating the possibility that the population in figure 6 was linked more densely than the configuration suggests. Therefore, when the number of dyadic relations for any individual are counted, in this figure the resulting statistics must always be presented in the form of *minima*. In the Baltic census generally, certainty in statistics of any kind ranges from very high for dependent male children to low for married older females.

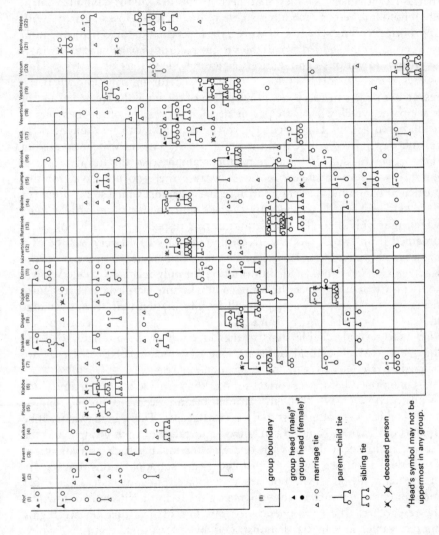

Figure 6 Kalitzen reconstruction
Source: Plakans, 1983: 184–5

group boundary
(BI)

▲ group head (male)[a]
● group head (female)[a]

△ — ○ marriage tie

△—○ parent—child tie

△▽△ sibling tie

✕ ✕ deceased person

[a]Head's symbol may not be uppermost in any group.

which depicts a maximal reconstruction of a relatively small serf estate – Kalitzen – in the province of Kurland in the year 1797. Communities much larger than Kalitzen of course become very difficult to represent diagrammatically, because the lines that need to be drawn to symbolize intra-household links cross each other so often that there is a loss of clarity. With appropriate coding schemes, however, the links can be stored in the memory of a computer and added as variables to the records of particular individuals or treated in various combinations as entirely new units of analysis. They always remain ready, therefore, to be tapped for information when the researcher makes the decision about which of them will be treated as ties of kinship and which will be used as signifying the presence of the members of a kin-based group. The extent to which such links can be thought of as reliable depends very much on the nature of the sources which are used in their reconstruction. We may note, for example, that the ties depicted in figure 6 will remain uncorroborated because there do not exist, for this particular community, a set of parish registers against which some sample of them can be checked. This will always be a shortcoming of domain linkage, which uses only a single source, and in this respect when such linkage is obtained from two separate sources the reliability could very well be of a higher magnitude. There is also the fact that a single-year soure such as the Kalitzen revision can provide information for only relatively shallow links, so that the extent to which the Kalitzen inhabitants did or did not recognize ties of greater genealogical depth will be information that always remains hidden from view. In spite of these problems, however, this reconstruction does take several reliable steps in the direction of the ultimate goal: the linkage of two structural domains, one of which involves ties that are defined by reference to common descent and marriage.

As mentioned before, historical sources that provide the raw material for reconstructions may, through various means, separate out kin-linked groups which were of interest to the record-keeper. This fact may in itself be used as evidence to weigh the relative importance of such groups, and the reconstruction provides us with one way for making such an evaluation. The groups identified by the record-keeper are subpopulations that remain in the data file as such, but are now placed side by side with other subpopulations extracted from the file on the basis of criteria laid down by the researcher. The consequences of this line of investigation are highly unpredictable, as can be demonstrated by reference to figure 7, which contains a diagrammatic representation of the detectable genealogical connections among residence group heads in Kalitzen (extracted from figure 6) and another, nearby, serf estate from 1797 called Spahren. In the original revision, the head of a residential group (*Wirth*) was always designated as such and the relational terminology attached to other people in the group

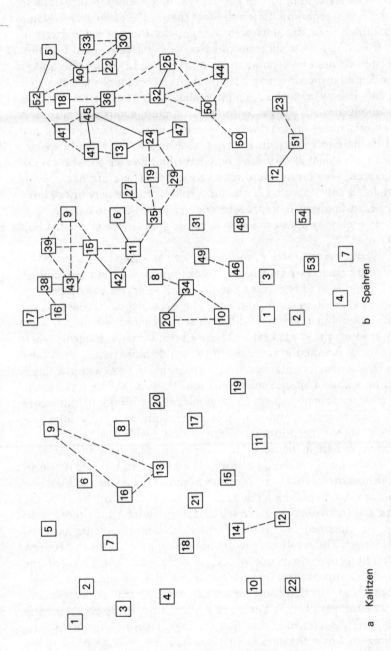

Figure 7 Genealogical links between group heads, Kalitzen and Spahren estates, 1797

a Kalitzen
b Spahren

——— ties between brothers
- - - - other genealogical ties

was always referenced to him. This format reflected the importance of these heads in the estate economy. Given the fact that in the estates the isolated farmstead rather than the nucleated village was the normal pattern of residence, it is always an important question how the residential isolation and dispersion of the estate population 'on the ground' should be understood. Residential dispersion may have been an important element in social relations, but it may have been counterbalanced by ties of descent and marriage among heads. The evidence for an unambiguous generalization remains unsatisfactory when the ties among heads of farmsteads are compared in the two estates. In Kalitzen, such ties were evidently sparse, suggesting that residential disperson may have had greater social meaning than in Spahren, where they were relatively dense. There are not enough data to provide a conclusive evaluation of such ties, but the network of links among heads in Spahren is impressive enough to suggest that residential dispersion by itself may not be the most accurate guide to the understanding of social activity.

Using the same reconstruction, moreover, we can demonstrate that even in a community such as Kalitzen, where examination of kin ties among heads results in one kind of picture, the choice of other ties and other units of analysis can result in quite another. The genealogical reconstruction remains the same, but this time a different set of connections is extracted from it to produce the configuration. Figure 8 shows what happens when the field of social interaction is redefined to include more people than only the heads. Here we are not asking about the meaning of links within a single farmstead, or within a special subpopulation. Instead, we are seeking the best way to formulate the question of significance of links for an entire community, when every member of that community and every subpopulation within it has been brought into contact with the genealogical reconstruction shown in figure 6. It is far from clear how in historical communities this question should be formulated, but certainly one way is to ask about the extent to which the farmsteads were linked when at least one person in each farmstead had relatives in one or more others. For the purposes of this discussion we have selected from figure 6 only those links which can be classified as 'primary' (that is, links involving parents, children, siblings). The result is a picture of a community in which very few farmsteads (altogether three out of 22) did not have some ties of the requisite sort that linked them into the total network of connections. A scan of this 'system' suggests that some farmsteads were 'central' in the 'system', while others were 'peripheral'. Yet if one hypothesized a 'message' entering this system, one can conclude that that message, entering at most points, and travelling only over the lines of communication formed by primary kin ties, could have reached nearly all other farmsteads in the community. There

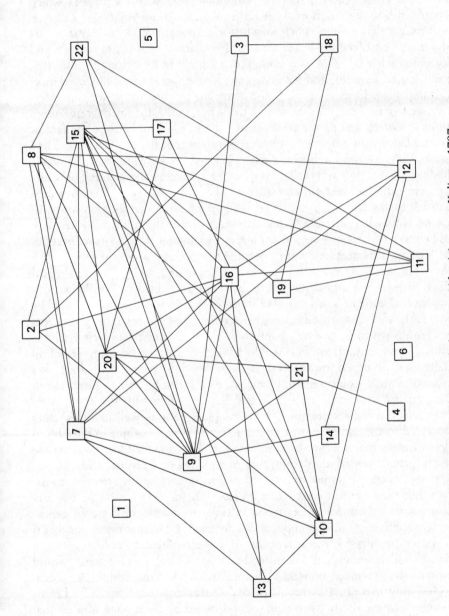

Figure 8 Primary kin ties linking co-residential groups, Kalitzen, 1797

would be good reason, therefore, to investigate in Kalitzen the factors which made for community integration, simultaneously with the factors which contributed to the isolation of each co-residential group 'on the ground'.

It is clear that even in as helpful a historical document as this Baltic census the major unsolved problem remains the relation between genealogy and kinship, between what we can take as analytically relevant links (the genealogical domain) and what we can assume were the socially used links (kinship ties). In fact, in the Baltic censuses, the only links we can safely assume to have been kinship ties are those that in the document were shown to have existed among the co-residents of a household, because the fact of co-residence would be a type of corroboration that the ties had been acted upon. Thus we can establish a tie between two males who are said to have had the same father as a tie between brothers, but strictly speaking only one of these – that between the co-resident father and son – would be confirmed as such by the fact of co-residence, while the tie between the two sons will have a somewhat different status. Although in the case of primary ties such as between brothers we would not hesitate to assume these to have been ties of kinship, this problem would become greater as we moved to establish more distant connections. While it would be possible, using the genealogical data, to establish a genealogical tie between an individual and his sister's husband's brother's son's wife, the status of this tie as a kinship tie would be in doubt. The same problem attaches to the use of the organizing concepts for groups which these data permit to be used: we might very well assemble all the likely candidates who would have been considered members of an individual's kindred, but the question of whether these people were ever treated as such would remain open. We might also be able to assemble all the persons who made up the several descent groups in this Baltic community, by using the mentioned genealogical data as well as other clues provided by the enumerator. But as long as there was nothing in the data to demonstrate that the group ever acted as a corporate unit, the exercise would remain one of simulation, even though of a very precise kind.

In reviewing the nature of interaction documents, I drew attention to the fact that they are self-enclosed universes and for that reason permit any individual in them to be examined in only one particular kind of genealogical configuration. The implication, not spelt out at that time, was that if a source permits the reconstruction of several different configurations, a better understanding of an individual's structural involvements would ensue. The enhanced household listings show that the additional genealogical information is sufficient to realize this goal only partially. Let us assume that the Baltic list was in fact produced by the linking of a normal household listing and information from contemporary parish registers, rather than being presented in the form in which it now stands. While this additional information certainly enables us to proceed much farther in reconstruction, at the conclusion of it we still do not have at hand completely reliable evidence about kinship. We can now examine individuals and households in the much larger genealogical contexts, but it is only within the household configurations that we have corroborated kinship ties. The conclusion that has to be drawn, whether we work from enhanced listings or from linked sources, is that domain linkage, when it involves a domain defined in large part by genealogical ties rather than corroborated kinship ties, does not carry the research to the ultimate goal. It is an absolutely necessary steps, but, having taken it, we are not yet entitled to assume that the linking process has involved 'the kinship domain' in a pure form.

A review of the circumstances in which genealogical links can be reconceptualized as kinship ties is therefore very much in order. In doing so, we should keep in mind the concept of the 'indicator' which, at least in the social sciences, is widely used when direct evidence about the phenomenon being studied is not available. There are no agreed-upon rules about what distinguishes a 'good' indicator from a 'bad' one, and much controversy in the literature of the social sciences revolves precisely around this issue. The value of the concept for the present discussion is that it permits us to continue to think of genealogical evidence as not entirely useless, even when the sources do not allow for an absolute identification of which ties in a historical community were recognized as ties of kinship. While a single genealogical link may not be the best indicator of a corresponding single kinship tie, it is difficult to envisage a better indicator for the entire kinship domain of a historical community than the totality of genealogical links among its members. To call this totality an indicator means precisely that it can be thought of as useful, that, in other words, in the absence of better system-wide evidence about a phenemon which requires some form of system-wide data to be discussed at all, the researcher makes use of that which he assumes to be closest to the evidence that is absent. It may turn out that large segments of genealogical evidence can be reconceptualized as kinship evidence on a perfectly sound basis. But we should also be prepared to conclude that the domain of genealogical links can never move out of the 'indicator' status.

4

From Genealogy to Kinship: the Concept of Kinship Roles

The Problem of Reconceptualization

An anthropologist has remarked that 'a society in which the great majority of persons who treated one another as close kin were not biologically related would be a very strange one' (Mair, 1972: 69). Such an observation, I think, would find little disagreement among historians who deal with the communities of historical Europe, where it would indeed be surprising to find, in case after case, throughout an entire settlement, that individuals who perceived each other as kin, and were so perceived by the community, turned out ultimately to have no genealogical connections to each other. In most cases we simply assume that when sources employ relational terminology of the kinship type, those preparing the source had access to genealogical information in some form, even when this remains entirely inaccessible to the subsequent analyst. Indeed, very frequently in discussions of historical kinship the genealogical substratum is not sought after it all, and the assumption is made that the record-keepers themselves, or the people about whom the records were made, knew what they were about when they employed relational terminology of the kinship type. In such studies, as was observed earlier, the conceptual transition from genealogy to kinship does not appear problematic: either the genealogical reconstructions used do not reach out far enough to create difficulties or the question is mooted by the unavailability of a record of connections independent of what the only available source reports.

It is impossible, however, to reason in the other direction with as much confidence, and to make the same assumptions about far-flung genealogical connections, because they may easily outrun the information available about social interaction. Even in a relatively successful domain linkage, as discussed in the preceding chapter, not all demonstrable genealogical connections can be referenced to demonstrable social activity, and such a shortfall immediately puts the question of what to do with genealogical links whose social efficacy cannot be demonstrated. The fact of co-residence of two brothers is an important clue about the utilization of the sibling tie, and in some sense corroborates, even if it does not ultimately explain, its social significance. But what is one to do with a third brother who is not in co-residence with the other two, but is clearly shown to be related to them through a genealogical reconstruction? In some sources, the contrast between analytically and socially relevant information is underlined in hundreds of cases of this sort, most of them falling beyond the somewhat less bothersome sibling range. We may still be somewhat confident in assuming that there is a match between genealogy and kinship – a permissible move from genealogical link to kinship tie and ultimately to a discussion of kinship roles – when the genealogical ties being dealt with are of the primary type (ego–father's brother, ego–son's wife, etc.). But if the reconstruction is successful and reliable (in the genealogical sense) much beyond these degrees, and supplies us with hundreds of links extending through space and time but still falling within a community's historical records, the question of the permissibility of the conceptual transition between genealogical tie and kinship link becomes a very pressing one indeed.

It does not seem likely that there will ever be for any of the historical communities that have yielded appropriate sources an easy way to establish, in a single and inclusive step, a complete inventory of the genealogical links that can be treated at the very outset as kinship ties. Some types of evidence – law codes specifying degrees of recognized kinship – can be an important clue, but they are not always available and in any case have to be tested concerning the extent to which they were being followed.[1] Such sources will be discussed more thoroughly later, but at this point in our effort to solve the problem created by maximal genealogical reconstructions they are not the help we are looking for. In a sense, at this point, we confront an important decision: to proceed very slowly and carefully, and not to allow into the discussion any genealogical links which cannot be clearly and unambiguously demonstrated as having created kinship ties (and kinship roles); or to relax the requirement for unambiguous evidence somewhat in order not to discard genealogical evidence that may be the only evidence of any kind we have about the historical community in question. If the former decision is made, then we will have recognized from the outset that all

---

1   An excellent example of the utility of law codes for the study of kinship information
     obtained from a living population is Farber (1981). In this study kinship terminology is seen
     to imply a 'series of rights and obligations pertaining to each relationship' without
     providing 'a clue to the relative strengths of these obligations to various kin'. Legal codes
     governing intestacy laws, on the other hand, are seen to 'express popular conceptions about
     priorities and "proximities" of relatives' and can therefore be used to assign degrees of
     importance or significance to various kin positions (all quotes from Farber, 1981: 3).

subsequent discussion of kinship will be a restricted one, for it is unlikely that there will be interactional evidence – proof that genealogical links were put to social use – for all of the particular links which can be identified. If the latter decision is made, and an entire genealogical configuration is reconceptualized as delivering information about kinship ties and kinship roles, all subsequent discussion has to be a complicated exercise in hypothesis-testing, because this reconceptualizing step will not by itself change the nature of the genealogical evidence. What it will accomplish, however, is to shift the locus of the empirical method we wish to employ. If, without this total reconceptualizing step, no kinship tie were considered valid unless proven to be such and all genealogical links about which such proof is unavailable were discarded, we would expect to be able to studh the 'analytically discriminable elements' of the kinship domain on a very piecemeal basis. If, however, we proceed to reconceptualize without direct evidence of the requisite sort, we would expect, in the subsequent testing of various hypotheses, to be able to make use of the untransformed links in the process of testing, and thus build a case on the basis of direct proof combined with inferences. Instead of discarding a non-co-resident brother from a set of three brothers because there is no direct proof that the identifiable genealogical tie between the two co-residents and the non-co-resident was ever recognized, in this latter approach we would make use of all three and test for the consequences of, for example, 'sibling solidarity' (Radcliffe-Brown and Forde, 1950: 23–4). We could not set up such a test, without having assumed, however tentatively, that all brother–brother links yielded kinship roles; nor, if the test could not be made, could we speak of the reality of the kin tie with the non-co-resident brother on the basis of inference, since he would have been put beyond the range of all discussion early in the process.

Genealogical Demography

There is a precedent for this reconceptualization step in the research of a subfield in the anthropological disciplines that has emerged in recent years. In 'genealogical demography' fieldwork information is used in conjunction with information from historical records of a particular locality, and the assumptions which the anthropologists have been enabled to make on the basis of the study of the living population are carried into the historical evidence, even when there is no direct historical proof that certain examinable genealogical ties had social efficacy (Dyke and Morrill, 1980; Swedlund and Armelagos, 1976). That is, if certain types of descent groups can be documented as being active in the living population, it is assumed that in the locality historical evidence that seems to be about descent groups in some past time can be dealt with as if it were about such groups in fact. In this work, the methodological analogies are with historical demography, because in both roughly the same techniques of reconstruction are employed. But historical demography differs from genealogical demography in that the former is concerned primarily with the demographic characteristics of communities, regions, or even entire societies covering stretches of historical time which do not necessarily extend into the present, whereas the latter is normally meant to illuminate the present of the people among whom fieldwork is being carried out. Thus the starting-point in genealogical demography is, for the most part, a living population, and the historical dimension consists of the immediate past of it: say, approximately the same time covered by the memories of the oldest members of the living population. Through the use of such historical documents as have survived, the researcher is enabled to test the accuracy of such memories and to draw at least an approximate picture of the immediate antecedent trends that made the living population what it is. The difference between the two is therefore a question of starting-points and time coverage, although obviously exceptions can be found to this general description.

Both types of demography share many concerns with kinship researchers, and in so far as the basic sources used by all three are also frequently the same, the work of the former two is of obvious interest to the latter. But consider the differences in the way in which genealogical data are used in the two approaches. Both start with a collection of raw data which require reconstruction of various kinds in order to be understood. The historical demographer and genealogical demographer, however, will be interested primarily in making use of only one aspect of the connecting information implicit in the relational terminology of the sources, namely, that which will permit the reassembly of groups pertinent to the study of marriages, deaths, childbearing, migration and population sizes, and to calculate rates of fertility, mortality, movement and nuptiality. In order to arrive at the population units which measurement of these matters requires, the researcher will need to use the relational language in the sources no further than is required to move certain people into adjacency with each other to form small clusters such as conjugal families. In some cases, all that is needed is an accurate record of the hundreds of dyadic ties which can be analysed for 'marriage' rates; in others, an accurate reconstruction of only the ties between mothers and the children they bore. For this kind of reconstruction, as we have said, all of the sources discussed earlier can be of use, even if they vary in the accuracy and specificity with which such ties can be established. Ultimately, research concerning topics such as these aims at a full description of the dynamics of 'population' considered as a biological rather than a social entity. This stress changes the way in which kinship is defined as well as the manner in which particular ties are interpreted.[2] Seen from the biological perspective, the facts of marriage and childbearing appear very different than when considered from the viewpoint of social relationships. They of course remain social regardless of what perspective they are considered from, but from the biological point of view they can be viewed as simply mechanisms that bring two people together for procreation and allow analysis of the results of the procreative act. Migration can be viewed as the inevitable movements of subpopulations in relation to each other, and death simply as the removal of some subpopulations from those which remain alive.

Nothing would be gained of course from drawing such distinctions too sharply. For very obvious reasons, the work being done in these two particular fields is of major interest to kinship research because the processes it examines bear directly on the question of the size of the groups that will be around to be labelled as kin, and may even touch on the question of whether changes in kinship systems are brought about by demographic patterns that have become a permanent feature of a particular society. Thus, for example, in a highly mobile society in which the sibling groups are scattered widely there may in fact come a point at which such kinship terms as 'uncle' may cease to be operative because, for generations, they would not have had an empirical content, that is, a person would never experience an uncle–nephew or uncle–niece relationship at all. Moreover, historical and genealogical demographers are not in principle limited to working with population units which are small; they can indeed move the entire range of analysis of small units into the context of large kin-based groupings, using these latter as the 'population' whose component parts have to be understood. Thus, for example, recent work has shown how demographic research of this sort can be of use in the understanding of such very inclusive populations as Chinese partilineages, when these are taken to be configurations with a time base (Fei and Liu, 1982). Thus a Chinese patrilineage may contain within itself some seven to nine generations of linked people, with hundreds of marriages and thousands of individuals, each of which can be used as units of measurement. The patrilineages over the course of time may undergo expansion and contraction, just in the same way as a non-kin-based population can experience such changes, and it may exhibit patterns of fertility and mortality that contrast with these attributes in other lineages. The important point about such studies, however, is that

2 A good introduction to these two different points of view can be found in the comments made on each other's conceptions of kinship by Gellner (1960), Needham (1960) and Barnes (1961), and in the discussion of human and primate kinship in Fox (1975a). See also Baker and Sanders (1972) and Zubrow (1976).

the reconstructions in which they are based are not of the sort that test every identifiable genealogical connection for its social meaning before absorbing such a connection into the total data base. If there is reason to believe in the reality of an uncle–nephew tie in one case, this reality is assumed for the rest of the ties that are found; and the hundreds of particular ties that exist in a reconstructed time-based lineage configuration are all assumed to have been relevant when there is reason to believe that lineages were an integral part of the social system. In other words, there are encompassing reconceptual-izations at work in creating data bases for research of this type, and the reasoning that carries the research from genealogical link to kinship tie to kinship role frequently starts with the genealogical tie as an indicator of a kinship role at the very first step.

Though the work of historical and genealogical demographers often begins with the same sources as that of the kinship researcher, the fact remains that at a certain point the interests of the two will begin to diverge (cf. Skolnick et al., 1976). While the focus of the former will fall more and more on the reconstructable units that are small and raise few doubts about role enactment, the interests of the latter will be drawn increasingly to the genealogical ties between these units: to the fact, for example, that the husbands in three conjugal families are brothers, or to the fact that the husbands of two conjugal families separated temporally by some 150 years stand in the genealogical relationship of Fa Fa Fa Fa to So So So So; and, correspondingly, to the question of what the structural significance of the links was, if all these individuals are linked by the records of one community. The fact that these people, in their own time, were members of conjugal families will not be forgotten, but this will be seen only as partial evidence of their structural involvements, because the same people will have been and would be in time members of families of birth as well as families of marriage. These large configurations, having considerable spatial and temporal dimensions, will have been reconstructed on the same materials as used for the reconstruction of any component units of them, but they will raise the question of whether they were more than simply the sum of their parts. Thus the question will be what conceptual equipment is needed to analyse them in this fashion, so that the analysis will take into consideration such multiple memberships. When questions of this kind come to loom large as the next steps in the analytical process, the researcher will have already moved to the very edge of the analysis of kinship, because he will have started to inquire about chains of genealogical links and their social meaning. If these genealogical chains are left in the domain of genealogy, all that can be accomplished is a measurement of their external attributes: how far from each other were the links in such chains, how do they cross each other and so forth. But this itself will not move the research into the domain of social meanings. What is necessary at this step is the adoption of conceptual equipment which invests these connected units (individuals, families) with the potential for having an impact on each other and provides the researcher with a tool for investigating this impact.

The concept that has been widely used for this purpose is the concept of social role or, the variant pertaining to our interests, the concept of kinship role.[3] It has been pointed out repeatedly that this concept is not an invention of social scientists, but in fact is used by people in everyday discourse to orient themselves in their social world (Nadel, 1957: 20). Its use in this fashion may be quite inexplicit and unrefined, but the fact that it is used is beyond doubt. Similarly, it is also a concept which is employed by 'traditional' historians in their writings, particularly at such junctures in their prose at which they shift from a host of examples about a particular social usage or custom to a generalization about the behaviour of persons. In the writings of historians this shift from descriptions of the activities of particular individuals to role language is usually quite direct, without much warning that it is coming or that a shift in focus has in fact occurred. Thus in his masterful description of the marriage and family life in English society in the period 1500–1800, after some dozens of examples of how parents and children addressed each other in their letters, Lawrence Stone concludes that 'these changes in overt marks of deference and modes of address are symbolic of a major shift in parent–child relations' (Stone, 1977: 415). The description that precedes this statement contains citations from actual historical actors; the statement itself shifts into the language of roles. In the social sciences, of course, the concept of roles has given rise to a significant theoretical literature (Banton, 1965), which we can now begin to tap for adaptation to our explicit needs to understand the nature of the genealogical ties in our sources.

Genealogical Links and Kinship Ties

As I have noted, the relational terminology in nominal-level sources always embodies several types of useful information. Drawing upon one of these types, the researcher uses the various clues about connections to reconstruct a genealogical configuration of greater or lesser inclusiveness, using princi-pally the given facts about who is married to whom and which children belong to which parents. Some sources may provide genealogical hints that go beyond parentage and offspringhood: residential sources, for example, may use terms for siblings, in-laws, grandparents and so forth. But the core of a genealogical reconstruction will always be marriage and children, the

3 The best introduction to this subject is Banton (1965).

married couple being, of course, the children of two other married couples, and the children in turn parents of other children. If the records provide accurate information about dates of birth and marriage, dates of the birth of each child, and dates of death for each individual, the historical and genealogical demographer will be in a position to research most of the subjects he is interested in, that is, fertility, nuptiality and mortality. Migration is more difficult to explore at this level on this basis, but some peculiar versions of household lists, as we have seen in the case of the Baltic soul revisions, do permit certain kinds of investigation of population movements at the local level.

To acquire usable information for these purposes, the researcher will not have had to make any assumptions about how the linked people behaved toward each other, how they addressed each other, or how they perceived their rights and responsibilities by virtue of being enmeshed in the demonstrable network of connections. Nor will it have been necessary, to accomplish the normal goals of historical and genealogical demography, to make much of the structure of the reconstructed configurations. Individuals enter these researches as participants in marriage, in childbearing or as decedents, and their unique structural involvements are largely irrelevant to the descriptions arrived at of the entire population in terms of various demographic attributes. We do not want to draw the line too sharply, of course, because even in normal historical or genealogical demography not all research deals with the consequences of biological events only: there is at least one social event – marriage – which is crucial to its success. But in general, I think it can be argued that the historical and genealogical demographer is interested in the relational terminology of historical sources to the extent that it brings him up to the point of being able to identify the smallest context beyond the individual in which certain biological activities take place: in this case, the conjugal family unit within which children were given birth.

Therefore, in order to invest these reconstructed genealogical configurations with maximum potential for having social meaning, we have to employ the concept of social role, or, in this case, a special type of role or a special system of roles designated as kinship roles. We assume from this point on that the clues about connectedness in the source provide not only material for genealogical reconstructions, but also for detecting the full structural meaning of this connectedness throughout the entire system of linked individuals. Every time we connect two individuals as spouses or as a parent and a child, and these individuals in turn to other individuals, the link becomes an indicator for the kinship roles we are assuming accompany such a link. The attribution of a particular kind of role to an individual means that we are enlarging in each case the field within which we shall explore that individual's activities. The systematic connecting of individuals into configurations having a spatial and temporal dimension of considerable scope, together with the systematic attribution of roles to the connected individuals, means that we change the nature of the entire configuration. Instead of it being a large system from which we select fragments (such as conjugal families) for particular attention, it now becomes a spatio-temporal stage over all of which any individual or any subgroup may have been active. In order to investigate the full meaning of kinship roles, we cannot therefore allow the historical document to dictate the range within which a role will acquire its full meaning.

At this point, historians tend to become uneasy, because the concept of social role appears to require a shift of description and discussion from the flesh-and-blood individuals they encounter in the sources to a level somewhere between individuals and such collective nouns as 'nation' and 'society' with which historians are also familiar. It should be understood that this is precisely what the role concept is meant to do. The idea of a social role is needed 'to bridge the gap between society and individual', and therefore it requires the researcher to refer:

> not to the concrete unique human beings living and acting at any point of time, but to individuals seen as bundles of qualities: the qualities are those demonstrated in and required by the various tasks, relationships, etc., that is, by the given specified, 'constancies of behavior' in accordance with which individuals must act; while the 'bundle' corresponds to a class or type concept, including any or all individuals exhibiting the capacities in question. We can express more sharply the variability of the actor as against the constancy of the contribution expected of him by describing the latter as a part meant to be played. (Nadel, 1957: 21)

While these matters may seem too intellectualized when stated in the language of abstraction, they are actually not that mysterious. As I have suggested, historical description employs the concept of roles widely when it moves from concrete examples to generalizations about entire classes of people for whom these examples stand. By adopting the concept of role as a heuristic device, we are not forced into descriptions of roles only, and we can maintain the constant back-and-forth movement in our descriptions between concrete cases and role language. But once adopted, the concept of social role (or kinship role) does force us to look at our data in a different way. We must now be very conscious of the fact that individuals may have inhabited a number of different role-creating contexts simultaneously and that the extraction from the evidence of only one of the contexts (and the individuals in it) may be only one of a large number of possible lines of inquiry.

This is particularly so in the case of kinship roles, because they fall into a general class of 'dependent' roles; that is, they require us to know a great deal about individuals in interaction with other individuals before they can be discussed. This can be explained by imagining a reconstructed genealogical configuration which we will have decided to convert into one from which the meaning of roles can be studied. We might then decide to abstract from this configuration clusters of husbands, wives and children in order to study families. But the husbands, in addition to having this role by virtue of being linked to their 'wives', might also be brothers to other individuals linked to them, and grandsons to still others. The extraction of them from the total configuration to investigate them as parts of conjugal families would leave these other roles unexplored. What this suggests is that in a complex genealogical configuration all individuals, because of multiple linkages, will have multiple roles, depending upon where the links leading to them start. The reconceptualization of genealogical links into kinship ties, which suggest kinship roles, therefore has the effect of complicating the entire system enormously. From being one point in a genealogical network, an individual becomes a point in many different networks partially super-imposed upon each other, with each of these networks presumably creating roles for the individual to enact. How many different roles an individual will be shown to have through such a reconceptualization depends very much on the spatial and temporal limits of the genealogical configuration which a particular source has permitted us to reconstruct. A genealogical configuration reconstructed on the basis of a transactional document might have only a few points, which would still translate into multiple roles for each of the individuals when the configuration is reconceptualized. A very elaborate reconstruction based on registers of vital events would contain many such points, and correspondingly a very large number of roles.

As we follow out the logic of this reconceptualizing step, two things should be noted. First, because the basis of the reconceptualization is a genealogical configuration, we shall not be able to move from it to a precise identification of other social roles which an individual may have had to enact. That is, the descriptive entries in many historical sources will contain various terms other than those dealing with the genealogical position of the individual, and in order to use these we would have to establish a very different kind of reconstruction. Thus, for example, if a person is also described as a 'servant', we would have to obtain the meaning of this role from a configuration which, presumably, would contain another person who has been described as a 'master'. If we wished to establish the meaning of sex roles, we would have to do so on the basis of yet another configuration. The meaning of kinship roles cannot be inferred from the reconceptualization based on these other configurations. We shall have to treat the genealogical–kinship domain as entirely separate from other role-creating and role-supplying domains, even though, of course, we are under no obligation to put the others aside permanently nor to claim for the genealogical–kinship domain any kind of primacy. At the very least, we are obligated during the course of this reconceptualization to take seriously Radcliffe-Brown's understanding (as explained by Fortes) that 'there are no determinants, let alone prime movers, of kinship institutions extraneous to the central core of genealogical connection' (Fortes, 1969: 69). In fact, this observation is useful to keep in mind for the entire undertaking of historical kinship study, until we learn what kind of evidence is available for its verification.

Secondly, it is this reconceptualization that creates the link between the phase of inquiry during which the evidence is, in a sense, being sorted, and the phase in which we have to begin to test various kinds of hypotheses about its meaning. What we eventually come to include as kin-role-yielding genealogical positions may be more or less than what is needed for a complete kin inventory, since some of the genealogical connections we trace will not have been recognized as socially significant by any of the historical actors, and some people may be designated as kin whose connections to a particular individual appear to lie beyond the genealogical clues in the source. This raises the question of how much reconstruction should be carried out, given the appropriate linking evidence. At this stage of development of kinship research on historical European communities it is advisable to follow the genealogical clues to wherever they may lead, because reconstructions which are stopped at a certain genealogical distance from an Ego have to presuppose that we already know where the actors in a particular historical community themselves drew the line. While in the case of some national societies the answer to this question is probably as clear as it ever will be, we do not have such knowledge for others. Consequently, in the reconstruction of examinable kinship grids it is safer to err on the side of excess rather than insufficiency, so as to ensure that we have at hand a maximum rather than a minimum position to test.

The problem is not likely to appear very serious in the case of sources which permit relatively limited genealogical reconstructions, because, as we have said, in these cases the relational terminology in the sources will make it clear from the outset that what the researcher is dealing with is a bona-fide kinship group. Hence the researcher, in making a genealogical reconstruction, will simultaneously be producing a record of kinship ties and a role inventory. But the discrepancy will emerge very sharply in the case of genealogically-enhanced household listings, for example, or configurations reconstructed from vital-events records, where more links may be made on the basis of the logic of genealogical connections than by reference to relational terminology in the source actually naming a link between two individuals. In these, the researcher faces something of a dilemma, which the reconceptualization is meant to solve for the purpose of pushing the research one step forward. The only way, in these sources, that the researcher will be able to obtain an accurate record of links is by following the genealogical clues wherever they may lead, but the farther away from the starting-point such links lie, the more dubious is the claim that the reconstruction is in fact producing a system of kin linkages. It is therefore better to suspend doubt about the ultimate usefulness of the more far-reaching links until they are in a position of being evaluated. Because at this point in the research no claims are being made about the ultimate structure of kin networks or kin groups, none of the genealogical positions identified in such a step assumes a permanent position for the final picture. If the genealogical links are present, however, their existence will have to modify any claims about the completeness of any lesser structure whose nature may have already been verified in the relational language of the source. These lesser structures may eventually turn out to have been embedded in more inclusive ones that also required an individual to enact kin roles.

The Properties of Roles

The reconceptualization of an entire cluster of genealogically-linked individuals as a system of potential role-producing positions draws all of the evidence we have about links into the sphere of analysability. The entire operation must not be thought of as the final step of the process of bringing kinship information to light, but rather as a preliminary step with which we assemble the evidence that is in the source for testing for social relevance. It may be that ultimately the positions that yielded kinship roles will turn out to be a subset of those which we assemble at this step. To make such a decision, however, we shall need to consider what investigations the use of the role concept entails so that we can introduce more certainty than we have at this step.

Theorists who have worked with the concept of kinship roles have identified the directions in which such an inquiry must move. But the main problem in these theoretical discussions is that they assume observability of enactment, since they are elaborated in the context of social sciences that normally deal with living populations. In such circumstances, the content of a particular role can be studied from many different points of view, but the historian cannot do other than start with the assumption that observability of enactment is impossible by definition. Thus the question for the historian has to be posed somewhat differently than for social scientists, namely, whether the minimal information available about role content is sufficient to make the assumption that a role has social relevance. In other words, at times the historian's acceptance of the social relevance of a role may have to be based on no more than the information resent in the very same document which contains the role label or the labels from which the existence of a role has to be inferred. If we start with the assumption that the concept of social role as such is useful at all – that social life in the past had roles as one element – we have to ask what the minimum evidence is to permit us to identify what the content of a particular role was.

This necessity, borne of the nature of historical evidence, is fraught with dangers for understanding social life in the past, because, as we have already pointed out, the evidence that is presented to the historian is always given from someone else's point of view, and normally from a single point of view rather than from the numerous viewpoints which are necessary to make the content of a particular role clear. In a household listing, for example, the decision by the enumerator to designate each person with a relational term that refers only to the head of the household allows us to abstract a set of role terms that cover only a minimal number of all the possible roles each individual may have enacted, and we have to infer the existence of others from these, rather than from terms that are actually given. This circumstance is likely to make much, if not most, of description a kind of argument for which there is in fact no empirical evidence of the sort that would be desired. None the less, the argument can be a controlled one, if it moves within the general characteristics of roles as social scientists have identified them in their writings about roles in living populations, where maximum observability is possible. The resulting picture may then be less empirically based than we would want, but it can still be within the bounds of credibility both with reference to the evidence we are making inferences from as well as the characteristics of the concept as it has been used in more informative contexts.

One very useful characteristic of kinship roles already mentioned is that they achieve meaning only in the context of reciprocity. That is, a set of descriptive terms given in the source will imply the existence of one or more correlative sets, so that if the source has identified one set, we can with some confidence proceed to talk about the existence of the correlative sets as well. When the reciprocal nature of kinship roles has been identified in work with living populations, we can make use of it to enhance the historical evidence we have at our disposal. If, for example, in our German-language source the enumerator regularly makes use of the term *Schwiegervater* to describe the individuals who occupy in relation to an Ego the genealogical position of wife's father, we have every right to complement our inventory of role terms in such a list with the correlative *Schwiegersohn* and *Schwiegertochter* and assume that these are the terms which would have been used by the *Schwiegervater* to describe his daughter's husband or son's wife (Debus, 1958). We can do so even if nowhere in our listings do these two other terms appear, and we can go further and assume that these positions in fact were socially relevant because of the use of the term *Schwiegervater*. This expansion of the role terms will not, of course, in and of itself, help us to discover the rights and responsibilities involved in the relationships, but it will signify that in this subset of relationships there was a cluster of roles which were identified in some special way other than simply by reference to the genealogical position. And it will signify further that, in addition to having to explore the nature of the role of father-in-law, we have to go beyond the given information and explore also the roles of daughter- and son-in-law. Moreover, if we have made this assumption with respect to one individual for whom the particular term is given in the source, we can also proceed to assume that the role would have had the same meaning, and imply the same correlative roles for other individuals in the given community, regardless of whether or not in the source other individuals are described with such terms or have such relationships imputed to them. This is, after all, what fieldwork anthropologists do in their work with kinship relations in living populations. They do not hope to be able to observe the enactments of every individual, but rather those which a subset enacted (presumably a satisfactory example of the entire population), and to generalize about the entire community from this less-than-complete inventory (Goodenough, 1970: 98–130). The reciprocity involved in kinship relations, therefore, can be made use of as an investigatory tool, with respect to historical evidence, in a way that could not be done with other kinds of role terms. If, for example, a source describes an individual as a shoemaker, we cannot infer from this label the existence of any particular other occupation, but the role label of 'uncle' indicates the existence of 'nephews' and 'nieces'.

Another basis for inference useful in the handling of historical information of this sort is the fact that kinship roles are enacted through time. That is, a relationship which is identifiable, at a moment in past time, between two individuals as being one of *father* to *son* can be assumed to have lasted throughout the lifetimes of these individuals, in a way that, for example, a relationship identified as *patron–client* (another set of dependent roles) cannot be (cf. Wolf, 1966). I say this even with the knowledge that it was possible in the past for fathers to disown sons, and for sons to reject parents, but in the absence of information about these extraordinary events the likelihood is that these two individuals continued to behave toward each other as father and son before and after that relationship was identified in the source with a particular set of words. This means that we can ask the question historically – covering the lifetimes of the individuals who are so identified – especially if subsequent sources no longer identify the same two individuals in that fashion. Thus, for example, two single-year household lists which are separated from each other by a stretch of historical time can easily reveal that in the second one the son in the first list has moved out of the father's household to establish a household of his own, and that in the second listing the son is no longer identified as his father's offspring, but as an individual in his own right. Assuming the presence of sufficient genealogical data still to link the two, we can proceed to assume that the son had a kinship tie with his father, even if now it might be subordinated to other ties he has established in the meantime. With respect to kinship roles, therefore, the assumption that they are lifetime roles is better than the assumption that they are momentary, so that their existence can be assumed to be continuous unless it can be clearly demonstrated that the tie has been severed. I say this in full realization of the fact that since we are dealing with historical time such assumptions are based on the notion of a 'steady state' of the general context in which such ties are said to operate. But in so far as, in this kind of work, we are always dealing with insufficient evidence about the persistence of ties, the opposite assumption that kin ties hold only at the moment they are detected to exist is equally bereft of proof. By and large, the findings of fieldworkers among living populations indicate that kinship roles are more satisfactorily explained when assumed to be persisting rather than momentary.

A third characteristic of roles, which has been identified in living populations – and which we also recognize in our own lives – is the fact of summation. That is to say, an individual can possess many kinship roles simultaneously – and enact them simultaneously and separately – so that we can assume that more often than not in the societies we are dealing with individuals are never satisfactorily placed in their total social context if only one or two role labels come to be attached to them. They can be, of course, but the more productive assumption would be to withhold judgement until there is some kind of evidence to explore the maximum possible number of relationships which might be there. Anthropologists, in talking about non-industrial societies, have come to expect of them such involution, and therefore are not at all surprised when they find the same individual having to enact a large variety of kinship roles with respect to a large number of people in the community. In connection with our historical data we should therefore be aware of the fact that any document in which an individual is described by reference to only one other person is likely to be misleading and not point directly to the total number of roles that individual actually possessed. The enumerator will have extracted from an individual's entire set of relationships only those which were needed for the particular purpose of the listing, and used only those in his description. The likelihood, however, is that, as an abstraction from concrete reality, such a list will only capture one part of it. Moreover, it also has to be kept in mind that this summation is not restricted only to those roles which an individual acquired through ties of descent and marriage. In fact non-kinship roles can also be summed up in the person alongside kinship roles, so that his enactment of some of them may not be fully a clue to what others he had to enact.

A final characteristic of roles which has to be recognized is concerned with the identifiability of their content: that is, what we earlier described as 'individuals' seen as 'bundles of qualities' (Nadel, 1957: 21). Simply put, we start with the assumption that in order to describe what the ascription of a particular role means we have to be able to point to what it required an individual to do or not to do with respect to those people to whom the links point. But the evidence for all the duties and rights which a role entails will not appear in the source in any one single place; or, in other words, we have to expect to do what anthropologists refer to as the 'piecing together' of a role, meaning by that that the significance of the possession of a kinship role will not be apparent from any one example of its enactment. If, for example, our source suggests to us that a marriage contract contains the provision that after the marriage the new son-in-law was required to provide his new brother-in-law (his wife's brother) with sufficient money to finish his schooling, we may very well interpret this as one way in which the groom expressed his willingness to enact some general understanding of his obligations toward his brother-in-law entailed in that particular role. But we cannot take this as the only evidence that is pertinent for describing this particular relationship, even though we recognize it as an important piece of evidence. We have to investigate the relationship in more than a single context in order to conclude that we have adequately 'pieced together' the content which the role of 'brother-in-law' entails. As in the case of the other characteristics of roles we have mentioned, there is a continuous need for open-endedness in the use of the historical evidence. At some point, of course, the search has to be judged complete – just as in anthropological fieldwork the gathering of evidence about roles must eventually be concluded – and the description of the role has to be made on the basis of what has been obtained up to that point.

In the foregoing description of the meaning of kinship roles I have mentioned only a few of the characteristics which roles are now understood to have, and which must be taken seriously by the historian, if he is to use the concept at all. As far as kinship inquiry in the past is concerned, I have argued that the concept of roles is inescapable: without it, all that the evidence can properly be said to contain is genealogical information which places individuals in clusters and permits at most a topographical description of their positions. But this alone does not permit us to assume that we are moving in the realm of social relationships. To make this move, the genealogical clusters of whatever size have to be reconceptualized as potentially role-generating. Thereupon we will have created a new collection of evidence with far more social meaning than mere genealogical clusters have implied in them. We henceforth assume that individuals are not connected only with lines, which are themselves neutral, but that each line points to the existence of two social roles whose content has to be understood if the relationship is to have some kind of social meaning imputed to it. At this juncture, however, with the introduction of the concept of roles, we pose a very difficult challenge to ourselves as historians, because of our knowledge that our data do not permit maximum observability of the people we are trying to describe. We have to make do with the evidence in the sources that permits us to make the reconstructions in the first place, as well as with whatever additional, and very likely scarce, evidence that can help to pin down the content of certain relationships.

Role Differentiation and Role Reduction

By reconceptualizing a particular genealogical configuration as a role configuration the historical researcher creates serious problems for further analysis, for now each point in the configuration is no longer a flesh-and-blood individual but a 'bundle'. Due to the reciprocal nature of kinship roles, and to the summation of roles at each point, each individual in the configuration ceases to be a single unit of analysis and is now considered as an indicator of the existence of roles. Since each individual enacts many roles, the procedure takes us from a universe in which the number of analysable units is more or less limited (to the number of individuals in a community) to one in which that number is immensely larger and to an extent open-ended. Each individual is a datum at one level, but each also yields many more data at another level. Since 'there are few human characteristics which are not, in some culture or society, elaborated into roles' (Nadel, 1957: 26), the researcher must face the implication of this reconceptualizing step, which is that there is almost no end to the types of roles which have to be investigated for the possibility of being separate and distinct. Thus, for example, if a genealogical reconstruction shows individual A to have three sons and two daughters, investigation of only the role of 'father' may not be enough. The inquiry would have to consider whether there is a difference between the roles of 'father' as enacted with respect to a youngest, middle or oldest son; with respect to a son and a daughter; with respect to sons born of different mothers; with respect to sons who are in the father's household and those which are living away from home, and so forth. When these possibilities are seen as implied in any combination of kinship roles which a genealogical configuration yields for examination, it becomes clear that moving from genealogy into roles, that is, into social life itself, presents all sorts of hazards. Identifiable roles which can quickly be found through investigation of the terminology used in the source become, as it were, only the first step into an analysable universe which is immensely complicated.

It is, of course, quite obvious that neither fieldwork anthropologists nor historians can ever complete this step and explore all of its implications. Historians have traditionally moved only a short distance from the starting-point, investigating fully only a few of the roles – usually familial roles – that the evidence suggests. Social anthropologists normally cast their nets wider, and sometimes look at long lists of roles inherent in any particular kinship configuration. How many steps into the world of roles should be taken is nowhere prescribed in the evidence itself, nor in any methodology worked out in practice thus far. It is, I think, true that there is always a tension between the roles which offer themselves for complete analysis and those which exist but do not permit themselves to be investigated. In fieldwork anthropology, there is a limit to such investigations that is set by the time which the investigator spends in the field; and in historical research, the inquiry may be blocked off from a full investigation of numerous sectors of such roles by evidence which does no more than suggest their existence, that is, their potential for being enacted. In the historical realm, we have to satisfy ourselves with the thought that, although it may be possible through genealogical reconstructions to identify roles which may have been enact-able, there will be no evidence about their enactment at all, thus leaving whatever analysis is carried out on the former in the context of a great deal of ignorance as to what precisely the latter implied. This is particularly true with respect to change-over time, an area in which structural anthropologists tend not to enter, being satisfied, as S. H. Nadel has assessed the situation, to think in terms of 'stationary states'. 'Stationary states' are understood to:

> include precisely the internal shifts and fluctuations with which we are concerned, produced by the appearance and disappearance of elements and by the forming and reforming of interrelations. . . . At the moment we cannot really assess the degree of this fluidity since, in anthropology, this field is virtually unexplored. Nobody has counted or is likely to count roles, relationships, and every kind of subgroup from moment to moment. (Nadel, 1957: 134)

These remarks should be sufficient to indicate the dimensions of the problem as it appears at the first step of reconceptualization of genealogy into kinship. But having made them, we must add immediately that social life itself provides some ways of reducing the size of the problem, both for social actors and correspondingly for investigators as well. The fact is that, in any society, it is not only differentiation of roles that is a dynamic feature of it, but also the reduction of roles, which works in the opposite direction. What this means with respect to kinship is discussed succinctly by Nadel, in a crucial paragraph which is here quoted in full:

> We cannot even indicate beforehand the potential maximum of any role inventory, save very roughly. Very roughly, it lies in the total vocabulary current in any given society and expressing its notions about differences of persons. The approximate nature of this clue is perhaps best exemplified by classificatory kinship terminologies. The names embracing a number of biologically distinct kinship degrees strongly suggest a corresponding coincidence or reduction of kinship roles; yet, as is well known, the persons all called 'father' or 'brother', or whatever the case may be, may well be differentiated by their respective rights and obligations towards ego, to a degree conceivably amounting to differences in roles proper. Conversely, kinsfolk differently named may yet be alike in their playing of roles. More generally speaking, actual usage would have to corroborate our assumptions about the potential maximum of roles inventories; and each named identity and difference would have to be tested for its true role character.... Again, I cannot imagine anyone proceeding in this way. ... Above all ... ambiguities would still remain, so that no role inventory can ever be really clear-cut or final. (Nadel, 1957: 61)

Nadel's remark concerning the difficulties involved in such a procedure – 'I cannot imagine anyone proceeding in this way' – suggests that in the analysis of roles, in a living or a historical population, the task of analysing thoroughly every role to which differentiation may have lead is probably impossible. This speaks directly to the problem we encounter immediately upon reconceptualization of genealogical configuration of kinship roles, and it justifies us in our decision not to require such minute analysis. To make the task feasible while still staying in the realm of kinship roles, therefore, we have to examine what precisely takes place in the process of role reduction, in which societies themselves diminish the number of roles which any individual has to enact. We have to undertake this exploration even though we know from the outset, as Nadel also suggests, that in a description of a reduced inventory we shall still not have obtained empirical information as to what the role terms mean as far as rights and obligations are concerned. None the less, in this line of inquiry we shall have moved backwards toward the social reality of the past, toward a position of working with the kin language current in a given population. In this step, however, we are using a procedure which social anthropologists seldom employ. In a paragraph which immediately proceeds the long passage cited above, Nadel observed that 'usually, we describe roles as they become relevant and as we proceed with the general analysis . . . no one would think of preparing a role inventory first, as a preliminary step before embarking on the study of relationships or whatever else a "structural" analysis entails' (Nadel, 1957: 61). It is quite obvious, however, that historians working with deceased populations cannot adopt this as a procedural guide, because Nadel's remarks are based on experience with living communities for which written records are only a subset of the total evidence that is or becomes available.

The fact is that in the study of historical societies, whose populations are unobservable, the compilation of a role inventory may have to be the first step to any subsequent analysis, whatever the difficulties and shortcomings of such an inventorial procedure. The types of historical evidence discussed earlier may each be the only evidence available about a particular community, and if we are to make any assessment of the meaning of kinship ties in that community, we have to make use of whatever material exists. Nadel suggests that even after we have compiled such an inventory, we still will not have a firm grasp over how roles were enacted, which can come only through observation: in the case of some roles, we shall have only labels, without enough evidence to say that the role was enacted identically by every individual to whom such a label applied; other roles may have no labels cited in the source, but may be identifiable through the use of genealogical ties. Even kin to whom the same labels apply may in fact have differentiated roles according to some criterion not known to us. In other words, role inventories are not to be interpreted literally. This general characterization of the significance of role information is helpful, however, since it clarifies the meaning of the types of evidence we have at our disposal. In transactional sources, as pointed out earlier, we shall have a limited number of relational terms, and some evidence about how the roles designated by those terms were being enacted. Yet this evidence will still not be sufficient to say with finality that the roles identified in it, together with the documented activities, is enough to arrive at a final characterization of the role; we would need, that is, examples of the same roles being enacted in other contexts in order to arrive at this conclusion. In enhanced household listings, we have very likely a much larger inventory of role terms, pointing to what enactable roles existed, but less information about how they were enacted. In configurations reconstructed from vital evidence, the list of role terms may be the smallest (for reasons discussed), but the absence of terms for distant relationships does not need to be taken as evidence at this step that these relationships were not recognized as having social significance. It is true, I think, that the move to roles from genealogical relations has the effect of equalizing all these types of evidence as far as potential usefulness is concerned. Unfortunately, this equalization is achieved by rendering each type somewhat less reliable, rather than by moving all of them to a greater level of reliability.

None the less, as Nadel has pointed out and as anthropological practice has shown, role inventories – the names with which people designate kin in conversation with them or in referring to them – constitute a field of clues which cannot be ignored. Whatever inferences we draw from this evidence have to be corroborated by observational evidence, or by what can be substituted in historical research for observational evidence. In certain respects, it is this field which for a long time has served for historians and for others interested in kinship systems in the past as the primary evidence about the phenomenon, and therefore it requires some systematic examination as to its usefulness. In making such an assessment, we have to remain aware of how far removed from kinship terms 'on the ground' in the past later historians really are, and not only in the temporal sense. Within the collections of documents generated by a historical community (itself already removed from the analyst conceivably by as much as several centuries), there may be several layers, each of which increases the distance vertically, so to speak, by representing a higher level of abstraction from the terms the members of the community were actually using. Even the layer closest to the historical actors – such as the Baltic revisions – may 'hide' important kin positions imply because of the way it was prepared, and contemporaries using such a document for their own intellectual needs may compound the problem, even if unintentionally. As in the case of our other evidence, we have to bring to this terminological information a maximum of scepticism, in the light of the complexity of the phenomenon we are working with.

5

The Languages of Historical Kinship

Kinship Terms in Documentary Sources

For historians using the approach being developed, the central question about kinship terminologies of any kind is whether they can help to bring clarity to other kinds of evidence about kinship ties. In the European past, kin relationships were obviously relevant to the understanding of the lives of *individuals,* as all biographies and autobiographies amply demonstrate. Yet when we put to ourselves the question of how best to describe the relevance of kinship to the social history of a *community,* an answer is not immediately apparent. The best historical records place before the analyst hundreds of individuals, each with a unique cluster of identifiable kin, with information in each cluster needing to be integrated with the information in all other clusters, if generalizations about the collective experience are to be reliable. The next steps, however, do not suggest themselves readily. We can appreciate in the abstract that the workings of kinship may have skewed common social activities, such as marriage, in identifiable directions and that consciousness of common descent may have created kinship groups, the members of any one of which had more to do with each other than with members of other groups. But to posit such abstract models of the consequences of kinship rules still does not answer the question of what to do with our individualized records. Should we sample the entire collection of records and then proceed to general statements on the basis of a handful of individual experiences, or would this procedure result in the discarding of valuable information? Indeed, is it possible that a simple summing up of the experiences of individuals, regardless of how detailed the information about them, would still not be sufficient to discuss the structuring consequences of kinship? These questions are particularly appropriate in the light of the discussion in the preceding chapters. There it was shown that the component parts of the historian's collection of primary evidence about kinship, and those of the data file gathered by fieldwork anthropologists, may at the outset be very different indeed as far as internal balance is concerned. The fieldworker will have obtained empirical information in the context of the varied activities that constitute the stuff of everyday life, with the collecting of genealogies, preparation of role inventories, and observations of role enactment all proceeding more or less simultaneously and reinforcing and perhaps redirecting each other as particular opportunities suggest. The order in which various kinds of information are written down will have been directed by the situation at hand, and the roles whose meaning is examined will have been suggested by the activity being observed or by the informant; these roles will have been dealt with, as Nadel says, 'as they become relevant' (Nadel, 1957: 60–1). It is therefore not likely that the fieldworker will have produced an excess of evidence as a result of any particular line of inquiry, because the various lines will have been controlling and validating each other.

The historian, by contrast, may have, early on in the research, a superabundance of information about certain aspects of kinship, as would be the case if an entire maximal genealogical reconstruction were reconceptualized as involving kinship ties, or a set of hundreds of discrete examples of a particular kind of transaction were prepared for analysis. Missing from such data bases, however, would be balancing elements: in the case of genealogical reconstructions, the actual observations of identifiable roles being enacted; and in the case of interactional sources, the genealogical contexts from which the participants of transactions emerged. In such cases, one possible stragegy would indeed be to return to the level of individuals, and search for further documentation of the experiences of a handful of people judged in some way to be repressentative of the whole population. This strategy may not work, however, in communities in which the population was, so to speak, anonymous so far as the documentation of personal experience is concerned. This approach in any case would result in the discarding of a considerable amount of evidence available in the entire data file, and this is to be avoided, regardless of how uncertain that evidence may seem at this phase of the research. Having reconceptualized a large collection of genealogical ties as kinship ties and having through this step created a large number of examinable kinship roles, we would be looking for a way to generalize about these roles across the entire collection, knowing full well that we shall never have sufficient information about the activities of the hundreds of individuals involved to produce reliable generalizations. Although the approach through the personal experiences of individuals always remains open, and can certainly be drawn upon for illustration, we have to remain cognizant of the community-wide information implied in the file, and for this purpose the individualized approach is not sufficient.

In an analogous situation, the fieldwork anthropologist is likely to begin to examine the information he has gathered by looking at the terms of address and reference used by relatives with respect to each other, in order to clarify how the latter are being used to sort out genealogical relatedness, and whether the people who are recounted as genealogical relatives are in fact recognized as such socially. This line of investigation may also be available to the historian in some cases, because historical documents at times contain the very terms which were in use in the community to describe various genealogical positions. If such a list can be abstracted from the source, we can assume that the numerous relationships depicted in a genealogical reconstruction can be sorted out by reference to a list of terms, and that this will provide us with at least the first steps toward identification of socially relevant positions. The utility of this line of investigation is underlined by the well-known fact that the list of terms used to designate imortant kin positions in any society tends to be short:

> To associate a distinctive pattern of behavior with each potentially distinguishable category of relationship would be impractical and intolerably burdensome and no society attempts to do so. The problem is solved in all societies by reducing the number of culturally distinguished categories to a manageable number through grouping or coalescence. . . . It is primarily through the liberal use of classificatory terms that all societies reduce the number of kinship categories from the thousands that are theoretically distinguishable to a very modest number, perhaps twenty-five as an approximate average, which it has everywhere been found practicable to recognize in actual usage. (Murdock, 1949: 97–9)

This step of extracting from the language that people used information about the structure of the society that they inhabited was not always an obvious one, and before the historian takes this step in this specialized field of inquiry, he has to note how momentous a discovery it was and how important a role it has played in the history of kinship research from the second half of the nineteenth century to the present.[1] If the historian expects to find in anthropological literature clear and easy guidance on how to proceed in particular situations, however, he will quickly find that the scholarly publications in this area comprise an entire literature with its own internal history of controversies, debates and disagreements, many of which have not been resolved, and with an accumulation of specialized concepts that have developed over time to deal with the original problem of the relationship between terms and structure. Extracting from this vast corpus of information a simple set of guidelines for use in the case of the historical

---

1 The intellectual history of this discovery is documented in Fortes (1969: 3–84); its current applications are discussed in Keesing (1975: 101–20) and Pasternak (1976: 124–47).

material from a particular historical locality is therefore no easy task, and it is made no easier by the historian reducing his requirements to the simple wish to know what to *expect* – roughly speaking – when dealing with a genealogical reconstruction. The historian, in fact, must be prepared to keep distinct three sets of terms in following this line of investigation: hence the use of the plural in the title of this chapter. There is, first, the language that was used by the historical actors to address and refer to each other, which may at times find its way into historical records, but may just as readily be completely inaccessible to the investigator. Second, there is the language used by the record-keepers, which may or may not be the language used by the historical actors, depending on the circumstances in which a particular record was created. Third, there is the analytical language used by several generations of kinship investigators, which has come to include specialized vocabularies in order to render comparative study of kinship structures easier. We shall look at these languages in this order and try throughout to keep in mind that what we are ultimately seeking are clues about genealogical reconstructions, when evidence about kinship roles and their enactment is minimal.

The Language of Historical Actors

At issue in this discussion are about 25 words in language that we encounter in the sources, and the recognition that, in conducting fieldwork, obtaining precise information about these terms is a perfectly reasonable goal. When the fieldworker confronts the informant or a set of informants directly, the preparation of such terminological inventories depends upon the degree of skill involved in the questioning; in principle, to acquire complete versions of the requisite list is not an impossibility. With historical records, however, the analyst stands at one remove from the direct information, and the skills he brings to the task have to involve scrutiny of the record-keepers' notations, rather than of direct information coming from the historical actor. Consequently one cannot escape the fact that, when this line of inquiry is followed, the analyst has to look at the status and history of the language involved in the sources, not only to establish whether the language of the historical actors may have been a dialect which remains hidden by the more 'learned' language used by the record-keeper, but also to determine, when a long stretch of historical time is involved in the records, whether the language has undergone changes during that time period. Moreover, the analyst also has to bear in mind the distinction between terms of address and terms of reference. If there is any chance of obtaining information about the language used by the historical actors at the time a particular record was compiled, it is necessary to establish whether, in the realm of kinship terms, somewhat different terms in the language were used when the historical actors were addressing each other than when they were referring to each other. Although information obtained in this way may prove to be immaterial, we cannot know this at the outset. Such fine distinctions may seem superfluous, yet in the final analysis they are only a part of the more general effort to bring together two realms of evidence in the historical past at the same level of specificity: the genealogical position which our source has permitted us to identify, and the terminology which the historical actors involved in the source would have used.

In order to ascertain that the language of the record-keepers did not disguise the distinctions among relatives drawn by the language of the historical actors, we have to pay attention to a variety of clues (Murdock, 1949: 101–6).[2] It is important to know, first, whether the two take into cognizance the fact that a particular relative is of the same genealogical generation as the individual who would have used a term in reference to that relative; whether the relative is of the same sex as that individual; and whether that relative is related to the individual through marriage or consanguineally ('by blood'). It is also important to know whether the two languages recognize in the same way the genealogical distance from the individual to a particular relative, and whether or not that relative is linked to the individual through a male or a female. Cutting across such distinctions may be the fact that though two relatives may occupy the same genealogical position *vis-à-vis* a particular individual, the term of address they use toward that individual may be different, in recognition of the differences in chronological age, or in the sex of the person doing the addressing or being addressed. It may also be of significance to know whether the two types of language take cognizance of the fact that persons *through* whom relatives recognize themselves as linked to each other are alive or dead. There are other points of comparison, of course, but to list all of them is not necessary at this time. What we seek to do in drawing up such a list is to make the point that the use of kin terms to identify socially relevant genealogical positions, in the realm of written historical evidence, brings with it certain problems with which the anthropological fieldworker does not have to wrestle. After the historical enumerations at hand are culled for what linguistic evidence they have to yield, the solution to these problems may entail the historian turning to evidence of an entirely different sort, namely, that of the histories of the particular language in question.

2 Murdock's discussion of these criteria is meant to clarify how terminological systems *in general* come to be distinguished from each other. The historian's problem of distinguishing the language of historical actors and the language of enumerators is a special variant of the larger problem.

Whether the histories of particular languages contain sufficient time- and place-specific information, particularly relating to kinship terminologies, is then a question of considerable importance.

What makes this seemingly over-cautious approach necessary is the fact that the sources from which genealogical reconstructions are obtained are invariably particularistic in character: they emerge from a specific historical situation in which the historical actors may or may not have been isolated from influences from the general society, the record-keepers may or may not have been local people replicating the nuances of the local language, and the format of the document may or may not have required emphasis on kin connections that ordinarily would be relatively unimportant. The terms present in a particular set of documents are used for genealogical reconstructions. These, in turn, have to be reconceptualized, with each position or cluster of positions examined as to whether they did or did not yield kinship roles. One line of inquiry for this purpose is to consider the relational terminology as a segment of a language code, on the assumption that an inventory of kin terms will yield clues about the kinship system being studied, which in turn will permit inferences about the relevance of particular genealogical positions. But when we examine the language of record-keepers closely, we find there are substantial grounds for proceeding with care. Relational terminology tied to particular events and reporting on dyadic ties could throw a curtain between the analyst and certain areas of kin relations; and relational terminology chosen to report only role relations created by, say, economic ties would remove from view completely the entire area of kinship relationships. Thus in order to obtain something like a complete inventory of kinship terms relevant for the examination of a particular local population, the analyst is forced to draw upon very generalized vocabularies, such as those being used in a society in which the locality is a part (Anderson, 1963; Friedrich, 1964). The extraction from these vocabularies of terms which could be assumed to identify important genealogical positions, however, creates an ever-increasing gap between the local source and the vocabulary that is to be used to examine it. The two kinds of evidence are thus connected very loosely, with minimal certainty that a generalized set of terms was in fact used in a particular locality. This creates persisting doubt, in the light of what we know about the social particularism of pre-modern Europe, where customs and presumably the language used to describe them varied considerably from locality to locality, and may have been different even in adjacent localities.

This reasoning with respect to actor language points us roughly in the same direction as recent work of anthropologists has been leading, because among them there has been a backing off from the earlier confident assertions about the usefulness of kinship terminology for the understanding of social structures. 'Despite a century of effort,' suggests the description cited earlier, 'no anthropologist has succeeded in producing a satisfactory general theory of the systematic relationships between kinship classification and social organization . . . [Recent research] seems if anything to erode the expectations that kin terms systematically reflect forms of kin groupings or systems of marriage' (Keesing, 1975: 102).[3] The best that can be said about the situation, the description continues, is that:

> scholars are far from agreed on what general conclusions to draw about kin terms and social roles from the complexities and variations that are coming to light from fine-grained studies. At least it is clear that the fit between systems of linguistic labels for kinds of relatives and systems for appropriate role behavior between relatives is not the simple matter anthropologists had come to assume. One cannot list the kin terms of a culture and produce a corresponding description of social roles appropriate to each kind of relative. The complex articulation between the system of labels and the system of roles must be disentangled carefully in each case. (Keesing, 1975: 128–9)

If, then, 'the complex articulation between the system of labels and system of roles' becomes the focus of inquiry, so that at some point during it we can become certain that we have a complete inventory of both, we have to make sure that the historical source does not allow some of the components of each system to remain outside our field of vision. Yet that is precisely what the most detailed historical sources do bring about, by presenting us with a potentially role-yielding position which cannot be ascertained to be such by reference to labels. Conversely, the use of a very general inventory of labels will not contain sufficiently persuasive evidence about how frequently a named role was enacted or about whether it was still part of the language, because language change had not been as fast as social change.

It would be foolish to conclude, of course, that nothing at all can be accomplished by this line of inquiry. The difficulties need to be emphasized, to be sure, if for no other reason than because in historical work along these lines they have tended to hover in the background of the discussion of evidence, rather than forming a logical step. Moreover, in light of cited descriptions of recent anthropological research, it is also necessary to remember that even when a reliable inventory of kin terms has been obtained, and the problem has been set up to proceed on the assumption that there is a congruity between actor terms and social structure, the next

---

3 Indeed, one line of thought among anthropological kinship researchers suggests that kinship terminology may 'serve to mask and counterfeit social relationships' (Murphy, 1967: 164) and may therefore have to be investigated as a kind of political idiom.

steps do not reveal themselves in an obvious fashion. Even if we succeeded in abstracting a set of terms that were, without doubt, those used by the historical actors involved in the source, and were thereby enabled to specify which genealogical positions were role-yielding, we would quickly become conscious of the fact that this was only a first step toward the kind of description and comparison that is the ultimate goal. More than probable, however, as the discussion of actors' language has suggested, the evidentiary base is unlikely to be 'pure' in this sense, since it would be shot through with terminology that came from the pen (and mind) of the record-keeper, whose contribution to the usable evidence has to be discussed more systematically.

The Language of Record-Keepers

In many instances historical sources seem to have a fine unity about them, and we have little reason at the outset to suspect that there are any serious discrepancies between how we ourselves would have recorded the described activity and how in fact a record-keeper reported on it. But this confidence must begin to wane as the requirements for precision become more rigorous, and we begin to ask numerous questions that need to be asked in order to assure that a source does in fact contain sufficiently precise information to minimize the number of assumptions needed to advance the inquiry. Certainly the most disquieting aspect about many historical sources (but not all of them) is the presence of the classifying mind of the middleman – the record-keeper – between the reality which is sought and the analytical routines we wish to use on information about that reality. The disquieting effect of such an intermediary may not be so obvious in the case of interactional sources that were created by a record-keeper who was identifiably a member of the same community as the actors participating in the activity, used the same language as they and presumably drew upon the same specialized vocabulary concerning kinship relationships. The French marriage contract used in chapter 2 would constitute a good example of a source of this type. Yet when we look at the Baltic sources – the enhanced household listings – we find that serious questions can be raised at the very outset. In the Baltic evidence, the German language terminology used in the source was distinctly not that of the Latvian-speaking historical actors; moreover, it is at least conceivable that, because of the language difference, the Baltic enumerators were unfamiliar with the customary ways of the peasantry, even when there was a strong desire to report relationships as accurately as possible. In the Baltic case, if we proceeded rigorously in seeking to obtain clues to the social structure of the peasantry from the kin terminology used in the source, we would have to add an additional step to the research, namely, some method to ensure that the kin terminology of the peasants (expressed in the Latvian language) was sufficiently like the kin terminology of the record-keepers (expressed in German) for the two to fall in the same general category of kin terms. Or, to put the matter in an even more demanding form, we would have to establish that these terminologies were sufficiently similar approximately 100 years ago for errors not to be introduced: a major obstacle indeed when we recognize that the Latvian language did not become a literary tongue until the second half of the nineteenth century, and the first fully reliable dictionaries of it were not available until that time. These observations about this ethnically heterogeneous area of historical Europe may well be generalized and translated into a requirement in historical kinship inquiry. Otherwise we have to proceed on the assumption that the same terms pertaining to kinship were in currency in all subpopulations of a historical society, regardless of differences in literacy skills and in the origins of the people who used them.

This problem is certainly one manifestation of the difficulty which Claude Lévi-Strauss referred to in his statement that ethnographers (anthropologists) and historians should not see each other's work as useless. 'What does the historian do,' he wrote, 'when he studies documents if not to surround himself with the testimony of amateur ethnographers, who were often as far removed from the cultures they described as is the modern investigator from the Polynesians or Pygmies?' (Lévi-Strauss, 1963: 17). The injunction in this statement is clear: record-keepers can be and should be envisaged as somewhat haphazardly trained fieldworkers who could have left exactly the kinds of records we would want, had they known the right questions to ask. But there is also the reservation that they are 'far removed' from the historical actors, not only through the fact that they may have drawn in their descriptions on a different language code, as in the Baltic case, but also because they may have been of a different social class or of a predisposition to describe things that did not exist or to miss those that did. An example can again be drawn from the Baltic evidence. The fiscal censuses from which our earlier illustrations came comprised a set of documents in which the thousands of residents of the Baltic provinces of Kurland and Livland were listed individually during eight years in the period 1782–1859. Yet in all of this welter of material, produced by hundreds of estate officials during these years, we have only the scantiest evidence about the terminology the surveyed peasants themselves used in their everyday lives for address and reference. Presumably there may not have been a great discrepancy between the German language of the sources and the Latvian language of part of the peasant population, but what of the differences between the German of the sources and the Finno-Ugric Estonian language of the other major peasant subpopulation of the Baltic area?[4] Moreover, there is ground for the strong suspicion that the German-using record-keepers were determined to employ one collective noun – the German term *Familie* – to sort out the population into various subcate-gories; yet the procedure, in retrospect, had the effect of raising more questions than answering them for the later analyst. In some of the documents, the term *Familie* is used to refer to what we would call a conjugal family unit – husband, wife and children – while elsewhere in the same document, and in others of like kind, the term is apparently used to refer to what analysts would now call a 'descent group' – all persons who had descended from a (recent) common ancestor. This usage, however, does not bring us much closer to what the described peasantry may have used to refer to such groups, though we know from folksongs and other similar material collected in this period that, for example, the Latvian peasantry did have a term – *dzimta* – for a patrilineal descent group, and another more recent term – *ǧimene* – for the conjugal family unit. We also know, however, that this latter term cannot be dated precisely on its entry into the Latvian language and that it could have both the meanings referred to (that is, a conjugal family and a descent group). Consequently, if it is terminology that we have to use to understand which genealogical positions were role-yielding, in this particular source we have to deal with very tricky interpretive problems from the beginning.

Admittedly, the Baltic example is an extreme one, but it does introduce us to one form of the problem that the use of written historical sources creates. In shifting from the genealogical to the social dimension in interpreting specific positions, we have to rely on the evidence left by these crucial middlemen, and the terminology they used cannot be taken in an un-examined form. As experience with these historical records has shown, there are two other difficulties to be faced, namely, the choice by the record-keepers of a system of notation that relied exclusively on terms describing dyadic ties, and their choice, at times, to use a relational vocabulary drawn entirely from role relationships which lay in the domain of local political and economic authority, rather than in the domain of descent and marriage. These choices meant that in the long run an interpretation of roles in this area may be blocked off by the evidence as it stands from certain relationships, regardless of whether or not the relationships existed. Thus even if the record-keepers and the historical actors were of the same language group, and would have drawn upon the same general vocabulary

4   It was not until 1918, with the establishment of Latvia and Estonia as autonomous states, that the language boundaries in the area of the Russian Baltic provinces were reflected in the political boundaries. Before that time, the Estonians lived in the province of Estland, the northern districts of Livland and the adjacent province of Kurland to the south. The principal language of all record-keeping, including population enumerators, was German until the late nineteenth century.

to describe kinship, the decision to use certain techniques of notation in preference to others had the effect of producing usable data about some systems of relationships which, though important evidence in themselves, would still not be the evidence we are looking for.

The problem involved in the use of a dyadic system of notations can be explained in the following fashion. A record-keeper who was obligated to describe the kin relationships among the actors in a particular social situation normally did so by means of attaching a term to each person in a cluster of persons, usually in reference to a central actor in the social situation. This was the case in all three types of records that we surveyed earlier. In interactional sources, such as wills, the relational term would state the tie between the person whose property was being bequeathed and the recipients of it; in a household list, between the head of the household and his co-residents; and in vital-events records, between the people named in the entry and the person who had been born (or baptised), the persons being married, or the person who had died. If the records were such as to permit the linking of individual cases to each other – say, two groups of heirs receiving bequests from two brothers who died at different times, or two separate households – the links between the individuals in these separate clusters would still be determined by reference to relational dyads, until a very much enlarged cluster of people emerged in which all the ties between the involved individuals could be ascertained. The point that has to be made, however, is that in following the notational system used in such records, the analyst would never arrive at what could be termed a natural boundary to such ties. That is, nothing in each particular tie, or in a chain of ties as it is reconstructed, would command the analyst to bring the process to a halt. Each particular additional tie would imply the necessity to go to the next step, which in turn would create the necessity to go a step further, and so on, while the entire sequence of linking steps would stay within the legitimate domain of personal relationships, as exhibited by the terminology of the notational system. If the record-keeper had not chosen at some point to stand back from the systems of individual relationships and posit a boundary to them, the analyst could continue such linkage until the historical material was exhausted and he or she would still be left wondering whether the entire network was not in fact a subsystem of some larger configuration. As this problem emerges in the historical records, it is recognizable as the same kind of difficulty that is presented to the analyst by bilateral kinship systems, in which kin ties are calculated through both the father's and the mother's line. Meyer Fortes has observed that:

> in these societies, kinship connections, whether taken in the narrow sense or in the wider connotation of including affinal relations, are potentially unlimited in range. *Structural boundaries cannot be gener-*

ated from within the kinship universe, and non-domestic corporate organizations delimited by kinship criteria, do not occur in such systems. (Fortes, 1969: 122; my italics)

We shall reserve opinion of whether or not 'non-domestic corporate organizations' occur within societies with bilateral systems, for at this point all we want to do is transfer Fortes's comment about the generation of structural boundaries to our sources. As long as we stay within the notational system used by the record-keepers, we will not be able to 'generate structural boundaries', regardless of how many people we manage to link together. The linking process has to be continuous because the terms used to link individuals in an initial set to each other recur to link them to individuals in other sets, and these latter to still others. But, to repeat, unless the record-keeper introduces at some point a different set of notations, by saying, for example, that from a certain point onward the dyadic ties will be falling into a different descent group, any limits of this sort that are used have to be introduced 'from the outside'.

What this means, I believe, is that the notational system used by some record-keepers is not, in and of itself, sufficient evidence for declaring that more inclusive kin groupings did not exist in the community with which we are dealing. Such evidence may exist in plenitude in other sources and, it should be added, as long as we are dealing with the *European* past we should not expect the emergence in the historical records of the kinds of corporate kin organizations which Fortes and other anthropologists have explained so well in the context of non-European societies.[5] In the kinds of sources which we have used to reconstruct genealogical configurations, we should not expect much help in making firm assertions about such groups. When the record-keepers, for whatever reason, settled on the use of a particular system of notations and followed that system throughout an entire document, this decision had the effect of removing from the analysts' field of vision an entire set of relationships by the use of which the population could have been described differently. To be more precise, we should say that such a system of notation left in these historical documents the kind of evidence which absolutely calls for the introduction of group terms 'from the outside', because the notational system itself enables us to compile only the personnel of such groups, which then becomes material for the testing of hypotheses.

We already have two examples in an earlier chapter of how an entire system of linkages can be transformed when group terms are introduced, as it were, 'from the outside'. In the case of the 1850 soul revision in the Baltic

5   Further discussion of this point will be found in chapter 8.

serf estate of Pinkenhof, the enumerator chose for reasons that are not entirely clear to add to the information in the revision a column of numbers headed by the term *Familie*. These numbers referred to patrilineal descent groups and the same number was used for all conjugal family units, regardless of where in the 150-page document they were listed. The point to be noted is that this linkage between family units could not have been accomplished with the same certainty as the use of the relational terminology found in the entries for individuals. These entries said very simply that a person was a son, daughter, father, etc., of another individual in the co-residential group; entries referring to the common descent of non-coresiding individuals were much less frequent. Whether or not these 'descent groups' whose existence is suggested by the *Familiennummer* were effective in some way remains to be shown. But there is no question that, in the presence of such linking information, the group membership of individuals which may have been role-yielding was expanded by the record-keeper, as he departed from his normal system of notation.

The second example is, of course, the patrilineage reconstructions in the German evidence, mentioned in chapter 2. These were based, as we have noted, on thousands of individual entries about birth, marriage and death in the parish registers of the Schwalm region of Hesse. These entries themselves were cast in the simple relational terminology that tapped the language, for the most part, of primary kinship. If, starting with a single entry, we followed this language wherever in the sources it led, in due course we would arrive at an immense reconstruction which would cease only when the records were themselves exhausted. But in the process, we would not come to any entry or set of entries that would suggest that the tracking process had to come to a halt because some kind of structural boundary had been reached. The structural boundary which the reconstructed patri-lineages (*Stammtafeln*) do have was introduced by the twentieth-century genealogists when they chose to organize this massive data collection in terms of patrilines: that is, when they decided to depict, on a single table, the connections between the persons who were descended from a male ancestor through a line of males, over some eight or nine generations. Even these reconstructions, however, were not 'pure' in the sense of closing off links that led from within the patrilines to other patrilines, because the genea-logists included with the symbols for out- and in-marrying females the number of the patriline they came from or went to. As with the Baltic information, these inclusive kinship groupings, which sprawled over several centuries of historical time, could not have been 'generated' from the simple notational system used in each and every component entry. Not until the Schwalm genealogists decided to introduce 'structural boundaries' did this mass of information acquire a semblance of order. But also, as in the case of the Baltic materials, the genealogist's enterprise cannot be seen as anything other than a major step in the creation of a hypothesis about the existence and effectiveness of unilineal kinship groups. In order to test the hypothesis, the reconstruction step would have to be taken in any case, and it could be taken only by means of introducing an organizing principle which the individual-level entries themselves did not suggest. Thus we arrive at the same conclusion, which is that the choice by the record-keepers of a particular type of record-keeping system effectively blocked off inquiry into structural boundaries until these were introduced 'from the outside'.

If the kinship language of record-keepers is to be used to separate the genealogical positions that were role-producing from those that were not, we must be sure that the language used in a certain type of record is not understood as the only possible one in the situation. The systematic use throughout the record of the terms appropriate for describing dyadic ties can never by itself lead to or entail the introduction of terms which would enlarge the role repertoire of each individual. This problem, which falls within the various uses of *kinship* terminology in historical records, is in fact part of a much larger difficulty pertaining to the use of any descriptive terminology. That is, a record-keeper may have decided at the outset to use only terms that describe the historical actors' economic or residential relationships, without at any time dipping into the terminological pool available for description of kinship ties. This problem is particularly noticeable in communities where enumerations of various kinds were carried out for a long stretch of historical time by different record-keepers for different purposes. Again, the Baltic area is a good case study of this problem, because the owners of serf estates needed periodic inventories of the peasant populations under their control, sometimes in order to specify the labour amounts each peasant household owed to the manor and sometimes to calculate a tax required by the Crown. Thus, for example, the estate of Pinkenhof found itself enumerated for a variety of purposes from the beginning of the eighteenth century to the middle of the nineteenth century, with the consequence being a long run of separate listings in which the enumerators' choices of terminologies become clear. In the earliest records, which were *cadasters* or land surveys, the residents of particular farmsteads were named, but the relations among them were not specified except for the notation about who was the head (*Wirth*) and who were the farmhands (*Knecht, Mägde*). Starting in the late eighteenth century, another terminology was added to that of economic relationships: namely, the use of terms that described the familial status of each farmstead resident. By 1850, in which year the last of the tax censuses was carried out, the economic-status terms had grown much more sparse, but the kinship terms much more plentiful and included the use of a notational system which permits the analyst to reconstruct patrilineal 'descent groups' involving people in different residences.

Any argument about the long-term importance of kinship relationships in this community, which is based on the presence or absence of kin terms in the various enumerations, is obviously bound to be problematic. It would hardly be satisfactory to argue without further information that the use of any of the available relational terminologies was closely related to long-term changes in the relations themselves, or else one would have an agrarian history that included the abolition of serfdom and increased geographical mobility, accompanied by growth in the importance of local kinship ties, that was so impressive as to force enumerators in 1850 to use kin terms to the near-exclusion of all others. The same problem appears in any of a number of single years during this stretch of historical time: in 1797, for example, in the 600 or so enumerated estates in the province of Kurland, only a handful used solely the economic-status terms, some (a larger number) a mixture of status terms and familial terminology, and a very few a mixture of status terms and kinship terms of the sort that permit the reconstruction of descent groups for that year. It is highly unlikely that, in that year, kinship relations in some estates were so insignificant as to eliminate the need to use kinship terminology completely, whereas in others it was so overwhelmingly impressive as to force a detailed use of it. Thus in the Baltic area, and very probably elsewhere on the European continent, the correlation between the language of the record-keepers and the relative importance of the various different systems of role-yielding relationships cannot be assumed from the outset. The predominance of one set of relational terms is not a sufficient indicator of the relative importance of the relations they describe. That predominance may simply reflect an initial choice on the parts of the enumerators of a particular notational system, which may systematically exclude from consideration other domains of relationships that may also have been role-yielding.

The Language of Analysts

In the historical sources available for a particular locality, the terminology of the actors may be inaccessible, or only partially available, and the terminology of record-keepers may be formalized in such a fashion as to prevent the record-keepers themselves from entering certain sectors of the kinship domain or to prevent certain group terms from ever being used. As long as only these languages are understood to be the proper evidence about kin relationships, it appears that all we can expect are data of an incomplete sort: genealogical positions whose occupants are never seen to enact roles, role terms which cannot be positioned by reference to a genealogical grid, clusters of positions and terms to which no group term can be attached. In order to overcome difficulties of this nature in kinship analysis of living populations, fieldwork anthropologists normally pass to a higher level of abstraction at the point in the research when there exists a collection of clues about what kinship principles are at work in the studied population. At such a point, the judgement is made that enough has been seen, heard and recorded for the analyst to begin to characterize the community in terms that are recognizable by other anthropologists. Sometimes the data-gathering stage has been successful enough for such terms to be made use of as descriptions, but more often than not they are used as preliminary hypotheses to guide further data-gathering. Exactly when the introduction of such terms becomes warranted is a question to which the anthropological literature does not provide a uniform answer. Whether the analyst has jumped to a conclusion too early, or whether the hypotheses which such terms constitute are proven or not eventually becomes a matter of acceptance by other specialists who may have done fieldwork in the same locality or are familiar with the evidence in other ways.

The complex language of kinship analysts developed over time to provide a common set of terms for kinship positions, behaviours and entire systems as these were studied throughout the world, primarily in terms of the living populations of small communities. The effort aimed at the development of generalized vocabulary, so that a particular community of a certain type, when characterized generally, could be expected to exhibit specific attributes which belong to that general type. The assumption is that, if a community can be on some basis classified as one in which kinship was, for example, *patrilineal*, the investigator will expect to find there certain kinds of kinship roles that are also to be found in all communities in which patrilineal kinship is known to be important, including the specification of importance attached to the same kinds of relatives. How informative such inferences are likely to be with regard to our central problem – attaching importance to certain genealogical positions in a historical community, when information about role enactment is minimal or absent – depends very much on the nature of the analytical vocabulary that is drawn upon. Some of them offer strong clues about this level of kin reckoning, whereas others have been created to have a maximum amount of neutrality. None of them, however, are of the sort from which we can extract information in order to make judgements on every single one of the genealogical positions revealed in the genealogical reconstructions.

The most neutral of these specialized vocabularies is based on distance to a relative from a particular individual (or Ego), and its categories are simply a description of degrees of distance. Thus the parents, spouse, siblings and offspring of a particular Ego are designated as *primary* relatives, and the ties between them and an Ego as primary ties. The primary relatives of these primary relatives, who are not also the primary relatives of the Ego, are designated as secondary relatives of the Ego, and the ties between them and the Ego as secondary ties. Thus, for example, a brother would be a primary relative, but a brother's wife would be a secondary relative of an Ego. The primary relatives of these secondary relatives, who are not also the primary or secondary relatives of an Ego, are designated as tertiary relatives, and so forth. Most clearly described by G. P. Murdock and employed by him systematically in his classic work, *Social Structure*, this system of calculation is different from a reckoning scheme that one would expect to identify from the languages used by historical actors or record-keepers (Murdock, 1949: 94–5). It is neutral not only with respect to the direction (lineal, lateral) in which the link between an Ego and a relative is traced, but also with respect to the question of whether, for example, a relative located at a quinary distance from an Ego was recognized as kin by that Ego; whether, that is, the indicated connection gave rise to two social roles. The scheme is based entirely on genealogical connections (including step-relations), and its use does not require the analyst to give greater social meaning to one tie as opposed to another. When such meanings are introduced, they have to come from a frame of reference which lies entirely outside the system. Moreover, it gathers into a single category relationships which common sense would tell us need to be distinguished: for example, the ties between an Ego and his father, and an Ego and his mother, both of which we termed 'primary'. In a sense, this system of labels of distances is a preparatory system; it permits us to arrange raw data (individual ties) in some fashion before we start to analyse the meaning of particular groups of ties that may include both primary, secondary and tertiary kin. It has proven useful in the historical analysis of kinship ties in areas where the basic rules of kinship are not known or are not known very well (Plakans, 1982: 66). Thus, for example, we can produce an inventory of the dyadic ties appearing in household listings by reference to such a system of classification, as well as the ties found in a transactional document; and, if these ties all fall into the primary and secondary categories, we can be fairly confident that we are dealing with 'kinship universes' in these documents, rather than simply sets of genealogical relationships. We can make similar inferences in handling maximal reconstructions, without expecting serious challenges to the analysis of primary, secondary and perhaps even tertiary ties as being role-yielding. But as a general rule, the further from the central Ego a particular connection falls, the less confident the inference that we can make, without introducing other criteria for distinguishing between a role-yielding tie and a mere genealogical position. Moreover, such a neutral system of analytical terms will not bring us any closer to understanding the contents of particular role relationships, even though it enables us to analyse groups of people whom we infer to be linked through such roles.

A second type of specialized vocabulary used by analysts characterizes customs, by underlining in the terms used the special relatives by reference to whom a particular custom obtains its meaning. Thus, for example, post-marital residential rules are described as *virilocal,* requiring a newly married couple to live with or close to the husband's kin; *uxorilocal,* requiring the couple to live with or close to the wife's kin; *viri-avunculocal,* residence with the husband's maternal uncle; and so forth. This specialized vocabulary with reference to customs is never entirely unambiguous. Thus, for example, the characterization of inheritance practices as *patrilineal* may not take cognizance of the fact that certain types of property may have been disposed of pre-mortem along different lines. If we wish to use such general characterizations of customs to specify whether particular genealogical positions were role-yielding or not, we shall find ourselves with relatively imprecise guidelines. Certainly, one problem of such characterizations, which is significant with respect to how well they can be used as predictors with regard to genealogical positions, is concerned with the lack of agreement about the frequency with which a particular custom has to operate in a particular way before the entire society can be characterized by reference to the custom of that type.[6] More often than not, in the historical record, a variety of practices can be found, and this means that an inference from a general characterization to a particular genealogical position may not be as accurate as we would like. Thus, for example, in the Baltic area it appears that most new marriages were in fact *viripatrilocal,* with the new couple moving into the farmstead of the husband's father. But uxoripatri-local and neolocal practices were also statistically significant in any gener-ation, and therefore raise the question of the appropriateness of the use of a single characterization (Plakans, 1975: 27). If we were to infer from the viripatrilocal characterization the significance of particular genealogical positions, there is no doubt that a substantial number of significant positions would be left out of the picture entirely.

A third type of specialized vocabulary is used in characterizing entire terminological systems, and it takes note of whether kinship terms used by the people in question group certain genealogical positions together or give to each separate designations. L. H. Morgan and his successors discovered that the ways in which the various peoples of the world designate relatives fall into a relatively small number of subtypes, such as those that equate a man's sister and his daughter, or those that equate a woman's brother and her son. For a very long time the expectation among anthropologists has

6   On this point see Pelto and Pelto (1978: 263–6) and Johnson (1978: 52–4).

been that a close study of these major types would yield a general theory from which one could predict, in a society characterized by a certain type of terminology, various other features of that society, such as forms of marriage and patterns of succession.[7] Presumably, were such a theory available, the historian could in fact make some headway with genealogical reconstructions, because the kinship terminologies in them would be a very important clue as to which of the positions could be considered role-yielding.

A fourth specialized vocabulary in kinship study is concerned with how the people in a living community use their various ancestors to classify themselves into distinct groupings. Traditionally, this vocabulary involved consideration, for most part, of societies in which groupings saw themselves organized along unilineal lines, that is, in a line of descent from an ancestor to the living population through a series of male links (patrilineal descent) or through a series of female links (matrilineal descent). More lately, however, no discussion of these principles can be complete unless it also contains consideration of alliance systems (especially the description growing out of the writings of Claude Lévi-Strauss); of cognatic descent, in which the distinct groupings in a living population sort themselves out by reference to a series of links that can be either male or female or a combination of both; and of bilateral kinship, in which reckoning is carried out not in terms of corporate descent groups, but rather by reference to nuclear families and personal kindreds only. Nor does the emergence of specialized vocabularies for analysing this basic question stop at this point. More recent work has tended to stress such concepts as the network (with its specialized vocabulary of analysis) in which kinship ties are seen as instrumental and less of a tool for placing people into one descent category or another.[8]

This sketchy inventory of the specialized terminologies of kinship analysis has attempted to point out that most of kinship research in social anthropology operates, after a point in the empirical research, by substituting for particularized descriptions of concrete terminological systems, customs and practices more general terms by means of which these phenomena are subsumed under general types. A case study is seen as contributing to the confirmation of general rules or to their modification, and this process of classification itself may help the researcher to 'fill out' the particularized description, when the general rules that already are known are used to assist in particular description in which not all the empirical evidence that is

---

7 The most impressive of these efforts is Murdock (1949: ch. 8); for an evaluation see Pelto and Pelto (1978: 147–52).
8 The best recent summary of the growing literature on network analysis is Burt (1982), but see also Boissevain and Mitchell (1973).

needed is available. This constant movement of analysis between the particular example and general type is characteristic of much anthropological writing about kinship, so that the terminology used in the description of a particular community will always be a mixture of such general and particular terms. In principle, there is nothing to prevent the historian from approaching historical reconstructions in this fashion. In the light of the problem that was stated at the outset – namely, which genealogical positions in a reconstruction can be assumed to be role-yielding – such an approach may indeed be fruitful, by allowing the investigator, first, to make use of such information as is obtainable to classify a reconstruction as belonging to a terminological system of society of a certain type and, second, to infer from this membership which of the genealogical positions that have been identified can conceivably be taken as role-yielding. With respect to the societies of historical Europe, this approach may in fact produce credible results, particularly as most of the systematic correlations of various social traits have shown societies to have a considerable degree of correspondence between such traits as terminology, rules of residence, rules of descent and forms of marriage.[9]

The problem for historians, when dealing with highly localized data sources and the meaning of particular links in them, is the appropriate point for introducing such generalized characterizations, the amount of evidence that has to be present for these characterizations to be allowed to remain descriptions, and the situation that has to obtain for such characterizations to be seen as hypotheses. How often, in other words, do we need to detect the presence of some important relative in a collection of interactional data, before we can characterize the locality in a certain fashion, and use that characterization to help assign importance to a welter of genealogical positions occupied by individuals who do not appear in the interactional sources at all, or appear only marginally? This is only one of a large number of questions that can be raised about the interplay between interactional data, genealogical sources, general characterizations and terminological evidence, but it summarizes well, in a quantitative fashion, the phase at which our reasoning has now arrived. The elements in the question and the uncertainties they contain argue strongly against over-hasty descriptions, and suggest that the introduction of general characterizations – a necessary and possibly very helpful step – be seen as the start of a process of hypothesis-creation and hypothesis-testing, in which the statistics that can be derived from the individual-level data available to the historian will play a major role.

9   It may also be possible to move in the reverse direction: see D'Andrade (1971).

6

Quantitative Approaches to Historical Kinship Evidence

Reducing Conjecture

The foregoing chapters have suggested that historical evidence about kinship often presents itself to the researcher as a large number of dyadic links, extending from a starting-point – an individual named in the source – to related people participating in an activity, co-residing in a household or in the community, or, in some types of reconstruction, living earlier or later in time. Some of these links will be named directly and others implied in the named links. When the researcher decides to make use of both types, the external boundaries of the population linked in this way will always remain somewhat ambiguous, because neither the language of the source nor external classifying terms will make it absolutely clear where the significant links of an individual have stopped. Although it is true that the researcher can choose deliberately to stop the links at some point, or a series of points, in an analysis of the closed population so created there will always remain a suspicion of structural involvements having escaped. These warning flags will definitely go up in the case of minimal reconstructions, as in the case of the Baltic examples, in which two communities living side by side may emerge from the analysis as having radically contrasting densities of inter-household kin links by virtue of the fact that in the record for one the enumerators systematically included genealogical information in each census entry, but excluded it just as systematically from the record of the other. These doubts will most definitely be present in maximal reconstructions, in which fairly good inventories can sometimes be compiled of all people born into a particular lineage over a long period of time. Whenever the researcher extracts a bounded set of links from a much larger un-bounded set, by reference to what is perceived to be 'natural' kinship groups in the locality or to definitions brought in from theory, the demonstrable but unused links will continue to pose the question of what else there may have been by way of role-creating ties now excluded from consideration by decisions regarding boundaries.

The discrepancies between the information given and the information suspected as having been disguised by record-keeping practices, and between the information given and the information actually used through the employment of boundaries not found in the actual data, mean that the entire enterprise of developing social statistics about historical kinship must involve continuous effort of hypothesis-constructiction and hypothesis-testing, at all the levels at which historians may eventually wish to make general statements or proceed with descriptions. Of course, the need for the work to have this character stands in inverse relationship to the amount of effort that has been focused on particular areas to date, and the tentativeness with which generalizations and descriptions can be made about historical populations in given areas will decrease in time, as such a careful procedure continues to be followed. At the time of writing, however, no area of historical Europe in which historians may wish to interweave the history of kinship with the history of other social forms will permit such a procedure without the historian having to make vast leaps between points in past time and in geographical space. This emerges quite clearly if we review the kinds of information it would be desirable to have, leaving out for the moment the very important factor of source survival. In table 2, I have summarized what to me seems to be the kind of information it would be desirable to have for a relatively 'non-conjectural' history of European kinship, or even a relatively 'non-conjectural' description of kinship at points in past time, knowing very well that such a data base will never be achieved and that it would be foolish to recommend that generalizations be halted until it is achieved. Research on kinship will continue, as it should, even on partial evidence, and imaginative propositions will be put forward even when the evidence, strictly speaking, is incomplete. Yet the table does make clear the limitations of such propositions, by reference to the data that may not have been examined to make them hold true over the time period or geographical area in which they are sometimes said to hold true.

Table 2 consists of a series of lists and is meant to be read from left to right. It starts with a list of the units ('cases') about which the analyst could conceivably wish to have kinship information, and continues with lists of the kinds of reconstructions from which this information would have to be extracted, the kinds of statistics that could be obtained from the information, the units of historical time over which the statistical information would be useful, and the kinds of geographical space the statistical information should cover. In the lists after the first, only some of the items would be relevant to the units in the first list; which of them become relevant, however, must depend upon the investiveness of the research design and the quality of the available data. The most frequently used line of investigation with nominal-level data begins with a group of individuals

Table 2 Desired information about historical kinship

Unit(s) of analysis	Genealogical reconstructions	Types of statistical analysis	Time frame	Geographical frame
Individual	Dyad, triad	Frequency distribution of ties	Cross-sectional: point in past time	Co-residential group
Cohort	Action set	Cross-tabulations		Community
Bounded group	Family unit	Topographical (network) measures	Longitudinal:	Locality
Activity	Co-residential group		developmental cycle	Region
Population	Kindred	Correlations	developmental course	National society
	Descent group		Time series	
	Lineage			

Reading from left to right, a particular entry in one column may imply more than one entry in the adjacent column.

(Egos) and seeks to identify the dyadic links among them, counts the frequency with which various types of kin dyads appear at a point in past time, and limits this analysis (usually because of the quality of the available data) to a community at that point. Sometimes, when a source includes multiple listings over time of the same population, such frequency counts become available in serial form for a stretch of historical time. It has been very difficult, however, to obtain such counts for various points in the lifetimes of particular individuals; and equally hard to identify dyads that did not involve people in co-residence.

Table 2 can be understood in a number of different ways, the first of these being as a statement of the lines of inquiry which a data base that does permit genealogical reconstructions may make possible. In minimal reconstructions, the limits to what in fact can be done will probably be reached very quickly and may turn out to involve no more than frequency counts and cross-tabulations (such as the number and types of dyadic links cross-tabulated with the household status of the person whose links are being investigated). Even so, an analysis of these will require the researcher to pay attention to the problem of representativeness and to consider how many local-level studies of this nature have to be carried out before the findings can be posited as having regional significance, and how many regions have to be investigated before generalizations can be said to be reliable at the national level. If dyads and action sets are investigated – two very common lines of inquiry with minimal reconstructions – there may also be the possibility of controlling for the age óf the most important person in such groupings, which would extend the relevance of particular findings over the lifetime of the individuals living in a particular locality; and, there may also be the possibility, as was said, of extending the analysis over a series of individuals over a long period of time, thus creating a data set that would be truly historical in character, that is, covering real historical time.

At the same time, table 2 can also be read as a presentation of those characteristics of past kinship which will remain unknown when one or several lines of inquiry exhaust the possibilities of a particular kind of data base. Here we return to the earlier observation that, because of the nature of historical data, research may have to focus on some aspects of the total phenomenon with full knowledge that other aspects will not be covered because the source simply does not permit access to them. Thus, for example, a maximal reconstruction on the basis of parish-register evidence may make possible several lines of investigation that involve specified links: that is, it might be possible to extract from the total reconstruction a relatively reliable inventory of familial kin of particular individuals as well as an inventory of various kinds of kindreds, and to study these by means of frequency distributions as well as topographical analyses. But no amount of data manipulation in such a reconstruction will permit conclusions about household co-residence: and whatever the researcher may want to say about post-marital rules of residence consequently would have to be based on the rather more uncertain evidence about in- and out-migrations in a locality. Without concrete evidence about who lived with whom in co-residentail groupings – without household lists, that is – that particular dimension of kinship behaviour will simply remain closed. With respect to hypotheses, therefore, the table can serve a kind of restraining function, by making clear in what form 'kinship' has entered a particular study, or what form the kinship 'variable' has actually taken. Since the kinship variable can take many forms, none of which is very likely to be present in a single data base, the table should permit the researcher to identify immediately what meanings of the kinship variable the data require to be omitted.

Thirdly, table 2 can also be seen as a kind of map on which to place the existing studies of historical kinship in Europe, a process which should suggest in a particular case both the strength and limitations of particular studies and the strength of the generalizations that can be derived from them. Consider, for example, a standard kind of analysis of household kinship which the Baltic data have permitted to be carried out (Plakans, 1975). In this, the reconstructions are all limited by the fact that no links between co-residential units can be established, so that the data base consists of several hundreds of closed universes in which all kin relations are presented as links to a central person (the head). Moreover, the data base contains information for only a moment in time (in this case, April 1797). As a consequence of such characteristics, therefore, analysis of these data will be constrained, both in terms of geographical space and historical time, as well as in terms of social space. Analysis of kinship in such a community by necessity will not be able to explore the question, for example, of whether the community had effective descent groups, nor will it be able to generalize on the basis of a series of findings temporally adjacent to each other in a series. Nor, if the study remains of only a single community, will there be sufficient evidence to claim for its findings any regional or national significance. Thus a data base of this sort will permit an exhaustive analysis of kinship in several lines of inquiry, but because of its nature it will simply bar the researcher from other lines. If the researcher then wants to attribute to such a study significance for the areas not covered in the empirical evidence, it will have to be done in the form of an argument that the particular lines of investigation for which the data are given are those which, because of their inherent importance, would have been chosen in any case, even if a better data set had been present.

Finally, table 2 can also be read as a statement of the varieties of informative descriptions and analyses that historical data make possible, both in an absolute sense and as prolegomena to an identification of the 'rules of behaviour' that gave rise to the data in the source. There is, of course, no inherent obstacle to the researcher of historical data positing 'rules of behaviour' as the objective to whatever lines of inquiry are undertaken. Indeed, the incorporation of this objective in historical research is one of the consequences of the increased contacts between historical and social scientific research. The table does make clear, however, that any claim that such an objective has been reached, on the basis of historical data, has to be examined very carefully, precisely because of the multiplicity of lines of investigation which a good historical data base makes possible. More-over, the table also suggests that there is the possibility of a large number of types of controlled descriptions and investigations which, though carried out with 'rules of behaviour' in mind, none the less need not present themselves either as suggesting the existence of such rules or as denying their existence. Indeed, a listing of all of the ways in which the kinship variable might enter a particular study, and of the successive and complementary studies that are needed to give to it greater spatial and temporal significance, has the consequence of placing the preoccupation of social scientists with such rules of behaviour – in this case, the preoccupation of anthropologists with the rules of kinship behaviour – at some remove from the particular studies which the data make possible, even though these studies would eventually become evidence for the corroboration or rejection of hypothe-sized rules.

An Individual's Kin: Boundaries, Frequency Counts and Cross-tabulations

The contrast between what we would like to know about the kinship past of European populations and what the data make immediately available is thus considerable. To test even the simplest hypotheses – for example, that industrialization reduced the importance of kin links – requires the bulk of the research work to concentrate as much on the preparations of the evidence by means of which a test can be conducted (as the research of Michael Anderson (1971) with industrial Lancashire has so clearly shown), as on the test itself. It is not only the difference between the readily recognizable relationships in uncomplicated sources and the more problem-atic ones in far-flung reconstructions that stands out so clearly, but also the fact that 'kinship' as a variable is capable of entering a particular study in many different ways, none of which is immediately identifiable as better than the others. If, then, we posit the additional requirement that the data about kinship be such as to allow for quantitative analysis and testing, we become aware immediately of how unprepared at this time historical kinship research is to make sweeping generalizations about even so fundamental a question as how many and what kinds of kin an individual had at any given point in the European past. It has become possible to simulate the numbers and types of different kin individuals had under certain kinds of demographic regimes, and this line of approach may in the end turn out to be more informative than the close study of real historical populations.[1] Until more work is done on actual populations, however, the informativeness of simulation exercises will have to remain in the realm of potentiality.

The question of what kinds of quantitative analysis historical kinship data make possible has to be answered in terms of the extent to which reconstructions permit us to use as evidence the contents of expanded 'kin universes', and of the extent to which we can make use of the individual components of such universes as well as their overall characteristics. This is the reason why, in the foregoing chapter, it was necessary to explore the question of the languages of historical kinship: we needed to establish the extent to which the terminology of the sources as such would permit us to distinguish between reliable and unreliable data in a reconstruction, and thus to make clear what, within a large body of analytically relevant evidence, we can actually measure. As was said in that chapter, this linguistic approach was judged to be ambiguous as far as historical data are concerned, that is, not entirely unhelpful, but at the same time decidedly unsatisfactory as far as drawing out the full implications of a genealogically specific data collection. The linguistic approach could not conclude with the guarantee that, in a data set consisting of given and implied genealogical links as well as of a set of terms describing given genealogical positions, we can draw upon the latter to sort out fully the former for social relevance. It was not the case that the linguistic approach could yield absolutely nothing by way of usable materials – some positions were, after all, clearly identified – but, rather, that the logic behind enumerations would not require them to make use of absolutely all kinship terms that the historical actors themselves would have used, nor all of the ones which the enumerators would have used, if faced with somewhat different data and a different assignment.

All of this means that the researcher has to proceed to make full use of the genealogical connections in reconstruction without, from the outset, having the assurance that the boundary problem will be resolved at any point in the research process. Put differently, the research worker will have to continue to consider the boundary given in a particular kind of source as a variable, rather than as an element of data definition which can be assumed to remain

---

1   These simulation studies have been conducted by James Smith, of Brigham Young University, and Peter Laslett, under the auspices of the Cambridge Group for the History of Population and Social Structure. See Smith (1983).

the same in case after case. Thus the boundary which is drawn by the source around a set of participants in a certain kind of transaction, or one drawn by the source around a set of co-residents, may, in the case of some individuals, include all of the most important kinship relations we would consider for that individual in any case; but we cannot assume that these boundaries accomplish this task for every individual, if there are genea-logical data to show that these latter individuals had kin elsewhere in the community or in the region who may have required the individuals to enact roles. In order to assume that the given boundaries of kin universes delimited all those individuals' relatives who should be considered import-ant kin, the argument has to be made by reference to the transaction which the boundary defines or the nature of the grouping which the boundary delimits. Now there is no doubt that a very good case can be made for the significance of certain kinds of groups which enumerators chose to draw boundaries around. By reference to kinship theory, we should be able to assume, for example, that a collection of co-residential groups, in so far as it can be made to yield information about such matters as post-marital residence of young couples, would contain important clues about the general nature of the kinship system in the locality.[2] But, at the same time, table 2 will suggest that an inventory of kin within the boundaries of the co-residential group is not the only form in which we would want the kinship variable to enter a final description. Although an inventory of household kinship will tell us more about 'rules' within a particular community, it will still not tell us much about adjacent communities, nor about the nature of more encompassing kin groups and their changes over time. To understand these we will be forced to return once again to the question of boundaries, to consider what measurements are possible when the needed boundaries are not those which the enumerator has provided, but rather those that would allow us to treat these larger groupings as role-generated units.

Such statements about source-provided boundaries should not be allowed to obscure the fact that working within them, and without reference to any other boundaries, has permitted researchers to move a long way toward a full understanding of kin ties within minimal reconstructions, through an

2   'The one aspect of social structure that is peculiarly vulnerable to external influences is the rule of residence. While a number of [scholars] have suggested that an alteration in the prevailing rule of residence is the point of departure for nearly all significant changes in social organization it is to [R. H.] Lowie that we are primarily indebted for establishing this point and for specifying how changes in residence rules can disturb the equilibrium of a relatively stable social system and initiate a series of internal readjustments which may ultimately produce a new equilibrium. This is by far the most important contribution of any modern anthropologist to our knowledge of the evolution of social organization' (Murdock, 1949: 201–2).

extensive employment of relatively simple quantitative techniques such as frequency distributions and cross-tabulations. Any examination of research on European household listings carried out in terms of the systematic tables recommended for this purpose by the Cambridge Group for the History of Population and Social Structure will show the wide variety of ways in which these techniques can be used, and the generalizations that can be derived from this usage (Laslett and Wall, 1972: 74–85). Over the years since these lines of inquiry were first suggested, moreover, they have been modified in various ways to permit application to listing sources which differ somewhat from those by reference to which the tables were devised, particularly through the inclusion of age data. Having comparisons as their goal, these tables have subsequently permitted movement to hypotheses about different rules of household formation in different areas of Europe and to a rudimentary typology of household types covering large areas of the European continent (Hajnal, 1982; 1983). So successful has this line of inquiry been in squeezing a maximum amount of structural information from seemingly limited sources, that it can serve very well as a basis for analogous explorations of larger structural units. For this purpose, of course, it has to be modified, particularly in so far as in many types of frequency counts and cross-tabulations within the given household boundaries the items that are actually counted absolutely and proportionately take on a specific meaning only by reference to a central person, such as a household head. A good case can be made, however, that larger structural units, inventoried for their content with the full use of frequency distributions and cross-tabulations, will yield at least as much descriptive material about other aspects of historical kinship as the household investigations have yielded about one sector of kinship domain.

Larger kin groups, when discussed by means of frequency distributions and cross-tabulations, as contexts of individual lives, involve far more uncertainties than inventories of units whose boundaries are given in the source. The fact is that nominal-level sources very rarely make it possible, in work with given information, to allocate an individual exclusively to one unit and no other, as this allocation is accomplished in household listings. Consider, for example, the descent group, the unit 'above' the household which is the most likely candidate for catching the eye of historical enumerators as having some importance and therefore in need of precise description.[3] In the 1850 Pinkenhof revision, which is the one instance

3   I am using the term 'descent group' to signify that group of people in a single-year historical census which, through internal evidence, we can determine as having been descended from a single ancestor. The term 'lineage', which is frequently used interchangeably with 'descent group' (Fortes, 1970: 78), I have reserved for use with time-based reconstructions, such as those discussed in chapter 9 of this book.

available at the present where a historical record-keeper gave data that were sufficiently precise to reconstruct the descent groups living in a particular community at a single point in past time, the information provided was less than direct. That is, the enumerator assigned a unique number to all families and individuals, regardless of which household they were living in, that made them components of this larger grouping, without actually spelling out that this larger unit, in the enumerator's view, was what we would call, by reference to the specialized terminology of kinship analysis, a descent group (that is, all persons descended from a common ancestor). Even seemingly precise information of this sort, which permits the analysis to draw a boundary around a subpopulation living in several different households, is not yet as precise as we would like, because the source does not make clear how far back in time the 'founders' of these groups are being considered. There is still, in this instance, a discrepancy between the information given and the role-yielding groups which were recognized by the historical actors, because the enumerator's reference point may not have been far enough back in time. None the less, even this one systematically supplied bit of information provides us with more inclusive units, so that an analysis controlling for membership in a descent group makes membership in a particular household a variable of the same kind as age, sex and marital status.

The difficulties presented by larger-than-household groups may of course be avoided by following a strictly limited strategy, in which only the individual is used as the unit of analysis. In this, only the dyadic ties which link him or her to others are considered, and the aim is to produce frequency counts of different types of ties that a given set of individuals had. Even with this relatively low-level approach important information can be obtained, particularly from maximal reconstructions which permit longitudinal analysis of the same individual's important kin over his or her lifetime. Without seeking at all to attribute group character to a particular set of kinfolk, this approach may still yield significant information. It is possible to tell from information gained in this way whether an individual was surrounded by kin in relatively close proximity who could potentially be interpreted as a group: that is, to produce an inventory of the correct personnel of a more inclusive kin group which can then become a basis for a hypothesis regarding the efficacy of that group. If, for example, sources in which maximal reconstructions should in principle be possible yield very shallow sets of kin ties (both in time and space), the conclusion must inevitably be that the workings of mortality, fertility and migrations were such as to remove continually from the community the requisite personnel for certain groups to have formed at all. A file of this sort would reveal a sharp contrast between kinship ideology and demographic reality, in the case of areas in which the kinship ideology stressed the importance and desirability of inclusive groups. Whether, however, the analyst takes the next step of moving to a discussion of groups depends very much on the quality of links.

The Kin Group: Contextual and Topographical Approaches

In the process of compiling an inventory of an individual's kin, or those of cohorts of individuals, the question must arise whether a group of people brought together in this manner had a describable existence as a group. We would not, of course, expect to have to deal with the question of corporateness in the case of most reconstructions, particularly when working with transactional evidence or with constructs such as kindreds, which are, by definition, impermanent. Yet at some point in the analysis, the question will become unavoidable of whether sufficient information is coming to the fore by mere inventories of kin of individuals, and whether, because of clues in the source or because of the demonstrable presence of the correct personnel of certain groups, the groups themselves were not a social reality and do not require analysis of their topographical features and their nature as persisting contexts. If a reason is found for proceeding along this line of inquiry, however, the researcher will soon recognize that the sorts of inventories we have been discussing how to be supplemented by other forms of measurement.

A number of commentators on the development of quantitative analysis in anthropology have pointed out that most of the analytical equipment still in use was developed through the study of small tribal societies in non-European settings and that, as the interests of researchers have recently come to include other types of societies, the strategies of inquiry have changed:

> In complex societies kinship characteristically remains an important basis for social cohesion and collective action. Kin groups may be significant social units in peasant communities or in the local groups – villages or castes or barrios – of complex societies. Where this is true, the kinship models derived from studying tribal societies have continued to be useful ... [But] traditional modes of analyzing kinship have been less easily adapted to the formal networks of interpersonal relations anthropologists have encountered in large scale societies, especially in urban settings. ... The recurrent problem, analytically, has been that the corporate kin groups of the sort familiar from tribal societies are no longer in sight. Instead each individual moves through

a world without neat boundaries, interacting with friends, relatives, business associates, and others in various roles and settings. Focus on individuals making choices, forming alliances, and temporary groups, advancing strategies, has been necessary. (Keesing, 1975: 130–1)

There is much in this description for the historian of European kinship to reflect upon, particularly since it is no easy thing in the European setting to draw the distinction between complex and simple populations. Most of the sources in which reconstruction is possible come from a period of European history when each of the component parts of European society was in some sense both 'simple' and 'complex', or in transition from one to the other. Even as late as the nineteenth and early twentieth centuries, some parts of the European continent could be described by analogy with 'tribal societies', while having to be understood as located in political units which also had 'complex' features (for example, Whitaker 1968). If we ask whether the dating of a particular source gives us a clue as to which research strategy to follow and which of several outcomes to expect, the answer in most instances will hardly be obvious. The fact is that we are as yet in no position to say unambiguously, with respect to kinship, at which point in the individual histories of the various European societies the 'corporate kin group' ceased to be a relevant model for kinship inquiry, although the fact that such cessation did take place cannot be doubted.

We cannot be in doubt either that a convincing demonstration of the shift has to be in some form quantitative, rather than simply derived from large-scale theory about the concomitants of economic development. As is well known by now, the different societies of the European continent experienced the processes of industrialization, urbanization and modernization on the basis of very different timing, so that two identical sources from the same period may in fact be documenting very different types of outcomes in the kinship domain. The same situation obtains with respect to documents within a particular country: thus behind transactional sources from a rural and urban area there may lie two entirely different worlds of kinship practice, even though the entire country may be, in terms of important indices, a non-modern society. Not only did different European societies develop at different 'speeds', but also *segments* within societies developed at different rates in comparison with each other. It is therefore very difficult to predict, from the date of a document alone, what the kinship practices were of the society or subpopulation which it enumerates. Moreover, as we have observed earlier, it is not at all clear that either written sources or the kinship practices that produced them are incompatible with the use of both strategies of analysis: that which focuses on individuals or that which focuses on groups. Following Fortes, we can say that an individual involved in a kinship group that has public recognition as a corporate group is perfectly free to follow various decision strategies in his personal field of kinship, even to the point of recruiting assistance along kin links that are not strictly those which make him a member of the group (Fortes, 1970: 82). Historical sources that are nominative reflect this dual possibility: we can analyse them with respect to other individuals who might have proved useful to an Ego, as well as for the groups to which an Ego may have belonged.

Among the inclusive social units, either entirely or partially based on kinship ties, which the sources offer for relatively precise measurements are conjugal families and family households. The stress here should be on the word *relatively*, because, as is now well known, even these simple formations are sometimes problematic to reconstruct, either because the enumerators left out crucial information about composition or the sources present them in the form of fragments which have to be pieced together. Thus, for example, in some household listings what the analyst has are names on a list grouped in a way that suggest co-residence, with no further evidence that such is the case; and in registers of vital events, the combinable entries may scatter the offspring of a married couple over many pages. Sometimes the clustered names are not co-residential groups, but rather taxable units; and in some relatively precise listings, it is impossible to say with any degree of finality whether such a cluster of people all lived under the same roof or had contiguous residences. Such lists may be very precise in the way they indicate the relationships between an individual designated as the head and others on the list, but these relationships may not be such as to permit an exact interpretation of the structural meaning of the group.

It has been adequately recognized by all analysts of these smaller units that the measurements the analyses make possible refer to only one part, albeit an important part, of the kinship domain – namely, a concentrated part of a dispersed kin configuration. Other kin of the individuals identifiable as members of a conjugal family or a family household may exist, but the nature of the record is such that they cannot be identified. This small concentrated kin unit, however, can still be important evidence, particularly with respect to such matters as post-marital residence of young people, the nature of the socializing group in which very young children grow up, and recruitment of relatives and non-relatives to assist in the tasks a household unit has to perform. In these various capacities, conjugal family units and family households have been measured in a wide variety of ways, with respect to size, generational composition, incidence of the co-residence of kin, as well as the dyadic ties represented in the household unit. Conjugal family units, in their capacity as kinship structures, are also important with respect to various demographic questions that clarify the emergence of kinship roles. Thus, for example, differences between areas, economic classes and generations in the age at first marriage constitute an important datum about the emergence of affinal kin with respect to the individual lifetime of an Ego; and relatively low ages at marriage, inso far as they trigger childbearing, are also an important clue with respect to grand-parental and grandchild roles. These kinds of measures, it should be understood, are not possible until and unless the sources permit the analyst to deal with reconstructed groups, small enough to make credible a claim that their members knew and recognized each other as kin, but large enough to provide a good selection of such behaviours as childbearing and marriage.

Assuming that there exists enough circumstantial evidence to hypothesize the existence of kin groups of the corporate variety in a particular locality, we can approach them with two different kinds of measurement techniques. The first of these seeks to describe them as contexts of the lives of individuals by focusing on whether various kinds of personal decisions were made differently by people in groups of different character; while the second attempts to state quantitatively the position of various individuals in the group, by focusing, for example, on whether certain people had more contacts with members of their own group than with members of other groups. With respect to measurements such as these, small kin-based groups such as family households have received most attention, particularly with respect to contextual measurement, whereas more inclusive groupings such as descent groups or kindreds continue to be uncharted waters. The reasons for this have already been alluded to: not only is it difficult to reconstruct more inclusive kinship units for examination and measurement, but there is also the possibility that a reconstruction, though entirely possible on the basis of genealogical evidence, may turn out to be of genealogical units that have no social relevance. None the less, until more is known about the more inclusive units such as descent groups, patrilines, kindreds and so forth, they must figure as important objectives in the task of developing a precise history of kinship forms. The information about them at the moment is so sparse that even successful measurement techniques modelled on the kind used for co-residential groups would bring a major gain of information. The chief problem in this regard, of course, is that with descent groups, patrilines, kindreds, etc., the sources do not offer boundaries. The demar-cation line which makes any measurement possible is therefore as much one of the goals of precise measurement as is the social space which such groups imply. This dilemma cannot be resolved in any easy way, and its resolution may have to depend on impressionistic evidence, or on the analysis of behaviour. This approach with historical evidence is not very different from the procedures employed by fieldwork anthropologists, who look at behavioural evidence in terms of pre-existing models of group structure. This is not to say that anthropologists already have their ultimate findings in mind, but rather than the behavioural evidence is interpreted within a relatively narrow range of structural possibilities. There is a constant interplay in such inquiry between normative evidence and behavioural evidence:

> The existence of a group of many members is easy to demonstrate normatively, if it is named and said by informants to have identifiable properties. For example, lineages in many societies are named and are believed by their members to regulate access to resources. But from a behavioral standpoint, demonstration of a group's existence requires that the members of the group behave toward one another in observable ways that distinguish a dyad within the group from a dyad between a group member and an outsider. For example, if group members address one another by exclusive terms, or if they cooperate significantly more with one another than with outsiders, then a group can be said to exist behaviorally. *Very few of the groups that occupy anthropological analysis have had their existence demonstrated behaviorally.* (Johnson, 1978: 102–3, my italics)

For historians the job is doubly difficult because of the near-absence of observational data. The normative evidence may in the final analysis be only statistical evidence, drawn from the same data base as the evidence about behaviour. Yet there is some comfort in the knowledge that much of the information which we now take for granted about the internal structure of kinship groups, and the significance for the membership of individuals in such groups, is the product of interplay between normative models and behavioural evidence. As far as anthropological research is concerned, this seems to be inevitable, because of the limitations placed by the fieldwork methods on the actual number of people and their behaviour that can be observed in a limited period of time. Thus the 'final picture' of kinship groups, approached from the anthropological side, is to be understood not as an inevitable conclusion forced upon the researcher by the behavioural materials he or she has gathered, but rather as a configuration which best seems to explain the patterns in the incomplete behavioural evidence that has been put together.

As far as topographical measures are concerned, the concept which is likely to be of utmost importance is that of a network; this has the potential of being used not only with data from societies in which corporate kinship is not important, but also with data from societies in which corporate kinship may have been important (Crump, 1980; Garbett, 1980). In the latter use, the concept becomes one of a number of different approaches to corporate groups. The network concept is an organizing concept *par excellence*, because all that we need to use are data that are connected to each other in some fashion. To demonstrate the existence of a network in the past we may have to perform reconceptualization of the data, but we do not have to attach to the results any particular terms (including a group term) in order to have success in the experiment. All that the use of the network concept calls for is data which can be arranged as points connected to each other with lines; as they stand, these terms – 'points' and 'lines' – are perfectly neutral and do not acquire any social meaning, even if we have demonstrated networks of great density. In sense, the concept allows the data maximum freedom, even after they are rearranged into the configuration called for, and for that reason the concept has come to be favoured by a line of inquiry which seeks to attribute maximal freedom to historical actors in their decision-making at any point in past time. The rearrangement of data in terms of normative rules implies that a demonstration of the existence of such rules places limitations on the direction of outcomes. But the rearrangement of the same data in terms of a network does not imply any such thing, but rather demonstrates whether the elements of the system were far apart or close together. It is a concept which seems to be very congruent with social reality, in so far as that reality implies that people in a society will in some fashion frequently or infrequently touch on each other's lives, that is, that their interaction will be network-like, if we transform those points of contact into points of a network and indicate that a contact has occurred by drawing a line between the points. The concept appears to be very useful in describing the positions people occupy *vis-à-vis* each other as a consequence of the operations of particular behaviours, rather than whether particular behaviours follow or do not follow certain rules.

The weakness of the network concept is that it is ill suited to the incorporation of the idea of time into the calculations, for it is meant to position evidence at a point in time, which may be a point in past time. We know, of course, that the relationships that do obtain among the points of a network are subject to change – they may grow more dense or more sparse – but the only way to make use of the network concept in order to establish this feature of change is to take a series of measurements of the same point in the course of a period of historical time in order to see whether the measurements have changed. On the other hand, it is a concept that can be made use of cross-sectionally, in that a network measure can be used uniformly to compare different segments of a single population at a temporal point. Thus what is gained in precision in the cross-sectional approach is lost in the longitudinal approach when the network concept is used.

Kinship Rules: Continuity in Variety

The concept of normative rules is useful for historical kinship research in two ways: first, as a means of organizing longitudinal evidence and, second, as a way of attributing greater spatial and temporal significance to the patterns found in cross-sectional (or single-year) evidence which, in terms of strict historical criteria, could not otherwise have such larger meanings read into it. Let us consider the first of these. A reconstruction based on a vital-events source might show that a surname group continued to reside in the community for many generations, at least one of the offspring of each generation marrying locally and staying there for his whole life, producing another set of offspring, one of whom married locally and stayed in the community, and so on. These interlinked families might then be conceptualized as a patriline, to be measured for size, concentration or dispersion, and consciousness of membership over the six or seven generations the data cover, as well as for the kinship circles which the development of that patriline over time created for the individuals in it at different points over the time period. The hypothesis would be that these interlinked successive micropopulations were conscious of membership in a time-based, kin-based group, and that the behaviour of each subpopulation followed rules that flowed from this consciousness of membership. Rules mean repetitive action, and therefore the task of the researcher would be to determine whether the behaviours that can be documented were sufficiently regular (rule-following) to designate this community as one in which there was a strong lineage ideology. The findings might show departure from norms occasionally, with the ideology persisting; they might also show a very high similarity in various crucial behaviours. The point is that measurement is made possible because the hypothesis creates a standard (or set of standards) by reference to which comparative measures can be carried out. It is not predetermined, however, what the results of such measurement might have to be in order for the hypothesis to be verified or disproved. Yet without the introduction of the idea of a 'rule', the data would remain a series of disconnected successive micropopulations, with the assumption built into the approach that each of them acted entirely by reference to matters within its own time period, without any consciousness of the past.

Historians have generally shied away from discussing the societies they study in terms of general rules of behaviour, preferring instead to describe what people actually have done in all its variety. There is in fact very little in the traditions of historical writing to require that historians seek to formalize explanations of this or that human activity in terms of rules. But contact with the social sciences has had the effect of requiring that the historian's thinking be sharpened in this area of historical explanation. The kinds of evidence which social historians have come to take seriously and explore systematically have also contributed to this requirement. Suppose that, for example, the historian is faced with an archival collection of a hundred testaments from a particular period in a community's history, which may contain valuable information about inheritance practices of a particular social class of urban residents. It is very unlikely that nowadays this material will be researched as it might have been in the past, namely, by the choice of one or two items from it to exemplify the inheritance practices of the group. Much more likely will be a strategy which examines all items in the file, notes what was done in each case, and then states the results in terms of a typology of actions. Also, it is more than likely that the historian will discuss such material in terms of inheritance 'rules' with statements about how firmly such rules were cleaved to (Goody et al., 1976). Throughout the whole range of contacts with the social sciences and the types of evidence that are now taken cognizance of, there are many areas that tempt (or perhaps require) the historian into rule language, at which point his description will begin to sound very much like that of an anthropologist, for whom rule language has been from the very beginning a stock in trade.

Similarly, the historian's use of evidence from a particular locality or community will require such rule language even more, if the research is question is meant to have – as it is often meant – more than local meaning. Even if the historian is very careful to disclaim more than local significance, almost inevitably such local studies will be drawn into the general historical description (written by others) as standing for larger areas than originally intended. That is, it will emerge as an example of 'rules' being followed by many more people than the original research focused on. While it is quite true that such a procedure is not strictly acceptable, it seems to be built into the ways in which historians think and work. The point is that for a number of reasons social historians who are working with past phenomena of a certain type must be very careful when generalizing, because the step from a generalization to the positing of a rule of behaviour is a very short one.

In the area of kinship research in the past, the temptation to state findings in terms of rules has been great, because the phenomena under discussion easily lend themselves to being organized in this fashion. The finding, for example, that an enumerator repeatedly attached the label of 'uncle' to people who were Ego's Fa Br or Mo Br has led to the formulation of a rule of kinship terminology; and the finding that, say, 60 per cent of the married co-resident relatives of a household head are the brothers of the head, can be restated as a general rule concerning patrilineal joint households. These steps from concrete findings to statements of such rules – or 'rules in people's heads' – are a normal procedure, and often a fruitful one at that. Presumably in the examples mentioned such regularities in the data may indeed have been socially meaningful, and their meaning can be best explored further if the finding is set up as a hypothetical rule to be tested again and again until it can be accepted as a general rule which the members of the community appear to have followed over long periods of time. The problem in such reasoning is that there does not exist at the moment any general agreement as to how frequently a particular phenomenon has to occur before the occurrence can be taken to exemplify a general rule. Indeed, there is even less agreement among anthropologists than among social historians as to what the positing of a 'rule' might mean cognitively. Does it imply that the population under scrutiny acted in terms of 'mental maps' or 'cognitive models', which informed them that a certain response to a given situation or problem was the correct one; or does it mean that the researcher has produced regularities only in terms of the research models he himself is employing? Moreover, if a rule is posited, how binding does it have to be to be accepted as a rule? Can it be assumed that a whole set of integrated rules served as a kind of straightjacket upon the population in question, or were they less compulsory than that? Furthermore, when change in such rules is noticeable, can it be assumed that the changes proceeded from wilful action on the part of the historical actors, or should it be assumed that the change came about for entirely extraneous reasons?

None of these questions can be answered in the abstract, of course, and to the extent that answers to them become available, they are not likely to be satisfactory unless they involve some kind of measurement. Yet the questions are important, because they involve the problem of the extent to which custom dictated courses of action. It is hardly satisfactory to assume from the outset that in every instance in past time when a decision involving kinsfolk had to be made, the decision was made with only short-run practicality in mind. That said, however, we are still left with the original question, which is whether and how the force of custom can be measured (custom is conceived of in this instance as 'rules' which people followed in their behaviour).

Unfortunately the history of anthropological research is not particularly helpful, because in anthropology, until recently, such matters were not discussed in terms of measurement any more than in historical research. Consider, for example, how anthropologists are described as arriving at the conclusion that patrilineages existed in a given community, with the implication being that such a society would henceforth be understood to be following the 'rules' that patrilineal societies employed in organizing their internal relationships:

[The evidence] impels us to state that a society has lineages, whereas it may only have certain values for lineages and tendencies to approximate what we conceive to be a lineage organization. Nonetheless, analysis proceeds upon the assumption that lineages do exist in the society and are fairly uniform within it, and that their existence in the ideal form can be analyzed relative to ritual and so forth. The concept is further hardened when this society is compared to other societies that have somewhat different lineage ideologies, but with which they are lumped because of a further reduction of typological criteria and a growing amorphousness of definition. (Murphy, 1971: 59, cited in Johnson, 1978: 16)

The point here is that what initially may have been simply a concept to organize evidence – the concept of lineage – may in the course of analysis, as it serves as an integrative mechanism, come to be seen as an attribute of the society, which henceforth comes to be understood as a lineage society, or more frequently, a 'patrilineage society' with corresponding 'rules'. What is likely to happen in the continued use of such an organizing concept is that, unless careful measurement is introduced at every step, the concept squeezes out all other possible descriptions of the society, and the rules which the concept posits as having existence become understood as the rules which almost without exception were followed by the people in that particular society. The point is that the desire to uncover basic rules may result in giving short shrift to exceptions and may lead to single-word descriptions from which further rules are inferred, sometimes as hypotheses to be tested, but equally as often as straightforward deductions from a rule which is now understood to have been 'established'.

The introduction of quantitative measurement in the various steps of this process of reasoning is meant to check unwarranted assumptions about 'rules' of behaviour.[4] The experience of anthropologists in this area of generalization should be informative for historians. There is no question that the kinship sources we have discussed are readily quantifiable, that is, transformed from words in the documents to various kinds of numerical expressions. But until we have more understanding of the connections between the research models which are so helpful as organizing devices, the ways in which people actually thought in kinship terms, and the frequency with which a particular phenomenon has to appear to be judged as having been produced by a 'rule' or a 'particular custom', the historian will be well served, with respect to the history of the 'various European societies', from drawing conclusions about rules too quickly. Thus, as was mentioned, in

---

4   The best introduction to the quantitative assessment of kinship is Buchler and Selby (1968).

the Baltic household-listing evidence, there is a dominant pattern of married co-resident relatives who are patrilineally linked to each other: for example, fathers, sons, brothers, etc. But a formidable presence is registered in the households as well by the son-in-law of the head and brothers of the head's wife. Whether these males recruited into the residential group through women constitute a stop-gap measure in cases where the heads had no sons, or none that could be judged as ready to take over the headship, is a research question of major importance in these communities. But the presence of these individuals as co-resident relatives means that we should hesitate before describing the Baltic kinship practices as straightforwardly patrilineal and patrilocal, without taking cognizance of the statistical exception to these putative 'rules'. Given the particularism of pre-modern European society, exceptions or 'negative cases' (Johnson, 1978: 44) may turn out to be very important as description shifts from localities to regions, and from regions to national societies. At the very least, they would prevent unwarranted assumptions about kinship on a culture-wide basis, by reference to the pre-modern and modern, pre-industrial and industrial modes of subdividing the past.

In spite of the growing scepticism about rules of behaviour – a scepticism which historians, given their generally weaker data, are likely to share – social science research on kinship has left a considerable legacy of trait attribution to entire populations and societies, notably the work of G. P. Murdock (1949 and 1967). The assumption in this work is that various social activities, carried out more or less regularly, produce characteristics in terms of which entire populations can be described, and that when these characteristics are cross-tabulated and evaluated (by means of the chi-square test), it becomes possible to view certain clusters of attributes as associated with each other and to expect that societies having one such attribute stand a good chance of possessing the others as well. At the start of the present chapter, in table 2, we suggested that one of the types of quantitative data on kinship which it would be desirable to have for the European past stands precisely at this relatively high level. Similar characterizations (or 'tendencies in domestic group organization') have been developed by Laslett, drawing upon the numerous studies of households in traditional Europe that have been carried out during the past several decades (Laslett, 1983). There is no doubt that in due course historical kinship research must also work in this direction, even though regional comparisons are by no means the only goal that it should be striving for. In any case, in both these attempts to transcend local studies of contemporary and historical communities, the effort to attribute traits to entire populations has come after a considerable amount of local-level research has been accomplished and more continues to be done, so that the macro-view explicitly proposed in both can also be seen as an effort to organize, in a tentative and impermanent way, the information that has been obtained to date and to point out the interesting trait associations on which additional work is yet needed. Historical research on European kinship, however, cannot draw on such a store of local studies and, indeed, still needs to determine what the geographical and cultural units in the past were to which traits can properly be attributed. In view of the many ways in which, as we can now see, kinship can enter as a 'variable' in historical studies, the question of what to attribute as a 'trait' to a particular historical people continues to be a problem. Whether we should characterize a society by reference to the personal experience of kinship or by reference to the features and internal organization of identifiable groups, and what evidence is needed to have these characterizations remain valid for long stretches of historical time – these questions come to the fore immediately and serve as the themes of the following chapters.

7

The Personal Experience of Kinship

Even a cursory survey of historical kinship literature will show that, to historians, how kin ties were experienced by identifiable individuals has been of greater interest than how the ties of many anonymous persons meshed and affected the social structures of the community. The reason for this, I think, has to do, in part, with the problems inherent in data aggregation: with the obvious fact, in other words, that an individual's direct testimony in such documents as letters and diaries about what it meant to have kin of various kinds is easier to deal with by the use of traditional history methods, in contrast to the time-consuming and often costly techniques that are needed for the kinds of data sources we are examining here. There is, it would seem, a qualitatively greater satisfaction in the researcher being able to stay close to the content of specific relationships than in dealing with relational systems, and in being able to cite descriptive statements of how a relationship had an impact on behaviour. In this approach, of course, the historian is not very far removed from the fieldwork anthropologist, for whom the questioning of a handful of informants over a wide range of personal experiences has been of primary concern. But the two disciplines have been, and, I believe, continue to be, different with respect to what they expect to do with their data beyond the study of the personal experiencing of kinship ties. Fieldwork anthropologists would not find it at all difficult to proceed from the investigation of the personal dimension of kinship to the analysis of kin-based groups, networks and entire systems. Among historians, by contrast, the simultaneous use of both lines of inquiry has taken place, if at all, primarily in those periods in which the sources make explicit references to kinship groups, most prominently in the period before the seventeenth century.[1] Later in time, as the principal sources took on the characteristics of census-like inquiries and

1 The most important of these studies are Flandrin (1979), particularly pp. 11–49; Heers (1977), particularly pp. 51–97; and Hughes (1975).

made minimal use of the terminology of groups, concern for the structure
and characteristics of kinship groups appears to have settled into the
background. In due course, we may find this redirection of effort wholly
warranted and the greater identifiability of individuals and family units in
the sources for the last three centuries wholly reflective of the diminution in
importance of kin-based groups. But, as I have noted before, the testing of
this proposition for the modern centuries is at this time very difficult,
because of the realtive scarcity of effort aimed at reconstructing the groups
that would have to be scrutinized for social meaning.

As research strategies, the two approaches need not be in conflict, since
there is nothing in the phenomenon of kinship itself to preclude the
simultaneous existence of kin-based groups and the personal experiencing
of kin relations within those groups. We shall discuss this point further in
chapter 9 in connection with lineages. At this time all we need to do is
mention it in order to provide the larger context for the present concerns,
which are indeed with the personal dimension of the kinship phenomenon.
It is particularly useful to understand from the beginning that the operations
which nominal-level sources permit us to carry out – in this case, to
surround historical individuals with kin of various kinds through reconstruction – are no more an argument for the primacy of individual
experience, than our inability to perform such operations in older sources,
which often mentioned groups but slighted inventories of their members, is
necessarily an argument for the primacy of groups. To put it another way,
there are at the present no theories of long-term development of European
society which permit us to predict, for any point in the long period we are
dealing with or for any community within that period, which of these
sectors of the kinship domain should be assigned primacy. The assignment
of primacy has to grow out of the particular study we undertake, and the
assignment cannot be made until the process of reconstruction is carried out
so that genealogical evidence can be properly tested for its social meaning.
As such testing is carried out, however, one line of inquiry within it has to
concern itself with the individual.

The Concept of Social Personality

In describing the methods appropriate to the study of pre-industrial English
communities, the historical anthropologist Alan Macfarlane observes that
in this kind of work:

> we are interested in human beings and their activities in as many
> contexts as possible. We shall see that the data about the English past
> is of such quality that it is possible to build up profiles of specific
> individuals which are, in many respects, as full as those which we

could construct for living individuals. The essence of the approach is the necessity that several different records bear on a particular individual at different points of his or her life. This concept will be familiar to those who have studied the 'family reconstitution' technique which links birth, marriages, and death together in order to build up demographic profiles of specific individuals. Extended to incorporate the tens, and often hundreds of other references to individuals, this approach is the basis of the method [used here]. An attempt is being made to practice 'individual reconstitution', using every record which survives for selected individuals. (Macfarlane, 1977a: 37)

Reviewed from another point of view, Macfarlane's method is an attempt to document what is referred to as the 'social personality' of historical individuals. Hundreds of different records may each mention the same individual, but describe him or her as participating in a very different activity or occasion. Thus in a parish register the individual may appear as 'husband', in a property survey as a 'landowner', in a court record as a 'witness', in a list of residents as a 'household head' and in a testament as an 'heir'. To use the language we have employed earlier, the totality of this descriptive terminology represents the way others classified an individual on different occasions; and this terminology can also be viewed as a description of some of the numerous roles which the individual enacted during his life as a member of the particular community. If all such roles could ever be brought together for analysis, we would have a complete record of that individual's social personality: a serial description of all the ways in which he or she acted in the hundreds of social occasions which community life involved. No record of this completeness will ever be available for any historical (or for that matter, any contemporary) individual, but it is this kind of 'reconstruction' of the individual's life that is involved whenever we seek to introduce the concept of roles in the analysis of social structure.

This is precisely what has to be done in the analysis of personal kinship, though in this effort we would set as our goal not to identify every social role that an individual enacted, but only those that could be traced by reference to descent and marriage. To focus on kinship roles is not a claim that these roles had primacy over others, or that an analysis of them is sufficient to understand the total social involvements of any individual. But it does mean that this specialized line of inquiry puts aside, for a time, whatever other roles there were in order to make clear what is involved in the kinship domain and what kind of quantifiable record emerges when such roles are identified. What we are doing is isolating one aspect of social-structural involvements for special treatment in order to be able to come to grips with the problem of how an individual's 'participation' in this domain should be measured and described. As will be seen, the matter is complicated enough to warrant such temporary isolation; and it would be even more complicated were one to attempt to carry out an analysis of all other social roles at the same time.

As with non-kinship roles, a historical individual possessed some kinship roles that were always being enacted, some that were being enacted periodically, and some that were real roles, but were not enacted at all. The totality of these kinship roles made up that individual's 'kinship personality', which, however, never received expression all at once. Certain of the kinship sources – notably the interactional documents – provide the researcher with evidence about moments at which some such roles were being enacted, but, by definition, these documents are not a complete record of all roles. Although with a set of interaction documents we can illustrate how an individual deployed roles in varying circumstances, we cannot use them, because of their built-in limitations, to reconstruct the entire repertoire of kinship roles an individual possessed. These documents are therefore strong and weak at the same time. They may be the only evidence we have about the enactment of kinship roles, that is, the only evidence of actual behaviour; but in each instance of behaviour, we can evaluate the importance of the role being enacted only in a limited fashion, lacking a record of the total repertoire of roles that could possibly be enacted. Thus, if it is possible in a testament to identify the heirs with respect to their kin ties to the decedent, we can certainly characterize this 'transaction' in an absolute sense by noting which particular kin are bequeathed which amount of property. But we cannot have a good sense of whether this universe of heirs is coextensive with the universe of all kin: whether, for example, the two nephews recognized in the document as recipients comprise all the nephews an individual had and so forth. Thus, by analogy to other statistical matters, we cannot in interaction documents – regardless of how many are at our disposal – get any sense of the population at risk in a particular interaction. A considerable amount of progress in the investigation of historical kinship can be made, even on the basis of these sources. But each one of them is, in a sense, a closed world of its own, carrying with it no clues about whether the people involved are a subpopulation of some larger unit. Very clearly, then, there is indicated here the need to place such a subpopulation in some larger context, and that context is the entire identifiable ego-centred collection of personal kinsfolk.

Personal Kinship in Cross-sectional Data

Most of the individual-level research on European historical kinship has concerned itself with data gathered at a single moment in past time. In the types of evidence surveyed earlier, such data are represented by interactional evidence and household listings and, as mentioned, the latter normally exist *without* the additional genealogical information present in the Baltic sources. I have suggested that in most sources of this kind the kinship terminology present in the source is uni-dimensional, that is, the relationships that are actually identified with descriptive terms are those between the members of the group and some important individual in tne group, such as the head. This format of recording has permitted analysis of a certain kind and this has been duly exploited for discussion of group structure and group characteristics; but the approach has normally not been used to investigate kinship from the point of view of *all* individuals listed in a given document. The individual's viewpoint has been used in these analyses for certain limited goals, but it has not been used systematically in an entire population, considered as an aggregate of individuals with kinship relations experienced individually.

If, however, we are going to explore the statistics of kinship with the individual as the unit of focus, we will need to try to go beyond a subpopulation of important people. We do not have to push special subpopulations out of the way permanently, of course, and indeed it would be inadvisable to do so if information about social rank (or occupation) is present uniformly throughout a data source. But it is only with the most democratic attitude from the outset that we can best evaluate the varieties of personal kinship experiences, because at this level of analysis the variety can be expected to be very great. Moreover, apart from the methodological requirement that subpopulations need a context, there is the fact that in historical communities there is no way of judging *a priori* which subpopulation of individuals had a 'typical' kinship experience. Consequently, there is really no satisfactory substitute for taking an entire community of individuals as the starting-point (if the data permit it), with statistics about subpopulations (even carefully drawn samples) labelled clearly as such.

Single-year censuses, as is now well known, provide information about individuals at a moment in their lifetimes. If the data are good, then it is possible to aim at an answer to the most important question, namely, how many kin did historical individuals or certain types have at a given moment in their lives, and how does this number compare with those which other individuals had. Even so simple a question has been very difficult to answer, yet it is questions of this order of simplicity that loom large, if, for example, we wanted to test, in the European context, such general hypotheses as 'the range of kin ties is inversely correlated with the degree of industrialization' or 'the attenuation of kin ties tends to occur in a politically centralized society'. Such propositions about kinship change sometimes imply the passage of historical time, as in the second example, and sometimes are

Table 3 Kin of Ego no. 12419, Spahren, 1797

KINSHIP LIST FOR 12419	AGE	LIFECON	SGSTAT	SEX	OCCUP	NAT	MAR	FORMRES	SGTYPE	CURRES	KINREL	CFUSTAT
(EG)12419	20	1	8	1	12	5	1	122	1	124	98	1
(FA)11313	54	1	13	1	13	5	2	139	3	113	71	2
(FA)11313 (FA)11314	99	2	94	1	97	5	98	139	99	999	98	99
(FA)11313 (BR)11318	70	1	1	1	14	5	2	142	3	115	1	2
(FA)11313 (BR)11318 (SP)11502	42	1	2	2	14	5	2	143	3	115	2	5
(FA)11313 (BR)11318 (SO)14023	30	1	11	1	16	5	2	115	1	140	98	2
(FA)11313 (BR)11318 (SO)14023 (SP)14024	25	1	12	2	16	5	2	139	1	140	98	5
(FA)11313 (BR)11318 (SO)14023 (SO)14025	3	1	16	1	16	5	1	994	1	140	98	8
(FA)11313 (BR)11318 (DA)11504	10	1	2	2	14	5	1	115	3	115	30	8
(FA)11313 (BR)11318 (CA)11503	14	1	2	1	14	5	1	115	3	115	30	8
(FA)11313 (SI)14220	30	1	12	2	16	5	2	139	1	142	98	2
(FA)11313 (SI)14220 (SP)14219	40	1	17	2	16	5	2	148	1	113	98	5
(MO)11315	50	1	94	1	13	5	2	124	3	113	70	5
(MO)11315 (FA)11302	99	2	94	1	96	5	98	124	99	999	50	99
(MO)11315 (BR)11301	43	1	1	1	14	5	4	124	3	113	1	2
(MO)11315 (BR)12401	54	1	1	1	18	5	2	124	1	124	1	2
(MO)11315 (BR)14501	40	1	1	1	18	5	1	124	1	145	1	2
(MO)11315 (BR)11301 (SP)11304	20	1	2	1	14	5	6	147	3	113	2	5
(MO)11315 (BR)12401 (SP)12403	50	1	2	2	18	5	2	118	1	124	2	5
(MO)11315 (BR)14501 (SP)14503	30	1	2	2	18	5	2	145	1	145	2	5
(MO)11315 (BR)11301 (SO)11305	18	1	2	1	14	5	1	113	3	113	20	8
(MO)11315 (BR)11301 (SO)11306	11	1	2	2	14	5	1	113	3	113	20	8
(MO)11315 (BR)11301 (SO)11307	7	1	2	1	14	5	1	113	3	113	20	8
(MO)11315 (BR)11301 (SO)11308	5	1	2	1	14	5	1	113	3	113	20	8
(MO)11315 (BR)11301 (SO)11310	1	1	2	1	14	5	1	113	3	113	20	8
(MO)11315 (BR)12401 (SO)14105	24	1	95	1	16	5	2	124	1	141	98	2
(MO)11315 (BR)12401 (SO)12407	12	1	2	1	18	5	1	124	1	124	20	8
(MO)11315 (BR)12401 (SO)12406	15	1	2	1	18	5	1	124	1	124	20	8
(MO)11315 (BR)14501 (SO)14505	8	1	2	1	18	5	1	145	1	145	20	8
(MO)11315 (BR)14501 (SO)14506	7	1	2	1	18	5	1	145	1	145	20	8

Table 3 continued

```
(MO)11315 (BR)14501 (SO)14507            3 1  2 1 18 5 1 145 1 145 20 8
(MO)11315 (BR)12401 (SO)14105 (SP)14107 24 1 12 2 16 5 2 152    98 5
(MO)11315 (BR)11301 (DA)11309           14 2  2 2 14 5 1 113 3 113 30 8
(MO)11315 (BR)12401 (DA)12408           25 1  2 2 18 5 1 124 1 124 30 8
(MO)11315 (BR)12401 (CA)10503           20 1 50 2  7 5 1 124 2 105 97 1
(MO)11315 (BR)14501 (DA)14508            9 2  2 2 18 5 1 145 1 145 30 8
(MO)11315 (SI)13214                     30 1  2 1 18 5 2 124 1 132 62 5
(MO)11315 (SI)13214 (SP)13213           25 1  2 1 18 5 2 132 1 132 60 2
(MO)11315 (SI)13214 (SO)13215            1 1  2 1 18 5 1 132 1 132 62 8
(BR)14415                               30 1 11 1 16 5 2 113 1 144 98 1
(BR)13020                               25 1  8 1 12 5 1 113 1 130 98 1
(BR)14026                               24 1 12 1  8 5 1 113 1 140 98 1
(BR)12616                               22 1  8 1 12 5 1 113 1 126 98 1
(BR)12916                               14 1  8 1 12 5 1 113 1 129 98 1
(BR)14415 (SP)14417                     34 1 12 2 16 5 2 394 2 144 98 1
(BR)14415 (SO)14419                      6 1 16 1 16 5 1 144 1 144 98 8
(BR)14415 (DA)14329                      8 1 10 2  7 5 1 144 1 143 98 1
(BR)14415 (DA)14420                      5 1 16 2 16 5 1 144 1 144 98 8
(BR)14415 (DA)14421                      1 1 16 2 16 5 1 144 1 144 98 8
(SI)13314                               15 1 10 2  7 5 1 113 1 133 98 1
```

After EGO, whose ID number and personal attributes head the list, each line of the printout identifies another person in the community standing in a particular genealogical relationship to EGO (Fa, Fa Fa, Fa Fa, Fa Br, Fa Br So, Fa Br Sp, etc.). The line for each relative also contains age, status in household, sex, occupation, current residence, etc. The full list contains all of those in the community who stand in any of 181 specified genealogical relationships to ego. Numbers in age and residence columns are actual numbers used in the source. Numbers in other columns refer to the code book for the Baltic project, e.g. nationality 5 = Latvian.

Lifecon = living or deceased	Occup = occupation
Nat = nationality	Formres = former residence
Sgtype = type of co-residential group	Kinrel = kin relationship to group head
Cfustat = status in conjugal family unit	
Sgstat = status in co-residential group	
Mar = marital status	
Curres = current residence (no.)	

better tested at a moment in past time. They are all put forward, however, as a major compilation of them suggests, as statements of relationships that are 'expected to hold in a wide range of societies and *historical epochs*' (Goode, Hopkins and McClure, 1971: xxv, my italics). The testing process then becomes a series of questions, each requiring a somewhat different treatment of the data at hand. If we proceed, for example, with the second proposition listed above, we would move outward from an individual identified in an enhanced household list, and the first inventory we could make with relative ease lists the number of kin in co-residence with that individual. One seemingly intractable problem in this respect is that compilers of household lists did not always use the kin relationships between head and co-residents to designate the principal tie between them; at times the kinfolk were farmhands or servants in the household and the relational terminology reflected this fact. Certainly a second line of inquiry will be the number of kin in the community at the moment of enumeration, and it is at this point that most such enumerations (as well as interactional data) create permanent and unbridgeable obstacles. For unless the specific ties that bind individuals living in different domestic groups are given, the discussion of kinship has to remain within the circle of co-resident kin. If, on the other hand, sufficient genealogical information is available, then it is possible to create a more complete kin list, as shown in table 3. The list in this table comes from the 1797 Baltic estate of Spahren and it has been produced through the use of the genealogical clues about relations between co-residents and non-co-residents. The column headed current residence suggests that in any exploration of personal kinship ties in this population, roles enacted within the residential group of individual no. 12419 have to be understood as only a subset of all kin roles, and cannot be used by themselves to discuss the 'attenuation' of ties.

A third step in this line of inquiry would be to ask how many kin an individual had in general, in and out of the community. The difficulties encountered in the second step will be compounded at the third, because here we will not even have the security of a listing of co-residents. If kin migrated out, even to nearby communities, it will be nearly impossible to identify them, unless a source appears which takes note of them in this fashion. The problem of identification, therefore, suggests that most of the time when we deal with personal kinship historically, the information about it will be restricted to kin ties at the local level. Whatever statistical summaries we end up making *vis-à-vis* local kin will include those who can be identified in the community within which an individual is living, and will not include those kin who have moved out.

If a source contains the requisite genealogical information as well as ages about all individuals, then it becomes possible not only to develop inven-

Table 4 Youngest male cohort (aged 0—4 years), Spahren, 1797

GROUP 1 MALE AGE 0—4, 19 PERSONS

PRIMARY	NO. FILLED	NO. KIN
FA	19	19
MO	19	19
BR	14	25
SI	13	17
SO	0	0
DA	0	0
SP	0	80

SECONDARY	NO. FILLED	NO. KIN
FA-FA	3	3
FA-MO	10	10
FA-BR	10	16
FA-SI	13	20
MO-FA	8	8
MO-MO	12	12
MO-BR	10	21
MO-SI	13	22
BR-SP	0	0
BR-DA	0	0
BR-SO	0	0
SI-SP	0	0
SI-SO	0	0
SI-DA	0	0
SO-SP	0	0
SO-SO	0	0
SO-DA	0	0
DA-SP	0	0
DA-DA	0	0
SP-FA	0	0
SP-MO	0	0
SP-BR	0	0
SP-SI	0	0
		112

GROUP 1 MALE AGE 0—4, 19 PERSONS

TERTIARY	NO. FILLED	NO. KIN
FA-BR-SP	9	43
FA-BR-SO	8	32
FA-BR-DA	8	17
FA-SI-SP	10	14
FA-SI-SO	9	33
FA-SI-DA	10	18
MO-BR-SP	8	13
MO-BR-SO	7	30
MO-BR-DA	6	20
MO-SI-SP	6	8
MO-SI-SO	6	27
MO-SI-DA	5	13
BR-SP-SI	0	0
BR-SP-MO	0	0
BR-SP-BR	0	0
BR-SP-SI	0	0
BR-SO-SP	0	0
BR-SO-SO	0	0
BR-SO-DA	0	0
BR-DA-SP	0	0
BR-DA-DA	0	0
SI-SP-FA	0	0
SI-SP-MO	0	0
SI-SP-BR	0	0
SI-SO-SI	0	0
SI-SO-SP	0	0
SI-SO-SO	0	0
SI-SO-DA	0	0
SI-DA-SP	0	0
SI-DA-SO	0	0
SI-DA-DA	0	0
SO-SP-FA	0	0

TERTIARY	NO. FILLED	NO. KIN
SO-SP-MO	0	0
SO-SP-BR	0	0
SO-SP-SI	0	0
SO-SO-SP	0	0
SO-SO-SO	0	0
SO-SO-DA	0	0
SO-DA-SP	0	0
SO-DA-SO	0	0
SO-DA-DA	0	0
DA-SP-FA	0	0
DA-SP-MO	0	0
DA-SP-BR	0	0
DA-SP-SI	0	0
DA-SO-SP	0	0
DA-SO-SO	0	0
DA-SO-DA	0	0
DA-DA-SP	0	0
DA-DA-SO	0	0
DA-DA-DA	0	0
SP-FA-MO	0	0
SP-FA-FA	0	0
SP-FA-BR	0	0
SP-FA-SI	0	0
SP-MO-FA	0	0
SP-MU-MO	0	0
SP-MO-BR	0	0
SP-MO-SI	0	0
SP-BR-SP	0	0
SP-BR-SO	0	0
SP-BR-DA	0	0
SP-SI-SP	0	0
SP-SI-SO	0	0
SP-SI-DA	0	0
		243

Summary table for all males in youngest cohort (aged 0—4 years) in status group no. 1 (household heads and relatives), showing the number of persons for whom a particular kinship position is filled and the number of persons (regardless of residence) filling the position.

tories for all individuals of certain types in the community, but also to introduce the age variable. With cross-sectional data this variable has to be used carefully, because its use can lead to generalizations about the long term that, strictly speaking, cannot be used to replace evidence about kinship ties of individuals actually gathered at certain phases of the life-cycle of those individuals. That is, we have to assume about the population of a certain community that the frequency count of kin for the youngest age-group is the same as that which would have characterized the oldest age-group in its youngest years (if we had the evidence), and that the frequency obtained for the oldest people will be the same as that which the youngest will have when they reach those years. The analytical difficulties as far as historical description is concerned in this procedure are well known: and they may be particularly misleading when the information about the community's migration history is lacking. It is possible, none the less, to use the age variable for comparisons, as long as one does not propose that the figures represent the life-course epxerience. There is certainly nothing wrong in comparing the distribution of kin by type for a 0–4 cohort (as shown in table 4, again drawn from the Spahren 1797 study) in one census with that of another. In this procedure, the propositions that are stated have to continue to take the form of statements about youth, middle age, old age, etc. in that community at the time of the enumeration.

If we remember that kinship ties are reciprocal and that we have reconceptualized them as involving individuals in role-creating relationships, then of course the next step in this inventory of kin by type is to proceed to the study of individuals as possessing what we have called social personalities, or in this case kinship personalities. This is no more difficult at the outset than demonstrating and summarizing what kinds of roles an individual had to enact, at the moment the source listing is created. In this line of inquiry, of course, we would not be describing the process of enactment – which could be done only when longitudinal data are present. But we will be enabled to make certain kinds of comparisons about the kin universe of the individual. We shall be able to establish the difference between 'generation' in the chronological sense and 'generation' in the genealogical sense, and thus obtain a more specific understanding of what it meant for an individual to belong to a 'generation' in the community in which he is living. We should also be able to obtain some understanding of the proportion of kin in co-residence and those not in co-residence, as in table 5. It would be possible to obtain a more concrete idea of the exact nature of marriage pools, because in marriage there was observation not only of appropriate ages, but also of appropriate degrees of kinship. We could also raise the question of whether at any age-group an individual is entirely isolated from kin in the community, and the meaning of residential

Table 5 Kin and co-residence: male cohort, aged 20–24, Spahren, 1797

MALE AGE 20–24 IN SPAHREN GROUP 1							
LINK	IN	CUT	TOT	LINK	IN	CUT	TOT
FA	11	0	11	SI	19	3	22
FA-MO	2	0	2	SI-SP	1	3	4
FA-BR	4	6	10	SI-SP-FA	1	2	3
FA-BR-SP	4	5	9	SI-SP-MO	1	2	3
FA-BR-SO	8	12	20	SI-SP-BR	1	6	7
FA-BR-SO-SP	0	2	2	SI-SP-BR-SP	0	3	3
FA-BR-SO-SO	0	2	2	SI-SP-BR-SO	0	6	6
FA-BR-CA	3	17	20	SI-SP-BR-DA	0	3	3
FA-BR-CA-SP	0	5	5	SI-SP-SI	2	4	6
FA-BR-DA-SO	0	5	5	SI-SP-SI-SP	0	3	3
FA-BR-DA-DA	0	2	2	SI-SP-SI-SO	0	8	8
FA-SI	2	10	12	SI-SP-SI-DA	0	3	3
FA-SI-SP	2	7	9	SI-SO	0	5	5
FA-SI-SO	3	12	15	SI-CA	2	1	3
FA-SI-SO-SP	0	1	1	DA	1	0	1
FA-SI-SO-SO	0	1	1	SP	3	0	3
FA-SI-SC-CA	0	2	2	SP-FA	1	1	2
FA-SI-CA	6	23	29	SP-FA-MO	0	1	1
FA-SI-CA-SP	0	2	2	SP-FA-BR	1	1	2
FA-SI-CA-SC	0	2	2	SP-FA-BR-SP	0	1	1
MO	11	0	11	SP-FA-BR-SO	0	1	1
MO-FA	1	0	1	SP-FA-BR-SO-SP	0	1	1
MO-MO	0	2	2	SP-FA-BR-SO-SC	0	1	1
MO-BR	3	3	6	SP-FA-BR-DA	0	2	2
MO-BR-SP	3	3	6	SP-FA-SI	0	1	1
MO-BR-SO	2	2	4	SP-FA-SI-SP	0	1	1
MO-BR-SO-SP	0	1	1	SP-FA-SI-SO	0	2	2
MO-BR-SC-CA	0	3	3	SP-FA-SI-DA	0	2	2
MO-BR-DA	0	6	6	SP-MO	1	1	2
MO-SI	0	15	15	SP-MO-BR	0	1	1
MO-SI-SP	0	13	13	SP-MO-BR-SP	0	1	1
MO-SI-SO	0	32	32	SP-MO-BR-SO	0	1	1
MO-SI-SC-SP	0	6	6	SP-BR	0	4	4
MO-SI-SC-SO	0	4	4	SP-BR-SP	0	1	1
MO-SI-SO-DA	0	1	1	SP-BR-CA	0	1	1
MO-SI-DA	0	28	28	SP-SI	2	4	6
MO-SI-DA-SP	0	4	4				
BR	16	2	18				
BR-SP	2	0	2				
BR-SP-FA	0	1	1				
BR-SP-MO	0	1	1				
BR-SP-BR	0	4	4				
BR-SP-BR-SP	0	1	1				
BR-SP-BR-CA	0	1	1				
BR-SP-SI	0	4	4				
BR-DA	1	0	1				

A summary table for all persons in male cohort aged 20–24, status group no. 1 (household heads and relatives), showing co-residence or non-coresidence of all living kinfolk found after a search of 181 different positions.

In = co-residence
Out = non-coresidence
Tot = total

isolation as compared to kinship isolation.

There is consequently a host of structural questions for which data can be provided by obtaining maximum information about the genealogical ties of individuals from a single-year source or cross-sectional data. But the most useful information obtained in this way has to be that which permits us to view each individual in terms of the maximum number of kin roles which he or she was enacting or could enact in the community. It is this ability to fill in a large portion of the 'social personality' of the individual which the kin search results in, and the identification of the roles and the attachment of them to specific individuals throws a new light on everything that we would want to say about the structural positions of these individuals, and everything that we need to explain about it. It may very well be that that same individual is described in the source with status terms that refer to his or her command over resources and authority. But when we can attribute to that individual a host of kinship roles, then the ensuing explanation of that individual's activities has to take place in terms of both or all of these known statuses. Indeed we can say – and this point will be pursued later – that with the uncovering of kin relations extending beyond the status of a person in a co-resident group, we place several sets of descriptions into possible conflict with each other. In table 6, for example, we have cross-tabulated the 'relation to the head' of all the Spahren residents with the types of kin relations (primary, secondary, tertiary) which the individuals in each 'relation to head' category had with other persons, inside and outside the co-residential group. The 46 'wives of head', in this instance, would have to be examined not only with respect to the meaning of the residential-kin category, which the enumeration assigned to them ('wife of head'), but also with respect to the other kin involvements which these wives had, most of which (1,145 in all) were in fact with persons outside the group in which the wives were residing. Similarly, the 11 'brothers of the head' had more of their kin involvements with persons outside their residential group than with persons inside. In the case of each of these 'wives' and 'brothers', therefore, a thorough analysis of personal kinship has to involve a recon-struction of the kind of list shown in table 3, and their involvement with the head of their group has to be interpreted in that context.

The retabulation of names in an enhanced single-year listing – in cross-sectional data – provides a certain amount of security in a way other kinds of data do not. Because all the individuals will have come from the same moment in time, we can be certain that their lives overlapped with that of the individual with whom the search begins. Thus there will be a good chance that the persons on the list will have enacted their kinship roles *vis-à-vis* each other at some point during the general time period in which the historical record was produced. In an enhanced household list, there is the

Table 6 Household status and kin ties, Spahren, 1797

SGSTAT BY KINREL FOR SPAHREN

CODE   02 RELATIVE OF HEAD

264

RELATION	PRIMARY I	PRIMARY O	SECONDARY I	SECONDARY O	TERTIARY I	TERTIARY O	TOTAL I	TOTAL O	N
02 WIFE OF HEAD	212	107	61	378	51	660	324	1145	46
03 FATHER OF WIFE	6	2	14	7	4	21	24	30	3
04 MOTHER OF WIFE	17	18	37	68	9	74	63	160	7
05 SISTER OF WIFE	5	1	9	4	0	18	15	23	1
07 STEPFATHER OF WIFE	0	0	0	0	0	0	0	0	3
20 SON OF HEAD	383	30	89	350	98	1036	570	1416	72
21 WIFE OF SON	7	13	15	13	2	32	24	58	4
22 SON OF SON	6	0	6	8	0	12	12	20	2
23 DAUGHTER OF SON	2	0	9	1	0	1	11	2	2
24 STEPSON	5	0	2	8	6	39	13	47	1
30 DAUGHTER OF HEAD	373	32	96	265	90	824	559	1121	73
31 HUSBAND OF DAUGHTER	1	1	4	0	1	1	6	2	2
34 STEPDAUGHTER	8	0	3	8	10	40	21	48	1
35 ENGAGED DAUGHTER	5	0	0	1	1	6	6	7	5
40 MOTHER OF HEAD	13	8	19	29	10	81	42	118	1
41 STEPMOTHER	1	7	9	26	3	51	13	84	5
50 FATHER OF HEAD	17	12	25	36	6	90	48	138	1
51 FATHER'S BROTHER	2	5	4	13	4	50	10	68	11
52 FATHER'S BROTHER'S WIFE	1	1	1	4	4	13	6	18	4
60 BROTHER OF HEAD	37	16	64	71	14	147	115	234	7
61 BROTHER'S WIFE	13	9	14	37	29	43	56	89	3
62 BROTHER'S SON	24	7	13	41	54	101	91	149	7
63 BROTHER'S DAUGHTER	10	0	6	41	15	34	31	43	1
70 SISTER OF HEAD	22	13	17	41	5	74	46	128	1
85 GRANDDAUGHTER	0	0	2	0	0	0	2	0	
98 NOT RELATED TO HEAD	0	1	3	0	0	0	4	1	
TOTAL	1171	284	522	1417	419	3448			

Summary of distribution of primary, secondary and tertiary dyadic kin ties for the 264 persons in the Spahren estate who were co-resident kin of household heads. Distribution categories are I (living in the same household as Ego) and O (living in a different household to Ego). Numbers are absolute numbers. The final column shows the number of persons.

Sgstat = status in co-residential group   Kinrel = kin relation to group head further evidence of co-residence, which makes personal interaction even more likely. However, this source, though permitting the researcher to surround an Ego with kin, is not as good as interaction documents for demonstrating social behaviour. The behaviour in lists is implied as a set of actions that were necessary to have brought the list in its present state into being. But the behavioural evidence will not be direct, as in the case of interaction documents, which by definition are evidence about activities.

Personal Kinship in Longitudinal Data

The entries in a parish register, made for an entire population of a community year after year, produce a total record from which, as I have observed, it is possible to reconstruct very elaborate genealogical configurations that incorporate large stretches of historical time. When presented diagrammatically, of course, these genealogical reconstructions appear static: all the symbols in them, standing for individual human beings, are shown in the genealogical positions each occupied *vis-à-vis* the others. But because the source includes birth, marriage and death data, each person in such a configuration is accompanied by evidence that tells us when he or she joined and left the configuration, and therefore in reality the configuration is not static at all. It can be thought of as a kind of giant framework which holds in a 'steady state' components that are in continuing motion: some are born, some die, some are married and thus render the linkages more dense, and so forth (Nadel, 1957: 134–41).

We shall say more about these configurations as social structures in the next chapter. At this point, however, what we want to understand is how, within these configurations, it becomes possible to examine personal kinship when, because of the nature of the data, we have a much less firm basis than is available with single-year listings. In the latter, only one moment in the lifetime of an individual is represented; in the genealogical reconstruction, however, if the information is uniform for all the individuals concerned, there is a chance of obtaining a genealogical history of each individual and, through that, a kinship history when the genealogical ties are reconceptualized in the manner we have suggested. The entry of an individual into such a configuration immediately connects him or her, through parents and through siblings who had been born earlier, with an entire network of relatives of various kinds. Let us think about this entry and the persistence of an individual in such a configuration on a step-by-step basis.

Suppose we are working with a set of patrilineage tables (*Stammtafeln*) such as those we have discussed in the area of the Schwalm. These have been reconstructed, through the linking of names in parish registers, first into familial units and then, through the use of ascending and descending connections, into patrilines, using the principle of surnames as the basis of patrilineage organization. At this stage of data preparation, the 'patri-lineage' is no more than a mechanism for organizing a vast body of micro-facts: that it can be so organized is not in itself proof that the patrilineage principle was followed by the historical actors themselves. There existed in the Schwalm community a large number of interlinked 'patrilineages', covering several centuries, and it is within them that we have to search for relatives of any given individual. Though the data are organized according to a lineage principle, the extraction of the personal relatives of any individual must follow more inclusive rules, because we do not know at the outset what principles of kin selection the historical individual employed. What we want to examine is as large a universe of potential kin as is practicable to extract, in the hope that all or most of these will turn out to be the individuals whom the historical actor will have recognized as kin. The results of one such extraction programme are presented in table 7, which tabulates all of the persons with certain specified ties to historical actor no. 20089 (Elizabeth Pfalzgraf, 1797–1876). Using a birth, marriage and death dates of all persons concerned, the tabulation sorts out the genea-logically related persons by reference to the lifetime of no. 20089, and uses symbols to indicate the certainty with which a particular relative can be assumed to have been alive at a certain point in the individual's lifetime.

Consider what happens when we 'introduce' this individual into a configuration prepared in this manner, through the fact of birth. Immedi-ately upon 'entry' she became part of an existing network of kin and, even if at that age she was not conscious of the fact, her appearance certainly altered the 'social personality' of the individuals who were related to her. Thus a sibling became a 'brother' or 'sister', parents of parents became 'grandparents', sisters and brothers of the parents became 'uncles' and 'aunts' and so forth. There were of course, numerous people to whom this infant was related genealogically who were not affected by her appearance, since they had already died. But the appearance certainly affected those whose lives overlapped with the life of the new child, and her appearance was also to affect those who were not yet born (but are shown in the reconstructed lineage), because she was subsequently present to be affected by them. In any case, we can make use of the biographical information we have about these people in order to establish who in fact overlapped with the life of our Ego and thus establish who stood in a relationship to her that was a role-creating relationship. Throughout her entire life, until she died, the role repertoire which this individual had was constantly changing, as relatives were born, died, married and had children. The point is that in such a file we can compare the lifetimes of numerous individuals of a certain kind (men, women, etc.), and study the personal networks which affected them and which, in turn, were affected by them. The question of boundaries is of course very important, but it can be solved (tentatively) by applying the boundary concepts known to be used in the culture. Moreover, it may be possible to draw upon interactional sources in order to confirm which of the roles that an individual was shown to have had was in fact a significant kinship role. For a systematic analysis of the entire network of roles, however, we have to resort to certain searching principles, which may have to be assumed rather than demonstrated at the outset.

It has to be said that only evidence of this kind can truly be called historical longitudinal data as far as the kin experiences of individuals are concerned. As was pointed out earlier, cross-sectional analysis controlling for the age produces a simulated life course which can be dealt with as long as there is certainty that the entire length of historical time encompassed by the lifetimes of the oldest and youngest individuals in the census did not contain major changes which might have altered the kinship experience of individuals. With a data file compiled from parish-register sources, however, we have the actual lifetime (or a collection of them) laid out for inspection, so that the impact of changes that diminished or increased the personnel to be categorized as kin will in fact be reflected in the numbers of persons to be linked to the individual through a kin tie. At the same time, however, with the life histories laid out before us, we can come to a more precise understanding of what personal kinship in a particular community consisted of as the individual aged, and as the individuals who were kin appeared and disappeared from the scene. We can in this manner obtain statistics about the duration of certain important roles, about which roles on average were most persistent, about major additions in kin ties that brought entirely new repertoires of roles (for example, through marriage) into being, and therefore about the changes in the social (or kinship) personality which an individual underwent. We can do this for individuals, and for cohorts, as well as for other groups of individuals we might choose to consider. And we can do this for individuals in different time periods, if the data continue to be good for a long enough stretch of time, and thus introduce comparisons in a way that cross-sectional data would not permit us to do.

We might raise in this context the question asked earlier: namely, what data are necessary in order to produce a non-conjectural study of the history of kinship? It would appear that with cross-sectional and with longitudinal data for individuals we have identified one of the kinds of analysis that would supply the information for such a non-conjectural study. In these two types of personal evidence we have empirical information about sequences of points in historical time, as well as about sequences of developments

Table 7 Kin ties of an individual over the life-cycle, Schwalm evidence

DYADIC TIES BETWEEN EGO AND RELATIVES OVER EGO'S LIFETIME FOR EGO 20069(FEMALE) LIFE SPAN (2/ 3/747 , 11/ 2/876)

I.D.|RELATION| 1797| 1802| 1807| 1812| 1817| 1822| 1827| 1832| 1837| 1842| 1847| 1852| 1857| 1862| 1867| 1872|
| IQ EGO | 0-4 | 5-9 |10-14|15-19|20-24|25-29|30-34|35-39|40-44|45-49|50-54|55-59|60-64|65-69|70-74|75-79|80-84|85-89|90+ |GEN

I.D.	RELATION
20090	BR
20091	BR
20092	SI
20093	EA BR SO
20094	EA BR DA
20095	EA BB DA
20096	EA BB SO
20097	EA BR SO
20098	EA BR DA
16051	BB WI
16054	BB WI SI
16056	BB WI BR
16057	BB WI SI
16058	BB WI SI
16059	BB WI SI
16062	BB WI BR
16063	BB WI BR
16064	BB WI SI
16065	BB WI BB
24172	SI HU
24177	SI HU SI
24178	SI HU SI
40081	HU
40057	HU SI
40092	HU SI
40901	HU BB
77092	BU SI HU
20094	EA
26191	MO
20065	EA SI
20066	EA BB
20068	EA BR
20070	EA SI
30954	EA BB WI
18558	EA BB WI
40901	HU EA BB
40421	HU EA BR
21225	HU MO SI

(Data matrix of X and Q symbols spanning the life-span columns not legibly reproducible.)

Table 7 continued

20037IEA_EA			X	X											2
21185IEA_MO			X	X											2
20025IEA_EA_BR			Q	Q				Q	Q	Q	Q	Q		Q	2
20029IEA_FA_BR			Q	X				Q	Q	Q	Q	Q		Q	2
21187IEA_MO_SI			X	Q				Q	Q	Q	Q	Q		Q	2
21189IEA_MO_BR			Q	Q				Q	Q	Q	Q	Q		Q	2
21220IHU_MO_FA															2
60062IHU_MO_MO	3	3	3	3	3	3	3	3	3	3	3	3	3	3	3
23908IFA_FA_MO	3	3	3												1
20125IBR_SO						X	X	X	X	X	X	X	X	X	1
20126IBB_SO					X	Q	Q	Q	Q	Q	Q	Q	Q	Q	1
20171IBB_SO					X	Q	Q	Q	Q	Q	Q	Q	Q	Q	1
20128IBR_SO					Q	Q	Q	X	Q	X	Q	Q	X	Q	1
20129IBR_SO						X	Q	Q	X	Q	Q	X	Q	X	1
20130IBR_SO							Q		X	Q	X	Q	Q	Q	1
20131IBR_SQ												Q	X	X	1
20132IBR_SQ							X						X		1
20270IBR_SO_MI															1
11766IBR_SO_MI													X		1
24533IBB_SQ_MI															1
24218ISI_SO															1
50901HU_SI_DA					X	Q	Q	Q	Q	Q	Q	X	X	X	1
59411HU_SI_SO					X	X	X	X	X	X	X	X	X	X	1
77261HU_SI_SO					X	X	X	X	X	X	X	X	X	X	1
77271HU_SI_SO					X	X	X	X	X	X	X	X	X	X	1
77281HU_SI_SO						X	X	X	X	X	X	X	X	X	1
77291HU_SI_SO					Q	Q	Q	Q	Q	Q	Q	Q	O	O	1
77311HU_SI_DA					X	X	X	X	X	X	X	X	X	X	1
77321HU_SI_SO					Q	Q	Q	Q	Q	Q	Q	Q	Q	Q	1
4078IDA															1
20165IBB_SO_SO						X	X						X	X	2
20166IBR_SO_SO						X	X			X	O	Q	Q	Q	2
20167IBR_SO_DA						X	X			X	X	X	X	X	2
20168IBB_SO_DA										O	Q	O	O	Q	2
37192IBB_SO_SO															2
20179IBB_SO_DA										X	X	X	X	X	2
20177IBR_SO_SO															2
20178IBR_SO_DA														X	2
16027IBB_MI_EA						X	X	X	X	X	X	X	X	X	2
27162IBR_MI_MO															1

TOTAL ALIVE															
SUM_OF_X_AND_Q	15	14	14	12	12	28	32	31	29	21	18	21	21	18
NOT CERTAIN															
SUM_OF_Q_AND_6	5	6	6	6	6	26	26	25	26	26	26	29	29	22

Table 7 continued

SYMBOL KEY
X: ALL RELEVANT DATES OF BOTH EGO AND RELATIVE AVAILABLE
#: TIE SHOULD START AT RELATIVE"S BIRTH DATE, BUT SINCE THIS BIRTH DATE IS MISSING, TIE STARTS AT RELATIVE"S MARRIAGE DATE
O: STARTING DATE OF TIE AVAILABLE, BUT RELATIVE"S DEATH DATE MISSING
&: TIE SHOULD START OF RELATIVE"S BIRTH DATE, BUT SINCE THIS BIRTH DATE IS MISSING, TIE STARTS AT RELATIVE"S MARRIAGE DATE;
    ALSO, RELATIVES DEATH DATE IS MISSING

    RELATIVES WITH WHOM DYADIC TIES MAY EXIST BUT MISSING DATA MAKES A DEFINITE TIE UNDETECTABLE

I.D.	RELATION	GEN.	MISSING
	TO EGO		CODE
4043	HU FA SI	1	4

MISSING CODE
4: DEATH DATE OF RELATIVE IS LATER THEN EGO"S BIRTH DATE BUT BOTH BIRTH AND MARRIAGE DATES OF RELATIVE ARE MISSING.
   START OF TIE CANNOT BE DETERMINED
5: DEATH YEAR OF RELATIVE COINCIDES WITH EGO"S BIRTH YEAR OR TIE START YEAR OF RELATIVE COINCIDES WITH EGO"S DEATH YEAR.
   MISSING MONTH OR DAY VALUES MAKE DEFINITE TIE UNDETECTABLE
6: STARTING DATE IS BASED ON A PRIMARY RELATIVE"S MARRIAGE DATE, MISSING FAMILY OR MARRIAGE NUMBER RESULTS IN NO MATCH BEING FOUND
7: TIE STARTS AT MARRIAGE DATE OF RELATIVE BUT THIS MARRIAGE DATE IS MISSING. START OF TIE CANNOT BE DETERMINED

In the final column, O = same generation as head; 1 = first ascending generation; 2 = second ascending generation; −1 = first descending
generation; −2 = second descending generation, etc.

I.D. = identifying number   Gen = generation

pertaining to a single individual or a collection of them. Starting with flesh-and-blood individuals and identifying their genealogical connections creates configurations, which, reconceptualized as kinship configurations, permit the use of the role concept to focus on what the experience of kinship meant in terms of concrete lives. When such demonstrations are possible, there is no doubt that in the historical community in question we have identified some of the features of a social structure of that community and the changes that social structure was undergoing. Moreover, with such information we are dealing with ties which do not lend themselves to being translated or reduced to any others. Even though we will not have a record of the self-classification of individuals, we will have a record of what someone close to the community produced when he classified the individuals in question, and that classification will have been carried out by reference to the facts of descent and marriage. This information, of course, can be used in other lines of inquiry: such as, for example, whether the kin adduced to have been present actually entered into social transactions that also involved the individuals under consideration. This, then, becomes the question of the frequency of kin use, or of the instrumentality of kin, but it is not the same question as that of whether kin existed. What these two types of data permit us to do is to fill the social space for individuals by reference to certain principles assumed to be in use.

Dyad and Triad Analysis

It should be noticed, particularly in the reconstruction based on the Schwalm *Stammtafeln* (table 7) that the analyst is not in a position to claim absolute certainty. Even with such a good collection as the Schwalm registers, in all phases of the Ego's lifetime, there are fewer relatives about whom it can be said with certainty that their lives overlapped with that of the Ego than there are relatives about whom such a judgement is less secure. The specific dates of birth, marriage and death are either missing or incomplete, and generalizations have to be controlled by this fact. More-over, just because people were alive at the same time did not mean close proximity of residence, so that we could not argue from table 7 that the related persons 'lived together', unless we were willing to assume that the registration of one's birth, marriage and death in the same community's records goes a long way toward suggesting permanence of place. For reasons of this kind, enhanced household listings provide somewhat greater security: at least in household lists there is very strong evidence about face-to-face interaction. It is not surprising that the analysis of Ego-centred (or Ego-headed) listings has preferred to stay with household lists, and with very carefully selected relationships about which there is little doubt.

In these analyses, it is the kin dyad that is focused on and discussed, and the reciprocities that are involved in dyads of various kinds. This procedure is well established in both anthropological and historical literature on personal kinship, not only because certain historical documents (such as diaries) describe in detail the content of such dyads, but also because through dyadic analysis it becomes possible to give systematic attention to the affective content of kinship relations over time. Then the fact that an individual may be embedded in a dense kin network becomes less important than the reciprocal ties with other individuals in it, each tie having to be isolated for careful inspection. One finds this approach used effectively in *A Black Civilization* (Warner, 1958: 41–95), for example; and in his work on social structure, G. P. Murdock recommends a series of particularly telling dyadic ties that must be at the core of any analysis of particular relationships (Murdock, 1949: 93). An examination of each of these requires an explication of the timing of its arrival into the lives of the participants, of the reciprocal rights and obligations the existence of such a relationship entails, and its meaning in relation to other such ties. Indeed, to take the broadest perspective possible, variations of dyadic analysis are present in nearly all the literature – quantitative and non-quantitative – that has been written about the *familial* dimension in the European peast. All such literature has involved comment on the enactment of familial roles *vis-à-vis* other family members, even when the description is not designated formally as dyadic analysis. Evidence about the meaning of kinship dyads can therefore be culled from a large number of primary and secondary sources, including folk proverbs in which specific roles are sometimes described with the other partner of the dyad implied (Segalen, 1983). The discussion of a particular kinship role, even though it does not mention two individuals, or the reciprocal role, is in effect dyadic analysis, because kinship roles always imply reciprocity.

The analysis of kinship triads, though less common, is an extension of this technique, and in it the roles created for three people are examined with respect to how one particular role affects the other two. There is no fine dividing line between triadic analysis and the analysis of kinship groups, and indeed certain kinds of triads (such as a family composed of a father, mother and one child) can already be the analysis of a family. But here I am thinking of small networks of ties which do not comprise a 'natural' unit – such as, for example, the impact on the father–daughter tie by the introduction of the daughter's husband, and conversely on the husband–wife tie in the same cluster by the presence of the wife's father.[2] This kind of

2 Whether a dyad, a triad or some other simple structure can be viewed as a basic 'atom' of kinship is discussed in Lévi-Strauss (1976: 82–112).

micro-analysis can be made to yield considerable information on the particular and affective nature of ties, and certainly belongs to the analytical procedures we are discussing here. Interaction evidence is especially well suited for this kind of examination, because it frequently involves very small clusters of people and reveals the affective content of ties between kin who do not form a unit that would otherwise be isolated by some boundary concept.

The refinement of this level of analysis can be as great as the researcher chooses and as detailed as the evidence permits. But it is most informative when carried out in terms of specific irreducible roles: thus, for example, the examination of a sibling–sibling tie in terms of this inclusive category will be less informative than that of a sister–brother tie, and this in turn will be less informative than examination of an older sister–younger brother tie. The degree of specificity is directly related to the degree of informativeness, because the more specific the tie is, the closer the analyst comes to how that tie was actually experienced in the daily lives of the people connected. Thus the ties between two offspring of the same parents, though classified in the source as a sibling tie and referred to as such, was experienced rather more specifically, because of the difference created by the order of birth, by the sex of the siblings, by the ages of them in relation to each other, and by whether nor not one of the siblings was married, and so forth.

A particularly good example of how the analysis of dyadic kin ties permits generalizations about kinship in the long term is the work of Joel M. and Barbara Halpern on the historical records of the Serbian village of Orašac. Here the kin dyads that can be studied are restricted to the co-residential group, because the basic data sources consist of a series of population censuses from the mid-nineteenth century to the present. Consequently, the sector of the kinship domain that is open for scrutiny is that around which household boundaries are drawn. In that context, however, the presence or absence of certain dyadic ties can serve as indices of the meaning of household kinship and its changes over time:

> [The] diverse clues all point the way to a transformation of trhe extended household from that of lateral extension across two gener-ations to one of lineal extension through three or four generations. Viewed in terms of dyadic relationships, the bonds that have not endured through time are those between married brothers, or between sisters-in-law, regardless of whether we are talking of the fraternal zadruga or the zadruga composed of a father and several married sons; these relationships within the household have, in effect, dis-appeared. However, the ties between a father and married son remaining in the household have proved stable, as have ties between

mother-in-law and her sole daughter-in-law. Indeed, as in the case of great-grandchildren, or the presence of a mother or even grandmother, these ties can exist across several generations within a particular extended family unit. (Halpern and Halpern, 1972: 30)

The ties which the Halperns have been able to identify and use as the basis of generalization are the product, of course, of several extractive steps. The first occurred when the membership in a household was recorded, and the enumerator chose to identify only those dyadic ties which linked the persons in the group to the head of the group. Secondly, the later analysis is itself extractive in nature, isolating only those relationships which are particularly telling with respect to the long-term changes of personal kinship experience within the household. But the procedure used in this case illustrates very well what can be done – and perhaps also the inevitability of extraction of and focus on specific ties – when the data base permits reconstruction to create a genealogical grid by reference to which kinship relations are examined.

Vulnerability of Dyadic Links and Kin Sets

From the foregoing discussion, we can surmise that the statistics pertaining to the personal experience of kinship are very vulnerable because the configurations on which they are based are subjected to continuous modification of several kinds. These configurations, regardless of how elaborate they are, include individuals whose membership in them is very tenuous; moreover, individuals in them may also be replaced by others, and this fact may escape the notice of the record-keeper and the subsequent analyst. Yet the existence of clues about genealogical connections among individuals in a community, when given for all such individuals, creates a temptation to assign to reconstructions a social reality which they may not have had. Evidence of the genealogical kind cannot be dismissed as irrelevant for kinship study, of course, because for the European continent at least we have every reason to think that calculations of kinship were always referenced to underlying genealogical connections. But thus there is good cause to proceed cautiously. We cannot jump to the conclusion that a set of genealogical links which an individual possessed meant *ipso facto* a clear map of the personal kinship universe; nor can we dismiss genealogical evidence as meaningless, because if individuals were aware of their kin at all, the kin they were aware of in all probability fell within the group of people pointed to by the genealogical reconstruction. Between these two extremes there lie all of the assumptions that historical researchers have made, and indeed are forced to make, when they set out to give meaning to the historical evidence at their disposal.

These assumptions have to consider the classification system used by the historical actors, demographic rates and a number of practices that were meant to resist the negative impact of demographic trends. Any set of kinsfolk of Ego, depicted individual by individual, was affected by the differential timing of births, deaths and marriages and by the unpredictable effects of migration. It would not be correct, however, to think of the size and composition of a kin set simply as functions of demographic rates. There was the fact of classification itself, which would have operated somewhat differently from individual to individual. Thus there is an interplay between demographic rates and cultural rules, and in order to understand the resulting configuration we cannot disregard either. Obviously the total impact of demographic changes in a particular society would have altered personal kin sets, but, even so, we still need to explain what the nature of the set was that was being altered. Moreover, there also existed countervailing cultural practices. The birth rate in a particular community would have had an impact on the size of the surviving sibling sets, and thus on the core of an individual's personal kinship group. But there is not likely to have been a direct relationship between birth rates (or fertility rates) and these sizes, because of the impact of adoption. Thus we cannot go directly from the one to the other and hypothesize a given size for a sibling group as a direct outcome of birth rates, because we have to take account of the fact of adoption, which could have changed the size and composition of the sibling group. Adoption would also have worked against a diminution of the size of the set through death. Mortality in the older generation may have been affected through remarriage, so that in addition to a set of kin who might be termed 'natural', an individual could have, in addition, a substantial number of step-relatives. Finally, the significant fact of migration, persisting at high levels over a sufficient number of generations, would have played havoc with local kin sets, decimating them to an extent that would have made existing rules of classification meaningless. Very clearly, then, demographic problems raise serious questions for the analyst, but even an initial survey of the factors does not permit us to conclude that understanding the operation of demographic events will permit us to explain all there is to explain about personal kinship.

These problems are particularly pressing when the evidence as we have described it exists in nominative form (that is, with individuals as units of analysis), and when the statistical focus we wish to use is the individual and the kin surrounding him. The problems increase when such individual-level evidence is too voluminous to sort by hand and we turn to mechanical means for processing the data, this being the only way in which justice can be done to the richness of the historical information. At this point, we no longer establish ties through the visual scanning of the evidence, but we rely on encodations of relationships for each individual to establish such ties 'in the machine' and to present us with configurations based on those ties. In this technique, the question of group boundaries becomes supremely important, because we have to guess at rules which the individuals themselves may have used to clasify others, in order to be able to provide rules for the machine for such classification. Thus it is no longer sufficient to proceed on the basis of one or two cases that permit us to pin down with great certainty a set of relationships, because we are then producing rules that 'generate' configurations ostensibly used by the historical actors in question.

In the context of European evidence, the problem is further compounded by the fact that we have to pay an equal amount of attention to all ties initially. If we were dealing with societies in which, for example, unilineal kinship groups were known, through overwhelming evidence from other sources, to have been the sole determinants of structural statuses and positions, then the job of characterizing analysable configurations would be easier. In such cases, the most important – and perhaps the only significant – links that would need to be made would be those between an individual and his father, his father's father, etc., and all the persons descended from these male ancestors. But since we are not dealing with unilineal societies in this sense, all directions of relatedness could prove to be important, and thus the search has to proceed from an individual lineally in descending and ascending direction, and laterally to include the spouses of siblings and cousins as well.

The problem with genealogical links, of course, is that by their nature they are endless. It is not clear, however, how such interconnectedness worked its way into the lives of individuals, unless we take the trouble to specify the ways in which people were related and suggest which of these ties actually was transformed into roles. To do this we have to know where to bring the search to a halt in the step-by-step recreation of links outward from an individual, because, clearly, such a boundary between kin and strangers must have existed. The question is a difficult one because, as I have indicated, we cannot necessarily look to the evidence itself to provide us with clues, nor can we assume that the historical actors were themselves always conscious of where the line was to be drawn. In the approach to kinship from the viewpoint of the historical individual, it is here that the unanswered historical questions begin. If we had clear answers to these questions for all historical actors, then the entire line of inquiry I am suggesting here would be irrelevant. We would then already know what kinship meant for individuals in the European past, and all that would remain would be to describe its various operations. It has been suggested that with respect to European kinship we are not operating entirely in the dark: that we have good reason to believe that most of the European societies in the past had kinship systems to which the term 'bilateral' can be attached (Goody, 1983: 262–78). But the use of this term takes place at the level of entire systems: it does not automatically translate into an inventory of the specific kinds of kin which any individual acknowledged, nor an inventory of roles which were important enough to be enacted. What we are after, therefore, is not only a characterization of individual kin sets, but also an answer to the question of when such identifiable sets should be thought of as kin groups, because this change of identity makes a great deal of difference in how individual ties are interpreted.

8

Group Ties: Bilateral Kindreds and Descent Groups

The Elusive Kin Group

Throughout all the previous chapters, regardless of what subject pertaining to the kinship domain was being discussed, the question of the kin-based group always hovered in the vicinity, demanding at least a mention, if not a full explication. To an extent this is inevitable in considerations of kinship that draw on anthropological thinking, because the social group based on kin ties has had a central place in most anthropological description of the societies anthropology has focused on. Yet it is also true that the question is implicit in the data available for historical kinship study: at times group terminology is present in the descriptions of contemporaries, and in at least a few instances group concepts have been used by enumerators – as in the Baltic case – to rearrange the nominal-level data. It is hardly surprising therefore that we should want to know whether the large quantities of the simple, discrete relational facts of historical sources might not make more sense when integrated by the use of some group concept, even when that concept is not part of the original data collection. Admittedly, there are many dangers in proceeding in this direction, yet these are rendered somewhat less threatening when we recognize that anthropologists, too, when studying kinship in living populations, do not expect to see kinship groups as if these groups were military units on parade. Rather, as was mentioned earlier, there is the belief that observable incidents involving kin ties, kinship terminology and long interviews with informants will permit inferences about rules of operation that can then be used to postulate the existence of groups. There will be few occasions on which the fieldworker will actually see an entire kinship group, however defined, presenting itself for verification as an entity. What will be seen are fragments of such groups, and what will be heard are the reports by the members of such fragments that they conceive of themselves as belonging to large kin-based units with a membership that may include substantial proportions of the community, perhaps even the entire community. This point is very important for the analyst who uses historical sources. The doubts that historians have about groups, because they cannot witness them in operation, have to be softened by the observation that anthropologists do not see such groups either. Because they do not, they conceive of membership in groups as being like a 'charter' that provides information to the members about the links they can put to various uses in everyday life (Fortes, 1969: 88–92). What a group in fact looks like 'on the ground' is a question to which few anthropologists have actually sought an answer through a complete inventory of all of its members. The evidence about such groups is therefore a combination of what people say about them, of how they are understood to affect people's behaviour in hundreds of different social occasions, and of how their existence is symbolized.

These remarks about how fieldwork anthropologists discuss kinship groups are helpful when it comes to historical evidence, because by definition historians are not able to observe any groups at all nor interview any members of them. All that exists is evidence from which inferences have to be drawn, and though this evidence is entirely a matter of written record and none of it is a matter of observation, it is at least somewhat similar to much of what the fieldwork anthropologist works with. Thus, in the matter of descent groups, for example, the fieldwork anthropologist questions a subpopulation of living persons about the reasons why they classify themselves as members of the same group, and discovers that they do so because they all believe themselves to have descended from the same individual, who may have been real, but can also be imaginary. In either case, that individual will be deceased, as will most of the intermediary individuals through whom descent is traced. This information is then the substance of the 'charter'. It is quite conceivable that the 'charter' will be perceived differently by each person who acts according to it: the element of human memory intervenes, and memories are not all alike. It is also possible that some people who consider themselves members of a descent group do so because they have been told by their peers that they are, without having in their minds actual information about what entitles them to be so considered. In the final analysis, what is significant for the fieldwork anthropologist is that the living people with whom he deals perceive themselves as being connected in a fashion strong enough to make a difference in the way they act. If it is a descent group with which the fieldworker is primarily concerned, then the most important persons in it, for the purposes of analysis, will be the several most recent generations. The deceased generations will not be as important, except as a retrospective linking mechanism. What has to be explained through the use of appro-priate and tried analytical techniques is the kinship domain participated in by the living individuals. This is done through an exploration of how the information about the past gives rise to various commitments, obligations, etc. among the living people.

There is, of course, no reason why historians concerned with historical kinship cannot follow this same approach by positioning themselves at a point in past time and exploring what knowledge the people alive at that moment had about their ancestry and how they made use of that knowledge to organize their contemporary affairs. This may in fact turn out to be the most common way of dealing with the problem at hand, given the nature of the kinds of sources that are available. The history of kinship in a locality would therefore consist of a series of such point-in-time studies, with those questions coming to the fore that are concerned with the retention of information about the group over generations, and the impact of this information on the activities of the moment. But the historian may seek another approach, if the data are available, and that is to explore the internal architecture of a kinship group over time, on the assumption that it had a persisting membership with an analysable and durable composition. This would tend to shift the focus away from the composition of the group at any one moment in time to the long-term composition of it, understood as a succession of populations coming quickly on each other's heels. Or, to put it in another way, this kind of study would ideally be able to analyse each succeeding generation in the group starting with the founding couple and leaving no generation out. It would concentrate in each generation on what its activities (marriage, adoption, etc.) added to the composition of the group, how these additions enlarged the number of 'lines' in the subsequent generation, how certain 'lines' disappeared, how the group 'segmented', and so forth. Each of the component parts of the group seen in this way would therefore be conceptualized longitudinally, with the 'lines' intertwined with each other. The quality of the historical record that would be needed for such a study would, of course, have to be extraordinarily good, but at this point we are discussing only the ideal situation and not the situation that actually obtains.

From all that we know about kinship groups in living populations this kind of study may seem irrelevant, because it has not been demonstrated (and is very unlikely to be true) that the minutiae of group history are actually remembered by all its members or actually have bearing on the way that a group behaves in a given moment in time. Indeed, as has been suggested, the only memory that may exist is some vague knowledge of a founder, without any exact knowledge of the intervening generations that

1   Who is likely to be remembered and for what reasons are questions dealt with in the Balkan setting by Hammel and Yarborough (1974) and Halpern (1977), on the basis of evidence from questioning and oral recitation.

the historian would like to know about.[1] Yet it must be pointed out that the historian's task could be different from the anthropologist's, and the question the historian will want to answer will require a different kind of evidence about the same phenomenon. Consider, for example, the thorny question of whether there are fertility differences between different kinship groups in the same community. The question can be answered by gathering the information of childbearing from contemporary identifiable groups of the community, but what we know of the varying patterns of childbearing over long periods of time suggests that a focus on the living population will not help us to ascertain whether the patterns identified in the present were attributes of the moment or were in fact long-term attributes of the groups considered as historical entities. This fact has been recognized by some anthropologists, who therefore have begun to use historical evidence in their work.[2] The question of persistence may not be the anthropologist's question, but it surely is the historian's question *vis-à-vis* kinship groups. Knowledge of membership may indeed be used as a charter, but this instrumental view of membership (which the actors themselves may take) does not invalidate the question that the historian should ask when taking a perspective that transcends the living population and the deceased population which are connected with it. The declaration that group membership is a kind of charter may explain much about the contemporary behaviour of a group's members, but it does not answer the question of whether a group had an existence in historical time and what the social consequences of such persistence may have been.

What we can conclude from this discussion is that there may be two principal types of kin-based configurations in historical sources to which the designation of 'group' can be attached. The first of these is a configuration which presents itself in the sources in sufficient detail to permit examination of its structure and social impact for a relatively short period of historical time, that is, for all intents and purposes, at a point in past time in the sense in which we have been using this notion. This type of configuration will be organized differently according to whether its membership is understood to have coalesced around a particular individual, in which case we will be discussing a *kindred,* or whether its membership will have coalesced because of some shared sense of descent from the same 'founder', in which case we shall be discussing a *descent group.*[3] Both of these groupings may have an extension in time, of course: that of the kindred being defined by the lifetime

2   A very good example of the use of historical data of this nature is Halpern and Wagner (1982). For a more general presentation of the use of historical evidence in anthropological research, see Hudson (1974) and Hodgen (1974).
3   For a discussion of the issue of who should be considered members of each of these named groups, see Freeman (1961), Fortes (1970) and Fox (1967).

of the person around whom it is understood to coalesce, and that of the descent group being defined by the combined lifetimes of the several generations which comprise it at the moment it is being analysed. The second major type of configuration is the *lineage,* the length of the existence of which supposedly is far greater than any entry about its constituent elements at a point in past time in the historical record. In the present chapter, we shall look closely at the kindred and the descent group, in order to establish in what form they might emerge from historical sources. A discussion of the lineage is postponed to the following chapter because, as far as European evidence is concerned, it is the lineage which gives us the best opportunity to explore what the study of kinship in the long term implies.

The Kindred

It was suggested earlier that European household listings do provide genealogical evidence for an analysis of the smallest of kin-based groups, namely, the conjugal family unit (CFU). Measurements appropriate to the conjugal family unit as a group have become well known, since much of the empirical investigation of historical social structure during the past several decades has concentrated precisely on this unit. These investigations have sought to understand the impact of demographic change on the structure of the group, and this thrust is relevant when the intention is to count individuals as well as relationships. The identification of members of the family group, and the exploration of the family group as a kinship group suggest, however, that to stop the analysis with the personnel of this group is an arbitrary decision, made for the analyst by the data (if they identify only ties appropriate for the family) or by the analyst himself, if it is family analysis he is seeking. The availability of additional ties suggests, however, that measurement can be carried out on groups more inclusive than the family, and must be carried out if we bear in mind that family groups, strictly defined, overlap in the course of historical time as well as at a moment in time, and entail roles for family members which are enacted *vis-à-vis* people beyond the strictly defined conjugal family unit. Thus in addition to enacting the familial roles, such as 'father' or 'son', an individual will also be enacting those of an in-law, and this suggests the presence in a particular population of clusters of people who may be candidates for being considered as kin groups. If the analyst is working with a data file in which genealogical relationships are systematically given for all members of the explored population at a point of time as well as over time, the group can be re-created, regardless of whether or not it is mentioned as a group in the source or other contemporary documents. But this kind of re-creation must

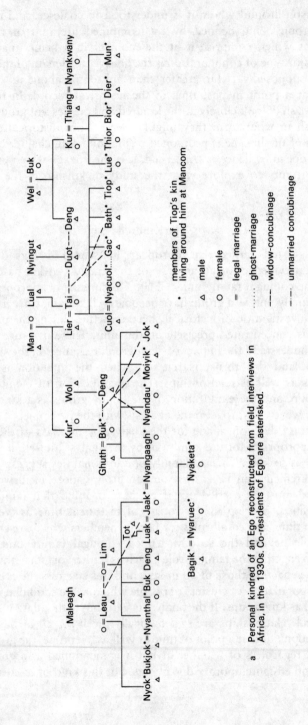

Figure 9 Reconstructions of personal kindred
Source: Evans-Pritchard, 1951: 105

a Personal kindred of an Ego reconstructed from field interviews in
   Africa, in the 1930s. Co-residents of Ego are asterisked.

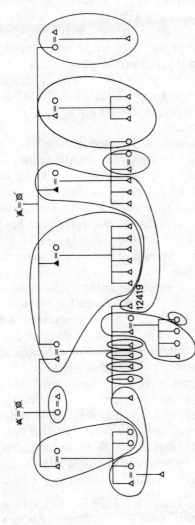

b Personal kindred of an Ego reconstructed from a single-year household list, Kurland, 1797 (see table 3). Circled symbols indicate co-residents.

12419

▲ head of household

✗ deceased male

✗ deceased female

Figure 9 continued

be tentative to a degree, because though we have the personnel of the group and knowledge of how the group was genealogically constituted, we might not have, in any final sense, evidence that the group acted as a group. Consider, for example, the two reconstructions shown in figure 9, the first of which comes from information obtained from fieldwork among the living members of the Nuer population (Evans–Pritchard, 1951: 105; 1980), and the second from a historical source which has already been mentioned, the soul revision of the serf Spahren estate in 1797 (see table 3). The start of the reconstruction simply followed available clues about kin relationships. But whereas, in the well-known case of the Nuer, we know by direct evidence that the individual around whom the reconstruction was made actually used the demonstrated ties in various ways, in the case of the 1797 Baltic serfs, as we know are the genealogical relations which raise the various relatives to the level of potentially significant people, but do not in themselves confirm that the ties were actually made use of.

It has been suggested that the most easily identifiable kin-based *group* (as contrasted with a set of relatives) in which historical Europeans were in some fashion involved beyond the conjugal family unit and the household was the *bilateral kindred,* a type of grouping that differed in composition from individual to individual, but none the less can be spoken about in terms of rules of formation and duration of existence.[4] The kindred was bilateral, in the sense that it was composed of relatives both from an individual's father's and mother's side and, possibly, also from affinal kin. In creating such a group for a specific purpose, the historical actor (and the later analyst) did not generally consider the father's relatives to be more significant than the mother's, but on either side not all of the people related to the father or the mother were included. Where the boundary was drawn remains unclear: that is, we do not know enough at this time about these groups in all of the different areas of historical Europe to be able to make a general statement about where precisely in the genealogical grid the line was drawn around all the people that were to be considered as 'kindred'. Moreover, even if we establish such a boundary and determine who fell within it, we do not have reason to think that the people within it saw themselves as comprising a group in any sense other than that they were all related to a specific individual. We know enough about the nature of such groupings, however, to say that the people in them ceased to be considered as part of a group when the central individual to whom they were all related

4 The disagreements over who is to be classified as a member of a kindred is discussed at length in Freeman (1961), and a detailed study of how kindreds operate in a European population can be found in Pehrson (1957). The most famous traditional historical examination of documentary evidence concerning these groups during the medieval period of European history is Phillpotts (1913).

died. What the size and composition of the group was during the lifetime of its central actor, and how these two attributes changed over the lifetime of the actor are the matters which we want to understand. But it also has to be remembered that this group is given a formal name for convenience's sake only, and is identified as a group because the analyst wishes to examine its properties, not because we can find it and other groups like it in continuous existence without reference to a specific individual.

If we bear in mind the main goal of the study of historical kinship, then this kind of group must be given an identity and its characteristics explored, regardless of how tenuous its existence was. The intention of the search for the meaning of historical kinship is not to identify only those groupings of people or subsets of a large genealogical set that had a corporate existence of their own beyond that of any individual member, but to describe the social consequences, whatever they may have been, of individuals classifying other people in terms of descent and marriage. This continuing classification, practised by individuals throughout their lifetimes, presumably had meaning not only for the persons doing the classifying, but also for the people being classified, in so far as classification eventually led to the recognition by both parties that they had roles to enact toward each other. As long as we remember that what we are after are the social consequences of social classification, and that in exploring kinship we are exploring a historical activity (analogous to work and other activities performed in the social context), then the bilateral kindred has to be one of the groups which we have to identify and measure. The kindred may not have had an existence beyond the classifications, but it had an existence at least for the lifetime of the individual; and conceivably, the relationships which existed between this set of persons and the person who had classified them may have come to be recognized only when the group came together to accomplish some specific purpose (cf. Karnoouh, 1979).

The identifiable personnel of a bilateral kindred can emerge in the sources in two different ways. First, they could be named in an interactional document (such as the marriage contract explained in chapter 2), that is, in a source that listed the participants of some activity at a particular moment in time. If the activity is such that we can assume the group as having been formed through recruitment by a central person, the resulting list would resemble the kind of record a fieldwork anthropologist would make after observing a similar activity in a living population. The list could be used to perform a minimal reconstruction, the participants in the group counted and, most importantly, their ties to the central actor identified as preliminary evidence to generalizations about who 'normally' participated and thus can be considered as 'members' of the bilateral kindred of the central actor. Such generalizations could come only after close scrutiny of many such individual records, because no single record would necessarily draw upon all the persons the central actor considered part of the kindred. Second, the members of a bilateral kindred would also emerge in such reconstructions as shown in figure 9 (and table 3 earlier); in these, however, the researcher would have listed not only the kindred, but also, conceivably, many other persons who fell beyond its borders. These reconstructions would give us the population 'at risk' from which the kindred was drawn; the inter-actional sources, on the other hand, would specify the participants without the context from which they emerged. In the one source, we would immediately encounter the boundary problem; in the other, there would be a shortage of evidence to answer the question of whether certain persons had been recruited into the kindred because they were the sole represen-tatives of certain kinds of kin in the population or through some kind of selection process directed toward a number of kin of the same kind. In neither kind of reconstruction, therefore, are we confronted with the best record we could possibly have.

The roles which the members of a bilateral kindred enacted toward each other, where they finally were brought together by a particular individual, may have changed somewhat when the relationships became known. To understand this, we have to remember that all individuals had roles to play, but that some of these roles were more readily identifiable and enactable than others. For example, it is possible that two distant relatives of an individual might not have recognized that they were related to each other by virtue of being related to the same person; but if that person acted so as to bring these relatives together by using the connection, they might thereafter have sought to define their own relationship more precisely, to define the roles implicit in it and to act on the basis of such roles. Thus the individual would have served as an agent for deepening the ties implicit in the bilateral kindred, by confirming and strengthening relationships which otherwise might have gone unnoticed and unused. In such an example, the individual in question would have served as a catalyst in making the kindred into more of a self-conscious group, in vivifying the genealogical relationships which did exist, but were not used. It is because of this feature of the kindred – that it needs a focus in order to exist at all – that we could call it a weak kinship group, as contrasted with groups whose existence was from the outset based not on the fact that they were connected to some living individual, but were connected because of common ancestry by all of the persons involved.

The bilateral kindred can be thought of as laying out the markers of a field of social activity that is not used unless activated for a particular purpose. But, once activated, the members in this field may act so as to bring to the surface the ties that existed, but were not recognized. More than other kinds of groupings in European history, the bilateral kindred suggests how necessary it is, in order to understand historical kinship, to explore not only the genealogical ties that stood behind it, but also the activities in which kinship ties were made use of. We might proceed a very long way in identifying and describing the attributes of kin groups organized on the basis of an explicit principle of exclusion and inclusion, even when we do not have strict evidence that the groups so defined ever acted as groups. We shall see how this is done later in this chapter, when we discuss the basis of descent groups. But with bilateral kindred, the weight of the evidence almost inescapably has to be on the activities in which such groups engaged, because it is most often through these activities that the groups themselves emerge.

Descent Groups

In the sources we have been discussing, enumerators frequently used relational terms, which permit conjugal family units to be distinguished from each other; and listing formats, which allow the assumption of co-residence. Precise measurement of these units therefore has been possible from the very beginning of the effort to analyse social microstructures quantitatively. But as soon as we move to the next step and look for equally precise information about somewhat more inclusive units such as bilateral kindreds and descent groups, the sources are, more often than not, silent. Although they may provide genealogical clues through which the analyst can reconstruct these more inclusive groupings, they will seldom provide even the barest of hints about the genealogical positions at which such a reconstruction has to stop, and little, if any, information on whether a particular reconstructed group ever acted in common – as a group – to achieve a particular end. None the less, in the study of historical kinship, terms such as 'kindred' and 'descent group' have been used relatively frequently, with the basic information about the former being taken from interactional evidence: from the group of relatives who participated in a particular transaction or activity; and the basic information about the latter extrapolated from general kinship information about the community. As far as descent groups are concerned, there have been, to my knowledge, no historical sources in which an enumerator used a designator for group membership for every person in the population of an entire community, so that each member of the community could be allocated to one or other such group in the same way that we would allocate them to one or other household. In principle, we should be able to measure, for example, the mean size of descent groups and discuss their internal composition in a manner not dissimilar to what is used with households, but in practice even this simple goal has been impossible to implement.

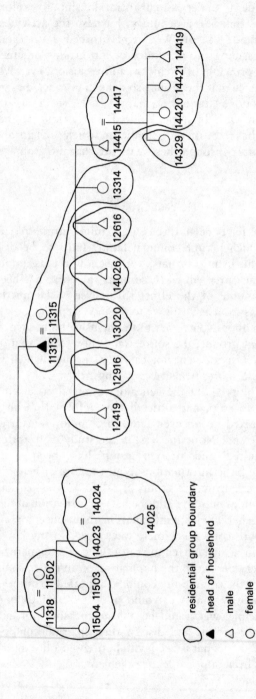

Figure 10 Ideographic representation of the patriline segment of Ego no. 11313, Spahren, 1797

Table 8 Patriline segment of Ego no. 11313, Spahren, 1797

	age	living/deceased	status in co-res. group	sex	occupation	nationality	former residence	current residence	kin relation	status conj.
EGO (EG)11313	54	1	13	1	13	5	2139	3113	71	2
MALES										
(BR)11318	70	1	1	1	14	5	2142	3115	1	2
(BR)11318 (SO)14023	30	1	11	1	16	5	2115	1140	98	2
(BR)11318 (SO)14023 (SO)14025	3	1	16	1	16	5	1994	1140	98	8
(SO)14415	30	1	11	1	16	5	2113	1144	98	1
(SO)13020	25	1	8	1	12	5	1113	1130	98	1
(SO)14026	24	1	12	1	8	5	1113	1140	98	1
(SO)12616	22	1	8	1	12	5	1113	1126	98	1
(SO)12916	14	1	8	1	12	5	1113	1129	98	1
(SO)12419	20	1	8	1	12	5	1122	1124	98	1
(SO)14415 (SO)14419	6	1	16	1	16	5	1144	1144	98	8
IN-MARRYING FEMALES										
(BR)11318 (SP)11502	42	1	2	2	14	5	2143	3115	2	5
(BR)11318 (SO)14023 (SP)14024	25	1	12	2	16	5	2139	1140	98	5
(SO)14415 (SP)14417	34	1	12	2	16	5	2394	1144	98	2
(SP)11315	50	1	17	2	13	5	2124	3113	70	5
OTHER FEMALES, UNMARRIED										
(BR)11318 (DA)11504	10	1	2	2	14	5	1115	3115	30	8
(BR)11318 (DA)11503	14	1	2	2	14	5	1115	3115	30	8
(SO)14415 (DA)14329	8	1	10	2	7	5	1144	1143	98	1
(SO)14415 (DA)14420	5	1	16	2	16	5	1144	1144	98	8
(SO)14415 (DA)14421	1	1	16	2	16	5	1144	1144	98	8
(DA)13314	15	1	10	2	7	5	1113	1133	98	1

54 = age	1 = living or deceased
13 = status in co-residential group	1 = sex
13 = occupation	5 = nationality
2139 = former residence	3113 = current residence
71 = kin relation to group head	2 = status in conjugal family unit

Even if the data were exactly in the form desired, measurements of descent groups still require certain decisions on the part of the analyst which are not entailed in, for example, household analysis. Consider, for instance, table 8, which presents the results of a reconstruction project designed specifically to extract from the Spahren 1797 census, mentioned earlier, all the persons about whom it can be said that they 'belonged' to a particular individual's descent group. This effort is similar to that which was used to extract information from the same census about bilateral kindreds of individuals, except that this time the rules of extraction were written to reproduce information only about those persons who, in 1797, were likely to have traced their descent to the most distant (in the census) antecedent male relative. Each of the three categories of persons in this group – males, in-marrying females and females not married – are assumed to have belonged to the descent group of Ego no. 11313, and their kin designations are referenced to the Ego. Transformed into an ideograph, as in figure 10, this descent group shows itself to have been quite dispersed, with most of the important component parts of it living in different farmsteads (households). Several decisions have had to be made to reach the conclusion that all the people depicted in the diagram were in fact 'members' of this descent group. We have had to assume, for example, that the wives of patrilineally linked males were, at the moment of the census, 'members' of the group, and that unmarried daughters (such as nos. 11504, 11503, 13314 and 14329) were also 'members'. Married daughters, who in such a process of reallocation would appear as 'members' of other groups, would not be counted in this one. There is, as mentioned, nothing in the census itself that instructs us to use these rules of allocation, but what we know of descent groups in other cultures permits us to assume that in-married and un-married females would have been under the 'care' of the males of this group. A preliminary assessment of this group would have to conclude that, at the moment of the census, this descent group had altogether 21 members dispersed among ten different farmsteads, and that at this point in time its structure was a three-generational one. Using the genealogical clues in the 1797 census and the principles of allocation already mentioned, we could classify each person in the entire estate in 1797 as a member of one or another group and, through a statistical assessment of these, arrive at a general characterization of the next most inclusve kin unit above the household. Whether the people shown in table 8 and figure 10 understood themselves as being 'members' of an even more inclusive grouping, as a result of the common descent the group shared with other descent groups in the 1797 record, there is no way of knowing. The genealogical clues, on the basis of which this reconstruction is made, permit linkages to be made over a maximum of three generations.

The important question is whether the group thus reconstructed had any social reality at all. Ordinarily, we would have no basis for making such a claim from the 1797 source itself, unless we could devise a means for showing that the behavioural evidence implicit in the co-residential patterns in the source revealed, for example, that the dispersed sons of no. 11313 normally were living in the households of more senior members of the descent group. This would be testimony for a certain amount of descent-group solidarity, but, as figure 10 suggests, no such pattern emerges here. Conceivably, in other interactional evidence from this community one might find other examples of such solidarity but this evidence is not at our disposal. Consequently, the analysis has to proceed, for 1797, on the basis of an 'as if' proposition: we can arrive at certain statistical conclusions about descent groups 'as if' they had social significance, but we cannot demonstrate unambiguously that such significance actually obtained.

There is one piece of evidence for Spahren later in historical time which is suggestive. In the final census in the revision series, in 1858, the enumerator himself carried out the kind of reclassification that we have done for 1797, evidently on the same basis which we have used for what would have been the grandparental generation of the 1858 population. Each of the seven census listings that were made of Spahren during the period 1797–1858 concluded with a statistical summary at the end of the list. The 1858 summary, however, contained an additional table in which the enumerator cross-tabulated what he called 'families' (*Familien*) with the names and numbers of the residential units (farmsteads: *Gesinde*) in which the members of these 'families' were to be found (*die Gesinde in denen die Familienglieder sich befinden*).[5] The German term *Familie* is therefore crucial for understanding what this retabulation really meant and, fortunately, we can analyse its use in another revision – the already-cited 1850 Pinkenhof document – where the same term is used as a column heading for a series of numbers (*Familiennummer*) attached to each conjugal family group and each individual not part of a conjugal family unit. These three documents – from Spahren in 1797 and 1858, and from Pinkenhof in 1850 – bring us a step closer to the social statistics of the descent group in the Baltic area. Even so, the term 'descent group' must still be used with caution, because none of the enumerators employ a direct counterpart of it, though all three documents suggest that concern for descent was as strong in the minds of the enumerators as concern for showing precise marriage ties and for delineating co-residential units.

These unusual data do permit us to obtain measurements of a type of kin-based group that is entirely different from the co-residential unit. But, because the documents are single-year lists, they clearly do not provide all of the information needed to reconstruct a strictly defined 'descent group'. The limitations in the evidence are shown in figure 11, which contains the reconstructed group we used as an introduction in chapter 1. The evidence comes from the 1850 Pinkenhof list. The genealogical reconstruction appears in the numbered blocks on the right side of the diagram, and the numbers here are those of the farmsteads in which the 'members' of 'family' no. 70 were living in 1850. This reconstruction and others for 1850 reveal very clearly that in the 1850 list the term *Familie* was meant to refer to, in the first instance, a group of males linked to each other patrilineally and, then, to their spouses and to their unmarried chldren. The document further shows that females who were married had changed their 'family' numbers from those of their fathers to those of their husbands. Yet the nature of the listing renders the information inadequate as far as a strict definition of a

5 This summary is to be found in the Central National Historical Archive in Riga, the Latvian SSR, in Fond 630, opis 1, d. 839.

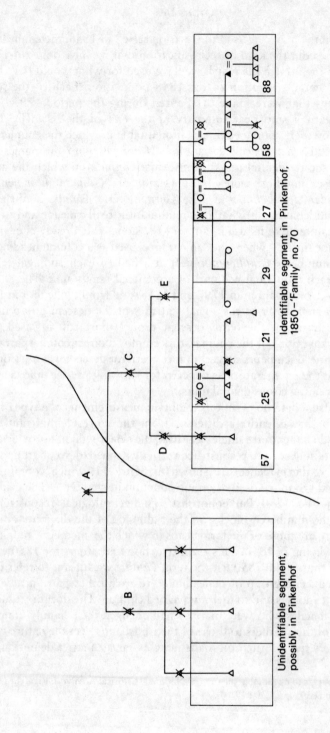

Identifiable segment in Pinkenhof, 1850 – 'Family' no. 70

Unidentifiable segment, possibly in Pinkenhof

Figure 11 Descent group: missing data, Pinkenhof, 1850

descent group is concerned. In the case of 'family' no. 70, the oldest person bearing the number (individual C) was already deceased, but was included in the source apparently to make the link between individuals D and E, both of whom were also deceased. It is thus the descendants of individual C who were still alive in 1850, and their spouses and children, who comprise the 'descent group' we are able to identify. What we do not know, and can never know from this document, is whether C had a brother (such as B) whose descendants were living in other farmsteads on the estate. The reconstruction is therefore limited to using a 'founder' (C) who may, in reality, have been only the point of origin of a lineage segment, so that the identifiable configuration in the seven numbered farmsteads can be viewed at best as a fragment or segment of a descent group. Any measurement we attempt must recognize these limitations of a single-year list.

It is only in the 1850 Pinkenhof document that we can make use of two types of internal clues: the genealogical information attached to each individual and the 'family number'. In both the 1797 and 1858 Spahren documents, the evidence is more limited than this. In 1797, the record-keeper supplied genealogical information for each person in the list, but did not use a 'family number'; by contrast, in 1858 we have no listing at all, but instead there is a summary of a listing that makes full use of the 'family number', but does not make available the genealogical information. The argument that in both of these lists 'descent groups' are being taken cognizance of by the enumerator therefore has to be made on somewhat weaker grounds. In the 1797 list, the fact that we can link dispersed brothers to each other, dispersed conjugal family units into their pre-dispersal formations, and married women to their fathers suggests that the enumerator, by providing the necessary information, could have had precisely this kind of operation in mind, though for reasons that we can only guess. In 1858, the fact that the 'family number' was used exactly for the kind of operation we want to perform with it (the recombining of residentially dispersed people into a non-residential unit), suggests that for the enumerators some value was attached to knowing which farmsteads 'belonged' to which 'family' (or descent group). The generalization which is true about all these unusual documents (though it does not bring us much closer to the reason for their existence) is that the surveys of which they were a part – the soul revisions – did not require details of this nature. The revision was carried out to determine which individuals in a particular locality (estate) were subject to the capitation tax, and this information could have been obtained from a simple list that contained no more than a person's name, household status, sex and age.

The concept of 'descent group' thus creates all sorts of problems, particularly if we wish to use it as a bridge between an ethnographically relatively poorly documented corner of Europe (with respect to the past) and the very rich literature on descent groups in the anthropological disciplines. The concept is useful for sorting the existing evidence, and it does seem to be close to what some of the nineteenth-century enumerators in the Baltic had in mind when using the 'family number' as an attribute of individuals. But it would be hazardous to use the concept to infer social consequences that are not documented in the listing record or other historical sources. That it could be used in this way is clear; we could, for example, easily surround our reconstructions with statements that a descent group was:

> a group of people who together act as *a single legal individual*. . . . [It has] a name or some other symbolic expression of the way it acts as a legal individual, an undifferentiated unit, *vis-à-vis* outsiders – however differentiated its members may be from one another seen from inside the group. Seen from the outside, in an important sense they are all One. . . . Its members can collectively hold title to land and other property. They can exploit resources by cooperative labor (even though members may garden in smaller family units and may own the actual garden plots, as opposed to the land, separately). . . . [Descent groups] are stable, since the corporation continues despite the death and replacement of individual members. (Keesing, 1975: 17)

Yet to proceed from our reconstruction to a full-fledged description of these Baltic estates as local societies in which descent groups were socially and culturally active would be inadvisable, because the information we have about them (lists and other material) is very ambiguous. Thus, at least in some cases, the 'outside' describers of them (the enumerators) saw such groups as 'One' by attaching a single 'family number' to a large number of persons who were residentially dispersed. By contrast, there was not in these estates peasant landownership of any kind: in 1797, all the Baltic peasants were serfs, working holdings which were 'owned' by the estate; by 1850 and 1858, the peasantry was no longer enserfed, but could at best occupy their holdings on a long-term basis only through labour rents; outright peasant ownership of land would not have begun until at least a decade after the last revision of 1858. There were two group terms in the Latvian language of this peasantry that suggest unity and collective action: the word *dzimta*, which refers precisely to a patrilineal descent group; and the word *talka*, which refers to a labour group that was gathered for undertakings too large for a single farmstead to carry out. The former, however, did not have the same status in the Latvian regions as the term *zadruga*, for example, in the South Slav areas; and the latter did not necessarily mean labour recruitment on the basis of *kinship* ties. It is, of course, conceivable that these population listings may turn out to be the only available inventory of descent groups in this semi-literate, historical population. But until that can be established, it is best not to require the concept to carry more weight than it has to.

Two different approaches are required to render the concept useful for analysing the Baltic listings. In the 1797 Spahren list, after each person in the peasant population is linked to the maximum number of others, each group so created has to be assigned a unique identifying number and is thereafter treated as an exclusive unit. The analogy in this step is with family reconstitution, though the 'family' here is defined as all those persons whom the list shows to have descended from the oldest identifiable male ancestor. Married women are assigned to the group of their husbands, unmarried women to the group of their fathers. In the 1850 and 1858 lists, the 'family' number was already supplied by the enumerator, so that in these lists the reclassification step uses existing grouping evidence. In tables 9 and 10, which summarize the statistics of the obtained groups, it can be seen that a substantial proportion of 'descent groups' in these three populations have only one member: one in every four groups in 1797, one in ten in 1858 and one in eight in 1850. This means that when the total peasant population in these communities is evaluated for the 'weight' of descent groups in them, a not insubstantial number of 'groups' can be expected to be tiny fragments, that is, the last representatives of their patrilines in the community and in-migrants whose stay was just long enough for them to be caught up in a single-year enumeration. The proportion of the total population that consisted of persons of this status, however, was not very large in any of the three years. These people, therefore, were 'solitaries' in a somewhat different sense than that implied in their residential position. Indeed, from the viewpoint of residence, such persons were not solitaries at all, for in all three years they can be found living together with other peasants in farmsteads that, in this respect, functioned as welfare institutions. But such persons were alone in the sense of the absence of patrilineal kin. While in the 1797 revision we might wonder if this solitariness is due to inadequate linking information, in the 1850 and 1858 documents the enumerators were certain enough about the unconnectedness of these people to assign to them 'family' numbers which absolutely no one else had.

Table 9 makes very clear that more than half of all groups in each year were in the size category (2–10 people) that meant that they were not much larger, if they were larger at all, than a conjugal family unit, including children. Here again, we are justified in thinking in terms of fragments of descent groups, with the various configurations in this size category including such structural types as an old married pair and a family with children, with perhaps a brother of the husband in each case somewhere in the population. A classification scheme analogous to those used for house-

Table 9 Group size and population in groups of different sizes, Baltic area, 1797–1858

Descent-group size (persons)	Spahren, 1797				Spahren, 1858				Pinkenhof, 1850			
	No. of groups	Percent-age of groups	No. of persons	Percent-age of persons	No. of groups	Percent-age of groups	No. of persons	Percent-age of persons	No. of groups	Percent-age of groups	No. of persons	Percent-age of persons
1	30	25.2	30	4.5	10	10.4	10	1.3	19	13.1	19	1.3
2–10	63	52.9	313	47.9	61	63.5	340	44.2	74	51.3	408	28.2
11–20	23	19.3	241	36.9	20	20.8	284	36.9	34	23.6	563	39.0
21–30	3	2.5	69	10.5	3	3.1	70	9.1	15	10.4	362	6.4
31–	0	0	0	0	2	2.0	64	8.3	2	1.3	92	6.4
Totals	119	99.9	653	99.8	96	99.8	768	99.8	144	99.8	1443	99.9
Mean size of descent groups	5.48				8.00				10.02			
Range of sizes of descent groups	1–33				1–40				1–45			

Table 10 Spatial distribution of descent groups and persons, Baltic area, 1797–1858

Location (number of places)	Spahren, 1797				Spahren, 1858				Pinkenhof, 1850			
	No. of groups	Percentage of groups	No. of persons	Percentage of persons	No. of groups	Percentage of groups	No. of persons	Percentage of persons	No. of groups	Percentage of groups	No. of persons	Percentage of persons
1	58	58.7	107	16.4	22	22.9	73	9.5	46	31.9	164	11.3
2–4	43	36.1	267	40.9	47	48.8	283	36.8	64	44.4	612	42.4
5–7	14	11.7	185	28.3	23	23.9	246	32.0	20	13.8	338	23.4
8–	4	3.4	94	14.2	4	4.2	166	21.6	14	9.7	329	22.7
Totals	119	99.9	653	99.8	96	99.8	768	99.9	144	99.8	1443	99.8
Range of number of places	1–12				1–10				1–18			
Mean number of places per group	2.4				3.5				3.0			

holds could clarify this point, but none are available for descent groups in a single-year census. Even with the relatively simple evaluation we are using here, however, some headway can be made in answering the question of what can be expected by way of measurable units when the *internal* evidence about descent in these sources is used to maximal purpose. Something like six or seven out of every ten reconstructed groups emerge as being about the same size or smaller than the groups we would have been dealing with, had we isolated conjugal family units. It is only when we come to the larger size categories, involving 11 or more people, that there come into view groups of the size we normally associate with the concept of a 'descent group'; the groups, that is, that look like the reconstruction presented in figure 11. About half of all persons in the three communities were involved in these larger, more inclusive, units and only about 10 per cent of each population were implicated in the very largest of them. If we were to identify the principles on which descent groups in these communities were based, it is only in these larger groups that there would exist sufficient evidence to identify the principles clearly. In using them, however, we would continually have to remind ourselves that we were looking at principles whose operation was being affected by mortality and migration, with the result being the emergence of many groups that were not at all close in appearance to what might have been the ideal.

The meaning of the groups in table 9 is enhanced by the findings presented in table 10, which make clear the fact that though in a substantial proportion of cases we can expect to find all members of a descent group in the same place (farmstead), in most cases we have to reach beyond the boundaries of a single residential group to identify all of a group's members. This is the case even with those groups we have characterized as fragments, because not infrequently members of a conjugal family unit lived apart from each other, particularly so if the offspring of the unit were old enough to be placed as farmhands in other farmsteads and the head of the unit was in the socio-economic stratum of *Knechte* (adult male farmhands). The dispersion of members of a reconstructed descent group was considerable enough to make the *average* number of places per group in all three communities stand above one. If we were to use the two lists from Spahren as evidence for the question of whether, over time, the process of dispersion intensified, the answer would be that it did so. Even though by 1858 the maximum number of places to which any single group had dispersed had fallen from twelve to ten, the average number of points of dispersal had increased from 2.4 to 3.5. This increase is an expected one, because in the period 1817–26 the Kurland enserfed peasantry was emancipated and their serf status abolished. Although the emancipation edict may not have improved the economic position of the peasantry to any substantial degree, it did permit, in the decades preceding the 1858 revision, much more movement of peasants within the estate of their residence, which, in turn, brought the statistical results shown in the table.

The internal organization of the revision sources was always such that the identification of the household structure in a given year was a relatively easy task. We do not lose this information by moving the analysis one step forward to identify what other groups may have been important for defining the social context in which individuals moved. This analytical shift for the 1797 document is more arbitrary than for the later documents, for in 1797 the enumerators might have provided the additional genealogical information in order to clarify the position of individuals, rather than to lay a basis for the reconstruction of groups. In the later documents, however, the use by the enumerators of the 'family number' was clearly an effort to point out the 'membership' of individuals in groups that were not the co-residential group (residential membership having been identified through other very explicit notations). Moreover, in 1858, another change had taken place which adds meaning to the use of the 'family number': whereas in 1797 the enumerators, judging by their signatures, were Baltic German estate officials and were therefore listing the peasant population, in a sense, from an outsider's perspective, by 1858 the enumerators were themselves Latvian-speaking peasants and co-residents with other peasants in the farmsteads they were enumerating. The 1817–26 reforms had succeeded in creating in the Baltic estates rudimentary organs of local county (*pagasts*) government, the offices of which were filled by the peasants themselves. In the last three revisions, therefore, the people who were entering detailed information, including 'family numbers', on the revision forms could be expected to have known existing kin ties between people not in co-residence with each other.

Kinship Groups as Role Systems

The quantitative assessments we hve made so far of kindreds and descent groups are only one kind of measurement. We could try also to show what additions and subtractions were made in the group over a period of time, and develop statistics about changing size during the 'lifetime' of the group, as measured from the appearance of a founder until the death of the last of its surviving members. An even more complicated form of measurement would be required if we were to view the kinship group as a collection of interrelated roles, remembering that each member in the group possessed more than one role (theoretically many more different roles than there were members), and that a proper measure would seek to encompass this diversity. Throughout this kind of measurement, however, we would have to remember that the unit of measurement was not an individual, but a group, and use measurements appropriate to groups and not simply measurements derived from individuals and applied to groups.

It is entirely possible to restrict measurement of any sort to a moment in past time as far as role systems are concerned, and take as the units to be measured only those roles which are being enacted by members of a living population. But the nature of social roles is such that this approach would not exhaust all the possibilities of measurement, and would in fact force us to consider the connections between living and deceased populations. Some kinship groups need not be considered in this fashion, of course. The bilateral kindred, for example, does not exist as a group with a structure other than that which is created by the fact that all living persons in the kindred perceive themselves as related to the same living individual. When that individual dies, then the reason for the members of the bilateral kindred to be considered as a group ceases to exist. But other collections of people tied together by kinship ties do have a unity that transcends the lifetime of any of its individual members. Let us take the simplest kinship group of this nature, namely, the conjugal family unit. When fully developoed, this group will be characterized by relations of consanguinity and affinity. But it will be more than this, because the roles which are created by it are exceptionally durable and are required to be enacted throughout the lifetimes of members of the unit. These roles will normally entail a certain separation from the rest of the community: the husband and wife are required to limit their sexual attention to each other, they are supposed to provide nurture to the offspring which their sexual union brings into being for long periods of time and the offspring, in turn, are supposed to be particularly deferential to the parents. No other kinship group will entail precisely these same roles. But, when such a group is considered from the viewpoint of kinship roles, it is clear that the individuals in it are linked to other groups through role enactment. Thus, for example, the 'husband' in conjugal family A will be enacting not only that role, but also that of 'son' in unit B into which he was born, and the 'son' in unit A will continue to enact this role even though he may become 'husband' and even 'father' in unit C. These roles will become obligatory in the course of his lifetime, and therefore in his lifetime he will be involved in at least three such conjugal family units and perhaps more. He will be, for a period of his life, son in one such unit, husband and father in another, and grandfather in the units of his offspring. The point here is that such kinship groups (in this example, the conjugal family unit) will in one sense stand separated from all others, but because of the persistence of role obligations they also will be connected to a great many other groups throughout a long period of time, as well as in a moment in time. To count and measure only the roles implied in a conjugal family unit will mean the separation of that unit from the others, in which its members are still involved, by a decision made necessary by the desire to measure. But 'on the ground' the separation will not exist, because the members of a conjugal family unit will be experiencing their multiple memberships by virtue of the roles which they will be enacting.

This view of kinship groups implies great continuity between successive populations in the same community, because it is a set of roles, rather than the physical human beings, which connect one kinship unit to another. All of the members of a grandparental generation of a family unit may have died, but we must still consider the links between the units, because the parents in the living unit will have spent a part of their lives enacting the roles of offspring in the earlier one. Even though the offspring roles will have disappeared after the grandparental generation has ceased to exist, the fact that such roles were enacted at one time, and that the carriers of the roles are still alive, provides us with the continuous linkage which gives considerable, though not infinite, time depth to the analysis. Similarly, the conjugal family unit in the living population may develop connections within the community with other living members. The spouses may have siblings in the community, as well as aunts and uncles; the children may marry and thus create ties of a similar sort with other conjugal family units; and with each marriage, such ties would increase exponentially, because of the numbers of additional links each such individual link creates. The upshot of this discussion is that from the viewpoint of genealogical connections, and the roles which such connections create, the various groups of people whom we want to separate out for the analysis of kinship groups will all be located on the same genealogical grid which extends backward and forward in time, as well as in space within the living population.

There are two ways in which discontinuities are introduced into this genealogical grid. Throughout the history of a community's population there will always be entire units which leave, thus creating certain 'holes' in the network of connections. The number of such departures may be quite large, as may be the number of new entrants into the community. Some of the new entrants may not remain as resident members of the community for any length of time, and may depart very quickly. Also, during the entire period under consideration, gaps will be introduced by natural death; some connections will be broken entirely, never to be recreated; some segments of the network will be severely diminished in density through the disappearance of a cluster of points, and so forth. Tables 9 and 10 depict the residual structures, which would of course, continue to change. But often this kind of demographic removal will be repaired by remarriage and adoption. There is an element of substitutability in the units with which we have to deal, so that biologically unrelated people may become considered as socially the same as those whom they have replaced and the roles which they have to enact become for all intents and purposes the same as those enacted by the people they replaced. The picture is not meant to slight the element of turnover in traditional populations, but it does suggest that we do not have sufficient information about mobility in all pre-industrial communities to assume from the outset that the picture we are sketching here is everywhere irrelevant. The data suggest that people were continually coming and going, but they suggest also that there may always have been a substantial core population which was bound up in continuous relations and that at a moment of past time kinship relations could be dense indeed, even if the turnover was considerable. The evidence of fieldwork anthropologists suggests that in non-European communities in which well-developed kinship systems operated, turnover could be substantial without affecting the system in force.

The point I want to stress here is that a reconceptualization of genealogically connected groups as role systems weights the analysis in favour of continuity by virtue of the way in which roles were enacted during the lives of individuals. I do not mean here simply that various roles, when they became sanctioned, remained a part of the community's repertoire of organizational principles, regardless of who enacted them and when they were enacted. I mean that the individuals in the sources were enactors of roles; and, in the same sources, kinship groups were clusters or systems of roles having to be enacted. This view of kinship roles requires that we start not with the roles themselves, but with their carriers, and deal with roles in so far as they are inserted into the collection by the carriers. The kinship group thus appears as a special collection of such roles, the enactment of which carries special meaning for the enactors of a kind that no other roles carry. But because people can have a series of roles throughout their lifetime, including roles of the same intensity (pertinent to the same kinship group), they provide the links between groups over time and space.

Kinship Groups as Hypothetical Constructs

As mentioned earlier, neither the fieldwork anthropologist nor the historian will ever be in the position of being able to observe an entire kinship group or the entirety of the activities of its members. In the one case, the fieldworker infers the existence of groups from the limited number of activities and relationships observed within the time-frame of the visit; and in the other, the existence and activities of the group have to be inferred from written documents which 'freeze' the participants in a particular activity or a genealogical configuration at a particular moment in past time. In both cases, therefore, the investigator is presented initially with a seemingly patternless reality, consisting of many different observations; and the patterns that come to be identified and described as the result of the activity of kinship groups must be understood as constructs the investigator imposes on the data. If the research were anything else but this, then fieldwork anthropologists would not disagree about the character of kinship systems, nor would historians debate about the presence or absence of kinship groups in the European past, for these would be obvious to all observers. The problem is that in neither case can kinship groups be analysed as if they were organizations with membership lists, with the task of the investigator being to interpret the list. In fact, in both cases, the chief assignment of the investigator is, figuratively speaking, to compile such a listing, or at least a sufficient sample from which the nature of the entire listing can be inferred. In no case do investigators of kinship begin with a prepared list beforehand, thrust into their hands by the actors themselves. Even when the actors themselves suggst the existence within their communities of certain groups, the investigators still have the obligation not to take the actors at their word, but to examine the population in order to establish whether their self-image is correct or is simply an idealization.

The advantage anthropologist have over historians is that most of the communities studied by fieldworkers do not interpose between the analyst and the actor a layer of evidence prepared by a third party, and therefore do not prescribe the way in which evidence about kinship becomes accessible. Historians, by contrast, are presented with already organized data and therefore face the job of transforming it to suit their research needs. It is ironic that the very same sources which more than any others permit historians to reach into this domain of social structure should, at the same time, create so many hindrances to a clear view, but this feature of the research is well nigh inescapable. When the historical analyst wishes to transform the received data so that the organizing concepts of the anthropologist can be made use of, more often than not the data will be found to be pulling the analysis in a different direction. This is particularly the case with household lists which, because of their plenitude and concreteness, at times tempt the researcher into treating co-residence as the sole basis for discussing kinship, rather than as one of a number of activities or behaviours in which kinship choices show up. All interactional sources present such temptations to a greater or lesser extent; moreover, it may be that, as research on kinship continues, we shall find that co-residence is the most important activity that needs to be studied if kinship is to be understood. As we observed earlier, such importance is accorded to residence by numerous anthropological investigators of kinship. Yet until this theory is corroborated further by concrete historical investigations in the European context, the focus on co-residence may also have the effect of foreclosing other possibilities. Therefore it makes a great deal of sense to submit the available data to the kinds of transformation which will enable the researcher to conduct the discussion over more inclusive concepts.

The role concept is very useful for this purpose, because it requires the researcher to hold open the possibility that a historical actor had to enact more roles than a particular kind of historical source identifies him or her to be enacting. We have already observed that the most useful manner of approaching relational terminology in household lists and other inter-actional sources is to see it as genealogical information, written down by the enumerator not so much because he wanted to preserve information about kinship practices, but because he needed to have some way of identifying people other than simply through the use of proper names. Thus kin-type designations in sources are clues rather than final information about kin roles which individuals enacted. The particular roles which interactional data permit us to discuss are likely to be different from others, because of the physical proximity of the persons they were enacted toward. The daily, even hourly, interaction between co-residents, for example, in the hundreds of activities that constitute everyday life meant continuing reference to norms of behaviour implied in roles, to the point that such behaviour would become routinized and automatic. It is quite conceivable, therefore, that behaviour towards others outside these small groups was different, because there was less of it. Historical information about small-group activities was more concentrated in the data than information about any other kin ties, but this has to be understood as the form in which the data were presented, rather than as concrete evidence about the existence or non-existence of more far-flung ties. It can therefore be misleading to draw a very sharp line around the small group as far as discussion of kinship is concerned. People may have had structural involvements in ways that may be difficult to establish retrospectively, but these difficulties cannot be used to justify the assumption that they did not exist at all. In this realm of expectations, we cannot subsume all regions and time periods in the European past to a common set of assumptions. As we have seen, all preliminary evidence about the serf areas of the Baltic would justify the assumption that such extra-group links were frequent and the roles they created real. Other preliminary evidence, particularly that from areas in which population turnover was much more rapid, might not lead the researcher to make this assumption. To a great extent the choice of assumptions on the basis of preliminary findings will dictate the further course of research on the kinds of data that are available. The point being made here is that a conclusion arrived at too quickly, without the requisite transformation of available data, may have the result of closing off entire areas of social-structural involvement, that is, of areas of enacted roles. Thus, for example, the anthropologist Jack Goody has written with considerable confidence about western areas of the European continent that 'patrilineal clans, where they existed, have mostly disappeared' (Goody, 1983: 262). Such a general observation, even if extended to the eastern areas it was not meant to cover, is no doubt correct: a researcher of European population data in the early modern period would be ill advised to expect individual-level sources to yield up formations of this nature for inspection. There is, none the less, a considerable sector of structural involvements between, for instance, 'conjugal family units' and 'clans', and it is precisely this sector that research should strive to open and keep open until more is known about it than at the present.

The analyst must bear in mind that the process of identifying kinship groups, wherever it is attempted, is in the final analysis a thrusting upon a variegated reality of the investigator's own constructions as to what the social reality was among the persons being examined.[6] This commonplace notion does not make any less real the kinship grouping and its significance in communities where the reality is very close to the construction created to explain it. For investigations of the past, however, the distance between the construct and the reality is likely to remain substantial, because the 'reality' is never accessible directly, but always through some mediating set of constructs: an enumeration, a description by some contemporary, a document created by the authorities for purposes of later reference. There is always the possibility that another invstigator viewing the same evidence from a different perspective and with different assumptions will arrive at different conclusions about the structures implied in it. The experience with the history of the family household is instructive in this regard, since much of the recent empirical research devoted to this particular social structure has invalidated what had been claimed by earlier historians about families and the nature of co-residence. This result obtained because assumptions had changed; the view that empirical data about social microstructures were not available was replaced by one that held that certain kinds of historical

---

6 Nadel's position on this issue (Nadel, 1957: 150–1) is summarized in the following statement: 'I consider social structure, of whatever degree of refinement, to be stil the social reality itself, or an aspect of it, not the logic behind it; and I consider structural analysis to be no more than a descriptive method, however sophisticated, not a piece of explanation.' This is, of course, one of the continuing matters of controversy, the passage cited above coming from Nadel's discussion of his disagreement with the ideas of Lévi-Strauss and Edmund Leach. The controversy, in its current manifestations, is documented in the work of such scholars as Kuper (1982), Barnes (1980) and Yanagisako (1979), who are all not only observers of, but also participants in the debate.

records could be treated precisely as the necessary data. The use by the historian of the group concepts of the anthropologists would thus constitute a similar change of assumptions: from that which holds that kin-based groups lost their social significance relatively early in European history to one which holds that through the use of group concepts we can determine whether, and how, such a proposition can be understood as true.

The constant with which analysts of European kinship have to reckon is that there was no time and place when Europeans were not engaged in the practice of classifying themselves by reference to common descent and to marriage. They classified people by reference to other attributes as well, of course, but the evidence is overwhelming that the facts of descent and marriage were always and everywhere used. Such classification was practised not only for the purposes of self-description, as when writers of various kinds sought to describe communities in which they were living, but also for purposes of social action, when it became necessary to know what relationship a potential heir had to a deceased individual or when it became necessary for an individual in high office to dispense favours. Such self-classification was carried out by people for their own ends, and it was practised as well by authorities whose job it was, again for specific ends, to keep straight the relationships among the persons under their charge. It is this broad range of classificatory activities which have to be kept in the foreground as we seek a credible starting-point for understanding kinship groups in the European past. Since the existence of such classificatory activity can be demonstrated, it follows that we have to explore its social effects across the widest possible field of evidence, which in our case is the genealogical evidence. In view of what is known about the social consequences of classificatory activity in non-European cultures, we cannot start out with the assumption that the only analysable consequence was the creation of the smallest kin-based group that historical records present for our scrutiny. To test for the presence of more inclusive groups therefore means the use of a wide range of constructs and of the acceptance of the possibility that the test will prove to be positive.

At the same time, we should be prepared to consider the possibility of failure: that is, the outcome that classificatory activity carried out simultaneously by residents in a particular community over many generations *never* had the consequence of creating kinship groups in the sense meant here, and that its only consequence, for individual after individual and generation after generation, was to allow persons to assemble, sporadically and temporarily, small groups of kin for whatever immediate needs had to be served. We should be prepared to consider that classificatory activity stopped at a short genealogical distance from Ego, that is, with biological parents and biological siblings and that, as a consequence, there was

considerable discrepancy between the various constructs of group organization which we may wish to use and the reality on the ground, even in
situations where prima-facie evidence suggests that the historical reality
resembled the contemporary societies in which the ideal types have a very
good fit.

9

Kinship in the Long Term: the Lineage

It would be easy to demonstrate that a kin set surrounding a historical actor had continuous, if finite, existence in historical time. This set would be considered as having formed when its members first became conscious of their responsibilities toward the common kinsman and having ended when that individual died. A similar time-frame would be appropriate to a bilateral kindred, which might in fact be encompassed within the total set of kin that a good genealogical record would permit us to identify. If, however, we sought to establish chronological limits to the existence of a descent group, difficulties would arise immediately. By definition, the descent group is a living kin-based group, all of whose members recognize the same ancestral 'founder' and, examined at a point in past time, its membership can be described relatively accurately when rules of inclusion and exclusion become known. But as the earlier discussion suggested, the analysis of a descent group starts with the decision to extract the group from its full genealogical context, that is, to sever temporarily the ties that link its oldest and youngest members to even older and younger generations and to declare that the people isolated in this fashion will be considered for the purpose of study as the group's membership. This procedure has to be followed in order to make use of the concept of kinship roles, which, after all, are not enacted toward people who have died in the distant past or who have not yet been born. For the fieldwork anthropologist who studies descent groups, therefore, the precise linkages among members of earlier generations are somewhat less important (though not unimportant) than the conception which a particular living and observed population has of them and which it puts to use to introduce order into its present relationships (cf. Lewis, 1968a).

Necessary as this procedure of extraction is for the examination of the descent group, it obviously does not do full justice to the entire corpus of historical evidence which certain sources – especially vital-events sources – place at the historian's disposal. If a set of three overlapping generations in a genealogical record are not isolated or extracted in this way, then they can be demonstrated to be three generations in a longer chain, no segment of which necessarily deserves to receive more attention than any other. When the genealogical record is good enough – as in some instances it clearly is – then we are confronted with an elaborate genealogical configuration with the internal links showing it to have had duration or persistence in time. Its 'members' are, so to speak, deployed over many decades and quite possibly several centuries. This 'membership' will have increased or decreased for various reasons, and it may have disappeared from the records entirely at a point in the past. We know quite clearly that only certain adjacent subpopulations within this 'membership' would have known each other and enacted kin roles toward each other; and we know also that it is such a coniguration that a person is likely to have in his mind's eye when making such statements as 'my family has been in the area for a long time', or 'I come from a very old family'. More often than not, in European history, these references to the 'family' will in fact be references to the lineage, or more precisely to the patrilineage. If, however, we change the vantage point from which the configuration is viewed, in order to make full use of the minute information a good genealogical reconstruction provides for us, the direction of further analysis is not necessarily obvious. This is particularly the case if the records of a locality provide us with reliable information about all or nearly all the lineages that ever existed in the locality for an extended period of time. Such a data file seems to have the exactitude for kinship evidence to be 'non-conjectural': at times it is possible to trace the exact connections between the earliest recorded members of such a group to the most recent members over seven or eight generations. But since the configuration contains 'members' whose lifetimes did not overlap and who could not therefore be pictured as having enacted kinship roles toward each other, what justification is there for treating such a configuration as a 'group' in any sense? Thus, although it is relatively clear how such anthropological concepts as 'kindred' and 'descent group' can be made use of with genealogical reconstructions, the methodology for analysing time-based configurations such as patrilineages has not been developed with the same precision.

The Long Term in Historical Kinship Analysis

When historians of the European continent think of the 'long term' in connection with most historical subjects, the general framework within which the long-term history of that topic will have unfolded is already known to them. This situation is a direct result of a century or more of systematic inquiry into the European past by archaeologists and historians.

Even if the exact history of a topic is yet to be written, the circumstances which might have influenced its development are already generally known and the significant evidence that needs to be taken into consideration has already been sifted. It is, of course, true that the opportunity for incontrovertible statements diminishes with the increase of the distance from the present. But if we set the definition of the 'long term' in Europe to include only the past thousand years, the ground which a description of any social situation will cover will never be entirely new. In the realm of social microstructures, we already know the general context in which they would have had to exist, as well as the constraining features of the general social environment in which they would have developed.

The societies which appeared, flowered and declined in the geographical space called Europe in this thousand-year period managed to leave relatively good historical records about themselves. In its totality, the European historical record stands in sharp contrast to that of the small-scale societies in which anthropologists have to date done most of their research on kinship. In these, the 'long-term' has had to be defined very differently. In order to place the directly observable and directly describable systems in historical perspective, anthropologists have had to combine fieldwork observations with relatively scanty historical documents, covering a relatively short period of time; or they have had to postulate an evolutionary framework within which the immediately describable systems are then said to be typical of a particular phase of such an evolutionary course (Goody, 1976: 3). These scholars have had to deal with research problems that are different from those presented by a civilization in which microstructures have been documented for an intermediary length of time (that is more than the two or three generations of a descent group, but less than the thousands of years which the evolutionary perspective implies). Anthropologists, of course, have thought about change in the short term, particularly when the culture they are researching has been undergoing changes associated with modernization (that is, urbanization, a decrease in fertility and mortality, the appearance of industry and long-distance markets, and the rise of centralized governments) (cf. Firth, 1956; Fischer, 1982). The long-term perspective has required speculative descriptions of change, starting at some postulated base-line period in the very distant past and carrying the story into the present. But by and large, the anthropological literature has not been overly satisfied with the results (cf. Hudson, 1974).

The European historical population record thus creates special problems. The record often covers long stretches of the historical past during which no major social transformations took place, so that we cannot find dramatic turning-points that would help to illuminate the problems at hand. Instead, the records contain information about communities that changed imperceptively. It is impossible to think about their human inhabitants, in every year, as comprising an entirely different population than in the year before. Without doubt, some segments of the population persisted, some left, some arrived, and because of this continuing shifting, the relationships between people were also changing. But it will do little justice to the available historical evidence to place such communities within a phase of a very long-term evolutionary process and to postulate that small changes constituted no change at all because no fundamental transformation occurred; nor will it be of assistance to try to focus on such communities only at a time when major transformations were in fact taking place. The long term in such European communities is more likely to be a stretch of several hundred years, during which kinship in them had a history in the sense of micro-events. The question that a historian facing data of this sort wants to address is whether there is a way of writing about this history, even if the result will not contain descriptions of major transformations.

Another way of posing the question is to use S. H. Nadel's formulation of structure and ask how kinship is to be studied in a succession of populations when one segment of a population is the same as a segment of the preceding one, and some other segment is identical to a segment of the next one (Nadel, 1957: 129–30). This formulation of the problem seems to me to be closest to the available historical sources. The problem of the long term in historical populations therefore begins with the image of a long chain of successive populations with the length of the chain being defined by the available sources. The sources might in fact document only an original population and then another somewhere toward the end of the postulated chain. Or they might document a short series within a longer chain, or three or four separated populations that did not overlap at all. What holds these successive populations in place, however, is the knowledge from other, probably non-structural sources that the population persisted over time. The question then becomes one of the central organizing concept for the study of kinship change in such a chain of populations.

Generally speaking, in the anthropological attempts to write the long-term history of kinship, lack of empirical data has made it impossible to produce convincing descriptions. In the nineteenth century, the efforts of this sort proceeded on the assumption that some forms of kinship were more advanced than others, which made it easier to allocate systems according to a time-line of development. It was against this kind of thinking, and its weak evidential base, as we have noted, that the structuralists eventually aimed their criticism, maintaining that most of it was what A. R. Radcliffe-Brown called 'conjectural history'. In explaining his criticism, however, Radcliffe-Brown noted that what he and other critics opposed was not the effort to produce a *history* of kinship, but that the histories so far produced went far beyond what existing evidence would allow. They criticized it for being conjectural, not for being historical (Radcliffe-Brown, 1965: 50). Behind this criticism, there seemed to be an assumption that there would never exist historical evidence for writing a history of kinship and, as a consequence, very little time was spent considering systematically the question of what kind of evidence would have to obtain for a reliable history of kinship. As can now be understood in the light of the historical materials considered in the earlier chapters, the question is a very important one, particularly when one type of historical evidence – reconstructions from vital-events data – draws upon the same genealogical data for its raw information as does the fieldwork anthropologist.

The Lineage Question

Social anthropologists have been writing about lineages for a long time, and consequently the ways in which they manifest themselves in the observable social lives of members of a living population are relatively well understood. What evidence should be looked for in the historical documents of a particular community for firm conclusions about the existence of lineages is a question that is not as easily answerable, however, particularly when it is asked not only about a moment in the past of a community, but also about a long period of its existence. Historians are still searching for the proper weight to attach to different kinds of evidence about lineages, and for the units of analysis that will yield the most accurate historical description of changes over time (Goody, 1983: 222–39). Almost all such historical research for the centuries after the sixteenth tends to assume that patrilineally organized corporate kin groups had ceased to play an important role in European social life by the end of the medieval period, and that the concept of the 'classical unilineal descent group' does not fit the data of the subsequent centuries. Such an assumption, however, if used to close off the entire area of lineal relations, will not help us to understand what the new role of lineality was. For surely the principle did not disappear entirely from the kin classification practised by Europeans.

The evidence from which information about lineal connections emerges is varied. One well-known type is customary and written law, and another type is the interactional sources describing activities carried out by reference to such laws; both suggest the existence in the medieval centuries of lineage groups functioning as corporate entities at the local and regional level.[1]

---

1 Various descriptions of corporate kin groups in European society in the medieval period can be found in Duby and LeGoff (1977), Phillpotts (1913), Heers (1977), Hughes (1975) and Flandrin (1979). See also Duby (1978).

Such groups were recognized as having corporate rights and obligations until increased migration diminished their numbers and growing state power assumed their regulatory functions. Thereafter, it is believed in the national societies where these transitions occurred that kinship reckoning became increasingly bilateral, and from the viewpoint of the analyst, the concept which most readily explains significant kinship relations in them is the personal bilateral kindred. The change was reflected in historical sources which no longer mentioned the presence of corporate kinship entities. The sources which gained prominence – such as parish registers and listings of inhabitants of particular communities – permit the researcher to make fairly accurate assessments of the personal kin networks; as these sources nearly always employed kinship terminology that refers to a central actor of a small group, analysis becomes the effort to understand the nature of ego-centred configurations and of groups understood as aggregations of individuals.

The argument that a change in the nature of evidence about kinship reflects a change in the nature of kinship itself has to be taken seriously. The disappearance of corporate kin groups as active elements of social life was bound to show up in the documents a society generated about itself. But the argument has to be assessed in the light of observations by anthropologists, cited earlier, concerning the temporal compatibility of kinship experiences of different kinds. In his analysis of kinship among the Ashanti, Meyer Fortes has pointed out that the full meaning of lineage organization among this people (and, by extension, in any society) cannot be fully understood unless the researcher looks first at the 'structural features and institutional forms that characterize the lineage as a corporate body in the politico-jural domain, in respect both to its external relationships and to its internal constitution' and, second, at 'what lineage membership signifies for the individual in his personal field of social relations' (Fortes, 1969: 196). The results of this two-pronged approach can be surprising. Among the Ashanti, for instance, the lineage as a corporate entity was organized matrilineally, but the 'personal field of social relations' of its members could not be described without reference to the element of patrifiliation. To understand the lineage as a publicly recognized institution, the analyst here has to take into account one set of genealogical ties; to understand its meaning for personal action, a somewhat different set of ties must be taken into account. We take this to signify, for the European past, that the availability of evidence about corporate kinship groups in the medieval period is not an argument in itself for a diminished importance of kinship in the personal sphere; nor that the much more plentiful information about personal kinship of the later period should be understood, in itself, as sufficient evidence about the relative importance of groups. In the earlier period, *were the appropriate data available*, we might be able to add to descriptions of corporate group activity what involvement in such groups meant for individuals; just as, later in time, we cannot assume that ego-centred data closes the door on the existence of lineage groups. In other words, the question of whether changes in record-keeping are a reflection of changes in kinship appears to require considerable testing.

In recent decades, social historians have probed the historical record of the European post-medieval centuries in order to write the history of various kinds of social groups and their functioning as contexts of individual lives. This thrust has produced the field of family history, which includes among its many interests kinship relations within the conjugal family unit and within the family household. In studying these, however, researchers have found the most readily available sources to be very restrictive with respect to traceable kin ties; consequently, the 'personal field of social relations' has had to exclude kin not in co-residence or not in very close proximity. Thus it has not been easy to contrast 'lineage membership' with 'personal field', simply because, in most localities and for most individuals, the empirical evidence has not existed to establish unambiguously the larger lineage context. This observation does not mean to suggest that lineages continued to exist everywhere in Europe beyond the medieval period, hidden from scrutiny by biased sources. It is meant to make the point that a great deal more work needs to be done to understand the timing of the transition in the various cultural regions of Europe, including the east. The sources for the post-medieval centuries make it very difficult to understand the social-structural consequences of lineality. Granted that this principle did not disappear (as can be shown), granted also that its workings did not everywhere bring into existence corporate groups and granted finally the evidence regarding the shift from lineality to bilaterality, we are still left wondering, in the light of Fortes's formulation of the two-pronged approach to lineages, what succeeded the corporately organized patrilineal kin group and how these successor structures, if they existed, coexisted with less formal groups.

There is evidence that this question has troubled not only historians working with evidence from the distant European past, but also anthropologists who have looked closely at the recent past of modern European rural communities. Consider, for example, the research of Robert Netting, who did his fieldwork in the Swiss mountain village of Törbel in the 1960s and 1970s. Netting concluded that the Törbel population appeared 'stubbornly sessile', with some 57 per cent of the surname groups which he found there in the 1970s having survived in the community for as long as 270 years (Netting, 1981: 71–3). These surname groups, referred to by Netting with the term 'patrilines', continue to work their way into the social life of Törbel:

Kinship relations within and among the patrilines seem to have been well known, though transmitted orally. There is little evidence, however, that patrilines functioned as corporate lineages, given the facts of residential dispersion, individual property as opposed to corporate estate, and bilateral partible inheritance that conveyed resources equally to male and female descendants.

Although patrilines in Törbel are not classic unilineal descent groups they do act as kinship statuses conferring distinctive and exclusive rights within a closed community.

Even after their primary responsibilities shifted to their own families of procreation it was expected that brothers would form a united front politically. Such bonds could be naturally extended to paternal cousins and because the majority of Törbel patrilines seldom had more than three to six adult males living contemporaneously, it is understandable that patrikin were likely to vote together and take similar stands on civic issues. (Netting, 1981: 74, 79 and 193)

A description not unlike Netting's of Törbel, but somewhat more emphatic with regard to the contemporary meaning of patriline groups, is offered by Joel Halpern in his researches on the Serbian village of Orašac, where Halpern began to do his fieldwork in the early 1950s. In the South Slav areas of Europe, it is the patrilineal co-residential group – the *zadruga* – that has always had pride of place in social description, but, as Halpern makes clear, the meaning of the social-structural involvements of the Orašani cannot be fully understood until the analyst pays attention as well to the *vamilija*, the common descent group, which:

> was not a lineage in the strict sense of the term since it was not a corporate group, nor livestock or landowing group. However, particular *vamilijas* tended to live in distinct neighborhoods, and even today [i.e., 1972] in Orašac the various neighborhoods generally reflect this fact and are identified as such. Geographic proximity, combined with a knowledge of relationships in the male line, has meant, and continues to mean, that the *vamilija* has a sense of solidarity reflected in work exchanges, mutual help, and lending, and a general sense of unity reinforced by common attendance at crisis rites such as weddings and funerals. Although vengeance seeking is more characteristic of the mountainous areas from which they originated, *vamilijas* very definitely function as common interest groups with respect to other *vamilijas* in the village and outside groups in general. (Halpern and Halpern, 1972: 22)

Were these communities the kinds that historians normally study – communities in the distant past with only census-type documents to supply empirical evidence about the social structures in them – it is not too difficult to imagine how the kin connections that permit Netting and Halpern to discuss patrilines and *vamilijas* could elude the analyst entirely. Brothers and cousins who lived in separate households would seldom be identified as relatives, and interactional sources about 'work exchanges, mutual help, and lending', while supplying names of the participants, would not always state the relationships between them. In the contemporary studies, it is observation and questioning that supplies the necessary links. The examples of Orašac and Törbel therefore raise a number of important questions about the history of kinship in these localities in earlier periods and in other localities of the European continent as well. If, in the mid-twentieth century, it is still possible to identify consciousness of membership in patrilineal groups that include a number of conjugal families and households, are we to assume that such a consciousness is of recent vintage or that it has been a factor in kinship relations for a long period of historical time? Or are we dealing, in these examples, with 'survivals', one in an atypical mountain community and another in a region of Europe which is known to be unique in many other ways? In asking these questions, we do not mean to be rhetorical, because we really do not have answers to them in mind. We do think, however, that these examples suggest the presence of prima-facie evidence, dispersed geographically and chronologically in the post-medieval centuries, for the lineage question to be pursued with greater precision than it has been. It may very well be that in due course, after such a searching review has been concluded, our picture of the European social past will not have changed substantially. But at least then we will know how better to generalize from evidence that is neither about the 'classical corporate descent group' nor about microstructures such as households and families, although it may involve the same principles as the former and affect the interpretation of the latter.

Reconstructing Lineages

A great strength of recent research on European social forms has been the insistence on reconstruction when the sources permit it. This approach not only permits the testing of statements made by contemporaries, but also forces the researcher at every step of data preparation to be conscious of classification: how the historical actors classified themselves, how they were classified by the record-keepers, and how the language of the records is to be transformed into the categories the researcher wants to use. Experience and the earlier discussion has made it clear that at times internal evidence in historical sources may lead to reconstructed configurations so elaborate that none of these terminologies appears to be sufficient for dealing with them. This is certainly the case with vital-events sources that permit maximal reconstructions. Consider, once again, the parish registers of the West German Schwalm area, and the lineage tables (*Stammtafeln*) that later genealogists created from them (see chapter 2). The parish records were kept by a succession of clergymen over a period of some 350 years, each man entering in the registers facts about births, deaths and marriages that occurred during his tenure. The result of this continuous activity was a set of historical records about some 50,000 individuals who had resided in the Schwalm villages for their entire lives or for shorter periods of time. When genealogists in the twentieth century undertook to reorganize this information, they created for each surname, when it first occurred in the record, a lineage table, without knowing at that point whether that surname would appear in the records again. As new individuals appeared in the parish records, they were linked to others of like surname, on the appropriate table, through the use of internal genealogical evidence. Some tables began with a clearly identifiable 'founder': others started *in medias res,* because the 'founders' predated the start of parish registers in the area. Some lineages had branches in several villages, others were concentrated in only one. Some continued through the entire registration period, and others began and became 'extinct' within the period. Consequently, the complete set of *Stammtafeln* contains lineage records of greatly varying lengths, because some lines were 'successful' in the sense of having had eight or nine generations of male offspring who remained in the Schwalm area, whereas in other cases no male offspring were produced in a particular generation or the males who were born died too early or emigrated.

It is important to recognize these genealogical configurations for what they are in the light of the approach we are using. The *Stammtafeln* are not 'genealogies' in the sense of ancestors' lists transmitted orally from generations to generation and referred to when members of a living population needed kinship information.[2] Rather, they consist of reconstructions from discrete historical data, which data were produced as the events they record occurred. These events fell into observable units, so to speak, only when it was decided, later in time, that reconstructions should be undertaken. Before that time, it is an open question whether any of the individuals who appear in the *Stammtafeln* knew who their ancestors were or even who all their contemporary kin were. We must therefore think of the Schwalm genealogists as informants who, when the need arose, presented kinship information to later researchers by using the lineage principle of organ-

---

2   See the discussion by Barnes (1979).

ization. This decision produced a set of lineage records with considerable extension in time and social space, but not, for any point in the time the records cover, a listing of residents containing an inventory of descent groups.

The differences between a time-based lineage table and a list of the members of a descent group are crucial. In the descent-group list, we have something close to the kind of record a fieldwork anthropologist would assemble to study, for example, residential rules. He would list where each member of a living population was residing and then obtain the kin ties linking persons within each unit and in different units in order to see whether patterns of movement based of kin lines corresponded with what people said about them. The population would be there 'on the ground', and movement could be followed in and out of actual residences. In the Schwalm, by contrast, 'co-residence' can be studied only as 'village co-residence' or 'regional co-residence', because the presence of a person in the parish was recorded at only three points in the life-cycle – birth, marriage and death – and the parish did, of course, include a number of communities. The descent-group record presents us with a static picture of relationships, and we can introduce a time element only by correlating the structural involvements of the individuals with their ages. Further generalizations along this line require the assumption that the structural involvements of, say, the youngest age-group were those which the oldest had had earlier, and those of the oldest those which the youngest would have in the future. That is, there has to be the assumption of absence of changes in the conditions that affected the community as a whole and the internal dynamics of its population. By contrast, each of the Schwalm lineage tables presents us with a time-based record of a particular kind of kin unit that gives empirical content to Meyer Fortes's suggestion that the descent group can be analysed as a 'continuing process through time' (Fortes, 1970: 90). To put it in another way, with this record we can distinguish that part of the population which persisted from that which did not, and we can examine some aspects of the internal organization of the former. The examination, however, has to operate 'above the ground', because we cannot tell from the lineage tables who was alive and living in the Schwalm at any given moment in time. We gain a time dimension at the cost of specificity in spatial information, whereas with historical records of descent groups we may lose the information that allows us to think of discrete households and families as 'groups' descended from the same ancestor.

The Schwalm record provides us with access to structural contexts which are not available from other kinds of historical evidence. The most telling ways to use aggregated lineage evidence have not yet been worked out, in part because social historians, to our knowledge, generally have not had data bases of this kind to work with; and anthropologists, given their preference for synchronic analysis, have not bequeathed to historians a methodology of the appropriate sort. We can certainly make use of Fortes's suggestion (mentioned earlier) and explore the members of a lineage in terms of what such membership 'signifies for the individual in his personal field of social relations'. But we also want to do more, because the lineage tables present us with configurations that can be used as 'units of analysis', even if we cannot tell from the outset exactly what kinds of units they are.

Suppose that the decision has been made to try to write a history of kinship in a particular community with exceptionally rich vital-events records, as is the case with the Schwalm communities. Furthermore, this 'history' is to cover a stretch of historical time in the relatively distant past, rather than a stretch anchored in the observable present. Let us say, further, that the decision has been made because, during this particular stretch of time, there are other good records – perhaps a good collection of household lists or interactional sources – which the researcher expects link the genealogical reconstructions. The objective of the inquiry is to understand how lineage relationships have to be factored into social-structural inquiry, and the first step has to be the extraction from reconstructed lineage tables, such as those for the Schwalm, all of the lineage information relevant for the selected period of time. Figure 12 suggests the problems that arise when this strategy is being followed in connection with the population history of one of the Schwalm villages – Merzhausen – which in the first half of the nineteenth century (1834) had a population of 700 persons. Each of the numbered vertical lines in the figure represents a lineage in Merzhausen, with the indicator of the presence of a lineage being the children whom the genealogists concluded were born 'into' a particular lineage (that is, into a conjugal family associated with that lineage). The beginning and end years in this example have been chosen arbitrarily to illustrate the data which the sources make available to study the problem in this particular community. The fact that a total lineage record extended throughout the entire period does not mean that all lineages began or ended in the two indicated years; and the total number of people who could be shown to have been 'members' of this set of lineages at any point in the century should not be understood as the total number of residents Merzhausen had. As can be demonstrated in the single-year censuses of these years, there were families in this community whose surnames do not exist in the registers from which the patrilineage tables were reconstructed. If, however, lineage kinship did function as one element of social structure in the community during this historical period, its presence would have to be demonstrated by means of hypotheses, for the testing of which, initially, the data would have to be rearranged in the manner of figure 12.

1750 1760 1770 1780 1800 1810 1820 1830 1840 1850

Each line represents the length of time each of the 124 patrilines was present in Merzhausen, from 1750 to 1850.

Figure 12 Patrilineages in Merzhausen, 1750–1850

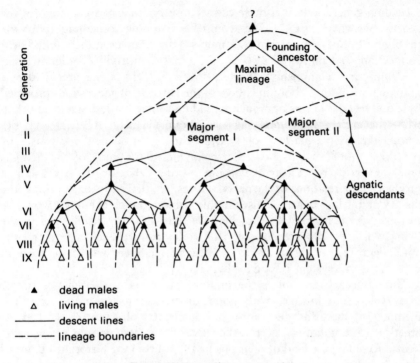

Figure 13 A patrilineage paradigm
Source: Fortes, 1945: 34

The data do not obligate the researcher to move in any one particular direction. We might, for example, attempt to extract from this welter of evidence sufficient information to deal with the question of the descent group, using for our gude the well-known lineage paradigm from Meyer Fortes's study of the Tallensi (Fortes, 1945: 34) (figure 13). The point of this would be to sort out living members of lineages in the census year 1834, for example, when one of the single-year censuses of the community was made. Among the Tallensi, lineage principles were undeniably socially important. But in the case of Merzhausen, we could not assume such importance *a priori*: the model would have to be used to arrange genealogical data in order for that data to be tested with the help of various kinds of interactional and residential evidence. The point is that before the genealogical data could be so tested, they would have to be reorganized in several of a number of different ways, and the lineage model would be one of these. In order to make sense of the 1834 Merzhausen population, which would be represented in the diagram by the living numbers shown in the most recent three generations, we would make use of the antecedent connections in the ascending generations as if these connections had meant something for the generations alive in 1834. We would be assuming something about the thinking of the 1834 populations, namely, that they used these antecedent connections as 'mnemonics' (Fortes's term) to introduce order in their contemporary relationships (Fortes, 1970: 37). Thus the precise demographic information about members of the antecedent generations provided by a *Stammtafel* in this approach would be somewhat less significant than what the entire *Stammtafel* suggests about the field of social activities among the people marked for analysis through a particular census. The paradigm would tell us how the 'behavior of the part [of the field] is regulated by its relation to the whole and the behavior of the whole is a product of the relations of the parts' (Fortes, 1970: 37). In approaching 'the history of kinship' in Merzhausen in this fashion, our chief interest would be to understand the people who, because their lifetimes overlapped in the living world of 1834, enacted kinship roles toward each other; and the antecedent relationships among non-living members would be used to explain the role system among the living.

This approach minimizes the importance of the earlier phases of the 'history' of the lineage, with good theoretical justification. After all, members of the 1834 generation did not enact roles toward their great-great-great-grandfathers, even if the existence of these persons as ancestors helped to define the field of relations in 1834. From the historian's point of view, however, this is not an altogether satisfactory situation, because the population which has been marked for closer inspection (from the viewpoint of roles) was selected more or less arbitrarily, not because it necessarily occupied an especially important position in the long-term history of this persisting social structure. Thus a second approach to these data – which can still be conceptualized in terms of the Fortes's paradigm – is to assign equal importance to all of the generations in the genealogical configuration, and deal with them as 'chapters' of the same continuing story, recognizing, of course, that when role analysis is used it can be used only for those generations whose lifetimes overlapped. Holding the entire lineage 'in place' would define a succession of generations or cohorts which we have some reason to think could have had a unity in the course of time. In this approach, the long-term connections between a succession of data sets would give the kinship domain an extension in time. Now we would be testing the persisting social relevance of a subpopulation within a persisting total population, and trying to establish whether a particular lineage (or indeed, a whole collection of lineages) can be thought of as having had social significance as a 'structure of long duration' (Braudel, 1972: 18). We would still have to select a starting-point and an end-point in past time, but we would not be assigning special significance to any particular generation by dealing with it as a descent group said to be representative of the entire kinship experience of the people concerned.

The exercise carried out in this fashion would have to be controlled and modified, however, by our understanding of the entire collection of lineages that existed in Merzhausen during the chosen stretch of historical time. This understanding would contribute three things to the inquiry. It would mean, as figure 12 suggests, that we cannot deal with lineages as if they all had 'histories' of equal length, and therefore, in using the paradigm, we would have to deal at times with the empirical information about groups containing only one or two adjacent generations. Thus the history of kinship, as pursued through the lineage paradigm, would have to describe what appear to be 'negative cases': the units which did not succeed in developing into long-term structures. Second, we have to remember that each of the unbroken lines in figure 12 represents the 'presence' of a lineage in Merzhausen as indicated by the continuing birth of children that can be associated with the lineage. The line therefore does not depict – nor can it depict – the structural history of a lineage. This means that the 'histories' of the various lineages shown in figure 12 and the end phases of them in 1850 (the chosen cut-off year) are somewhat misleading, in that they do not show the process of segmentation at work in the long run, having disregarded it for the sake of diagrammatic representation. Third, it also has to be remembered that figure 12 does not depict, though it does imply, that lineages were connected to each other through intermarriage. Indeed, it is one of the most interesting aspects of the Schwalm lineage reconstructions that the data file permits the linking of any one lineage through its entire 'history' to numerous others, because of the fact that the wives 'coming into' a lineage can be traced to their parents and the daughters 'leaving' a lineage can be followed 'into' their husbands' lineages. The terminology of movement employed here, of course, pertains to the manipulation of data. It cannot, at the outset, be assumed that, just because the genealogical reconstructions permit us to follow certain individuals from one data subset to another, 'lineages' in the Schwalm should necessarily be understood to hae 'exchanged women', to use Claude Lèvi-Strauss's conceptualization (Lévi-Strauss, 1963: 61).

How these warnings work out in the Merzhausen example can be discussed quite concretely. Suppose we choose for close analysis a lineage which supplied children to Merzhausen during the entire designated period from 1750 to 1850. Lineage no. 265 (the Korell, or Corell, family) was a prominent one in the Schwalm area in the early modern centuries, but its history during the 1750–1850 period in Merzhausen, when juxtaposed with that of the other lineages in figure 12 during the same years, indicates that it cannot be seen as typical. If we were to use it as a case study, we could speak of it as an example of what could happen with some lineages, but not what did happen with most of them, even during the short time period we are covering. The full history of kinship from the perspective of lineages would have to encompass not only those such as the Korells, who were present continuously, but also the many lineages whose tenure in Merzhausen, or indeed in the entire Schwalm population, was very short. Moreover, if we look closely at the entire lineage record of the Korells (which encompasses, as a small segment, its history in Merzhausen from 1750 to 1850), we would find that the Merzhausen Korells were only one segment of a larger configuration, the other branches of which had been supplying children to other Schwalm villages: to Gungelshausen from 1675 to 1804, to Loshausen from 1601 to 1857, to Wasenberg from 1603 to 1905, and to Zella from 1621 to 1873. The Merzhausen Korells had been supplying children to Merzhausen itself from 1607 to 1905, including the 1750–1850 segment we have examined in figure 12. A full understanding of the context of the Merzhausen 1750–1850 segment, however, would carry the research beyond this village and the time we have indicated, to encompass four more of the nine Schwalm villages in the file and nearly the entire period of the parish records. It would have to consider carefully the process of segmentation during the seventeenth century when, in the period between 1601 and 1675, the lineage developed branches in a total of five villages (including Merzhausen) and continued to supply children to each of them for periods of 100–200 years.

Even if we were to limit our exploration of the Korell lineage to its 100–year presence in Merzhausen, the activities of lineage members would require that the field of investigation be widened. The entire Korell lineage record contained 141 marriages, spread out in time from 1601 to 1905. In eight of these, 'Korell' males had married 'Korell' females, and in 42 the Korell males had taken wives from outside the Schwalm area. But in 91 cases either Korell males had married women from identifiable Schwalm lineages, or Korell females had married into these Schwalm lineages. In the 1750–1850 time period, the Korell lineage was linked through marriage to 43 (or 34.9 per cent) of the other 123 lineages present in Merzhausen during that time, some of these links having been established before, some during and some after the time period in question. Moreover, in addition to these links with 43 other Merzhausen lineages, the Korell lineage had also established marital links with 34 Schwalm lineages which do not appear in the 1750–1850 Merzhausen record. Consequently, a full history of the Korell lineage would have to account for the structural involvements of its members, with something in the region of 10 per cent of the lineages which had made an appearance in the Schwalm area during the period the vital-events records had been kept.

Intertwined Lineages

Researchers using structural metaphors have often argued that such terms should not be taken to connote static states, but actual demonstrations of how synchronic and diachronic analyses fit together in historical time have been few and far between. This is a particular pressing issue with historical evidence of the sort we have just surveyed. This evidence calls for the understanding of individual social structures (lineages) that undergo various kinds of changes in the course of historical time and establish and maintain connections with each other (intermarriage), and are, at the same time, social contexts of individual human beings, these contexts being analysable as descent groups whose members enact roles toward each other. In principle, the lineage should be an easily measurable unit. When analysed synchronically, it contains linked subsets of persons, all of whom are alive at the same time, recognize that they are descended from the same ancestor or have been brought into such a group by marriage or adoption, and express this sense of corporateness through common activities, rituals and behaviours that separate a particular subset from similar groups in other lineages. Analysed diachronically, the lineage (patrilineage, in this example) is understood: to have a 'founder'; to persist in time either in the form of a single line, when each generation has only one male offspring, or in the form of branches, when there are several male offspring; and either to become extinct when males are no longer produced or to continue as a fixture in a community's population as a result of continuous production of males. In both cases, as long as we stay in the realm of pure form, delineation does not seem to present major difficulties. But, as we have seen, particularly when the chronological placement of the population prevents the use of interviews, the evidence presents many problems. On the one hand, we can continue to use traditional structural images; on the other, when we are discussing lineages the metaphor which seems to be most apt is that of a thick rope (the entire community), having great length (historical time) and being composed of many strands (lineages) which are intertwined (through intermarriage). Each strand consists of many threads (individuals, family households) which also have extension, though never as long as that of the strands or the rope itself. A cross-section cut from the rope would show us the position of strands (now seen as descent groups) and the position of threads (individuals, households) *vis-à-vis* each other, but this cross-sectional view would not give us much of an understanding of the entire length of the rope itself, or the process of intertwining, or of the discontinuities in the various collections of shorter threads. Whichever images turn out to be most helpful, it does seem fairly clear that the intertwined lineages of the Schwalm data present us with the most inclusive field of historical-genealogical evidence, over which hypothesization about kinship should take place. Interaction evidence in its many forms in the Schwalm area provides the least problematic evidence for raising hypotheses, but, as we have said, this is evidence presented to us in the form of self-enclosed small universes. If we were to conclude from such evidence that no larger and more inclusive groupings existed, we would be allowing the *form* of the evidence to dictate our findings.

The evidence we have cited for the twentieth-century communities of Törbel and Orašac suggests that the inhabitants of these places were conscious of membership in groups that were in some sense less transitory than their own families of birth and marriage and the households in which they were living. The Baltic and Schwalm data from the earlier centuries suggest further than in some localities of Europe there is sufficient empirical evidence for the reconstruction of more inclusive configurations, which, at this juncture, can be viewed as having had potential social significance. Thus, Fortes's suggestions, cited earlier, on the lines of inquiry in the study of lineages, can be adapted for our purposes, as long as we remember that we are involved in a testing procedure. We cannot assume from the outset that the lineage reconstructions (unlike, for example, reconstituted conjugal familes) are proven to have had social relevance by virtue of our ability to pull their various elements together. We should think of them, neutrally, as surname groups, with the surnames and the appropriate genealogical evidence being devices with which to extract certain subpopulations for further examination. Then following Fortes, we can look at their structural features: how, for example, a surname group was distributed among several farmsteads; or how the several segments of a *Stamm* (lineage) were distributed among several villages. We can also examine the external relationships of each surname group: whether, for example, there was a pattern of more frequent intermarriage between some of the patrilines than between others. In some cases, it is possible to study patterns of placement of young people on farms different than those in which parents resided, and to establish whether a group of farms occupied by persons of the same descent group exchanged adolescents with a group occupied by members of a different one. We can also deal with the demographics of these surname groups in certain ways suggested by recent research on lineages in other societies. John Fei and Ts'ui-jung Liu have shown that it is possible to generalize about long-term patterns of demographic expansion and contraction in Chinese patrilineal clans through the use of a 'hierarchy matrix' of males (Fei and Liu, 1982); Netting (1981) and Wachter and Laslett (1978) have worked out methods of measuring rates of patriline extinction in Törbel and among English baronetcies. Although the demographic approach does not need to take up the subject of corporate identity, since it uses only the variables of birth, death, marriage and genealogical position, its findings regarding probable extinction rates and size-change patterns are certainly pertinent to the evaluation of the varieties of descent-group sizes and lineage persistence in our documents.

Certain kinds of analyses of historical lineages have to draw on other evidence to complement the genealogical information. For example, still following Fortes, one might ask about the institutional forms, such as whether members of a lineage were traditionally baptized in a particular church or were buried in a particular cemetery. There is also the internal constitution of a lineage, whose provisions – most probably customary rather than written – might have to be detected in the devolution of property, naming practices, choice of godparents, and so forth. In the Schwalm, for example, some farms (*Bauernhöfe*) had remained in the same patriline from the mid-sixteenth century to the present, and the Christian names of their owners showed an equal degree of continuity in being repeated generation affter generation (Schoof, 1977: 41–3). Though the representativeness of these individualized farm and name-histories remains to be determined, they do suggest, among the peasantry of the Schwalm area, a similar high degree of consciousness of lineage membership as was exhibited among the nobles in Hesse, the German state in which the Schwalm villages were located. In a detailed study of the transmission of property in Hessian noble families, Gregory Pedlow showed that:

> even. the division of a family's estates among several heirs was not necessarily permanent, for many lines died out within a few generations and their estates fell to relatives. There was thus a constant flow of estates between the different branches of a family as lines died out and new lines were created. As a result, few families passed on their estates from father to son to grandson until the nineteenth century (when child mortality declined substantially and a larger percentage of noblemen married), but most families were able to keep their estates in the family and preserve the family name from extinction, thereby achieving two of the nobility's most important objectives. (Pedlow, 1982: 350)

We do not know which of these types of evidence, or which combination of them, would constitute sufficient proof that the configuration we have been able to reconstruct did or did not enter the consciousness of their members as entities transcending time and place. Whatever the outcome turns out to be, it should not be forgotten that without the reconstruction no testing at all would be possible, and we would have to carry out our analysis of kinship in these areas as if the only memberships that individual historical actors were conscious of were summed up in statistics concerning the conjugal family unit, the household and perhaps the descent group. But the reconstructions can be carried out and their internal arrangements, emerging gradually as one piece of evidence is connected to another, are neither functions of any individual's memory nor the results of anyone's desire to depict the past in some idealized fashion. As evidence about lineages, these reconstructions contain both the negative and positive cases – both the lineages tht 'worked out' and those that did not – and this fact alone strengthens the case for testing them both as contexts of action and time-based units of analysis.

10

The Network Concept

Total and Partial Networks

Any group of historical actors can be analysed as a network when they are represented as a set of points and the relationships among them as lines drawn between the points. This manner of thinking about social relationships in the past was never entirely absent from the reasoning in the earlier chapters of this book, and at times the discussion in fact used the language of networks. But it did so sparingly, in part because this type of language can no longer be used figuratively or metaphorically, and in part because its use in any case raises a host of issues that are best treated together in one place. The fact is that a set of kinship relationships almost begs to be transformed into an analysable network and to be measured for such attributes as density; its component parts – the individuals between whom lines are drawn – in turn stand ready to be characterized as central or peripheral to the system as a whole. We can easily find network conceptions implied by non-formal descriptions of historical kinship ties. Thus, for example, the historian Jerome Blum, in his description of rural areas of pre-modern Europe, speaks of peasant villagers as 'often related by blood and marriage' and therefore desirous of keeping their internal quarrels from landowners and other 'outsiders' (Blum, 1978: 115). The French scholar Jean-Louis Flandrin, in observing that in modern France mere residence in the village community appears at times to be sufficient for an individual to be considered a kinsman, speculates that this 'might be because the peasant has been accustomed for centuries to being related to all inhabitants of his village' (Flandrin, 1979: 35). A testing of these propositions would require, as an initial step, the reconstruction of a kin-based network of persons and, as subsequent steps, some form of measurement of the frequency with which quarrels did or did not involve people outside such a network; also, with respect to Flandrin's description, some assessment of whether peasants in the past in fact were 'related to all inhabitants of his village'. Thus before we could accept these descriptions as containing some measure of truth about historical communities, we would have to go through the entire process of identification, sorting and reconstruction that we have discussed up to this point, in order to work out who was or was not related to whom and who did what with whom.

In the historical sources from which materials for such an exercise would be drawn, we would discover very quickly that kinship relationships (now lines between points) were not the only relationships that could be set up for analysis in this way. Some lines, defined by reference to descent and marriage, could indeed be extracted from the entire collection, but there would be other identifiable relationships as well, the non-inclusion of which in the exercise would now have to be justified. In a marriage contract, some lines could be drawn from the bride and groom to witnesses of the contract who were kin, but others would run from the central actors to others (presumably 'friends') who were also present. In a household list, some lines would flow from the head to his co-residing relatives, but others from the head to co-residing servants who were not related to him. A segmented lineage might connect two subpopulations of two villages, but the two could also be connectted by a line signifying that the one was a market for the other. In due course, as the small populations and the social entities they created were scrutinized in this fashion and positioned *vis-à-vis* each other, the isolation of the kinship tie as the linking mechanism could come to focus on only a very small proportion of all possible ties; this, in turn, would raise the question of what the relationship was between the ties of kinship and the other ties. At this point, the researcher would have to begin to think of the kinship network as a 'partial network', analysable as such, but also implicated in some fashion in the 'total network', defined as containing all possible relationships among individuals and between entities composed of individuals (Barnes, 1969; 1972).

Traditional descriptions of the kind cited earlier were not produced on the basis of data files, treated in this manner, but rested on a number of assumptions about the nature of pre-modern rural and urban communities. Thus, a high density of kin-connectedness was presumed to be a consequence of low in- and out-migration, which in turn was held to be the result of local prohibitions against movement, strong attachment to land, lack of opportunities for other employment, and simply loyalty to the group. If a sufficient number of people in each generation married and died in the community into which they were born, and this pattern was repeated over many generations, the result, naturally, would be that each member of the community at a particular point in past time was related in some fashion to all other living members. But how close were these assumptions to the social reality of the distant, or even near, past of European rural peoples? What was the chance that in a particular pre-modern rural community kin links, however measured, would have been dense? What was the likelihood that these kin links, if dense, were still not as important for social life as the idea of density would seem to imply, and that, if analysed together with other links of a non-kinship sort, they would become diluted because they were now a part of a 'total network'? In his pioneering study of kin and neighbours in thirteenth-century Suffolk, R. M. Smith warns us against always expecting, at least in medieval England, 'survival of durable networks of high density', and he adds that 'in many discussions of these issues precision has not been easy; families have not always been distinguished from co-resident domestic groups; kin have not consistently been clearly differentiated from heighbors' (Smith, 1979: 248, 220). To these observations one might add the following: *types* of kin have also not been distinguished; it is still an open question what levels geographic movement had to reach for the density of kin links to be changed noticeably; and it has not been clearly established among which of a number of possible units of reckoning connectedness, or the lack of it, has to be sought for any hypothesis to be tested. The historical data will not always yield the same kinds of units for testing. For example, Smith has researched the extent to which certain kinds of ties (between kin and between non-kin) entered a large number of discrete social transactions, and his work is a good example of how far the question can be pursued when evidence about social relations is 'wrapped up', as it were, 'in the particular occasions in which they [i.e., the relations] emerge' (Fortes, 1969: 60). By contrast, kin information from vital-events reconstructions or from domain-linked evidence may take the form of constituent units of a system whose outer borders are the borders of the community rather than of the small universe delineated by a particular activity. In such a case the entire system – the 'total' network of relationships – may appear to change very little in its size and essential form, even if there is a rapid turnover of some of its components.

In recent years, the analysis of network-like social configurations has been greatly formalized, and researcher working along these lines have all pointed out that among the types of social relationships on which the network concept can be used to good effect, relations based on kinship appear very promising, because kinship is articulated in a network-like fashion. The concept has been used widely in the social sciences, but, as we have found with other ideas, its application to historical data, particularly kinship data, has only barely begun (Burt, 1980; Mitchell, 1980; Rutman, 1980). Even so, the start is a promising one, because the early work has shown the concept to be sufficiently flexible to be applied to a wide variety of evidence. Thus, for example, we cannot investigate a lineage (as understood in the last chapter) on the basis of the evidence present in interactional data, or descent groups on the basis of vital-events reconstructions. Moreover, domain-linked data are inadequate (though not entirely

uninformative) as far as time-based lineages and a large variety of interactions are concerned. But these three types of evidence can be scrutinized
by means of the concept of the network, because among the organizing
concepts we have discussed so far, that of the network is the most neutral as
far as specific content of relationships is concerned. We can look at a
kinship network as a context in which individuals make decisions, or at a
number of related networks as subpopulations of a community. We can also
try to understand the entire community as a kinship network, but, whichever of these directions is taken, the analyst must always keep in mind that
the analysis is dealing with partial systems of relationships and that the
actual content of these relationships frequently has to be proposed by the
analyst.

Kin Networks as Contexts

As many investigators have noted, the 'community' leaves much to be
desired as a unit of observations for kinship in the past (Macfarlane,
1977b). Even in the pre-industrial communities of Europe, turnover appears
to have been high, succeeding in some areas (such as England) in transforming up to 60 per cent of a local population in as short a time as twelve years
(Laslett, 1977: ch. 2). Moreover, persisting exogamy, even at relatively low
levels, would create for many members of a local population many kinship
links with populations of surrounding communities, and could even remove
significant proportions of people from observation entirely, if they moved to
distant points. Statements about historical kinship have to be made in
recognition of these facts, and on the basis of precise definitions. In some
respects this places a limitation on the kinds of kinship structures which
investigators might wish to study. For some subpopulations, such as nobles,
place was a less important factor in kinship ties; for others, such as
peasants, it was very important indeed. The identification of a kinship
network for an adult nobleman might involve a large number of different
places and different records from these places; for enserfed peasants,
however, the entire kinship network could be identified from the records of
a restricted locality. The exact content of the kinship networks in these cases
might not differ greatly, and therefore the observation that communities are
not a particularly good unit of analysis of social-structual involvements has
to be modified with respect to the social standing of the people involved.
Even so, the use of the community as the universe remains problematic, and
for this reason the researcher might choose to employ the network concept
in order to arrive at a general characterization of the social context of
decision-making, rather than at a precise description of either the networks
themselves or the community from which the network data are taken. This

less ambitious strategy at times makes a great deal of sense. The identifiable components of a network are not treated as ends in themselves, to be submitted to various kinds of precise measurements, but rather as means to general statements about groups of people who were likely to be making decisions in segments of a community characterized by differing kinds of network relationships.

This is the approach taken to the recent work of Robert Ostergren with kinship networks in nineteenth-century Swedish villages. Here, network reconstructions serve as a stepping stone to a discussion of migration. Ostergren believes that it is not sufficient to locate only the kin links between migrants themselves in order to generalize about the importance of kinship in the migration process, but that 'studies must define the kinship networks extant in the population at risk and then relate patterns of migration to them ... the challenge is to find the mechanism by which kinship is relevant to the selection of migrants' (Ostergren, 1982: 294). The historical sources from which the networks are reconstructed are somewhat different than the principal types we have discussed so far: catechetical registers which were continuous records of all the events that affected a particular household, or a collection of households, over a delimited period of time. Ostergren began with a record of the migrants who left four villages from the parish of Raatvik in the Swedish province of Dalarna, beginning in 1866, and then reconstructed the kin networks from which these individuals emerged as they became emigrants. The data used for the reconstruction were limited to the 20-year period before 1866: thus the characteristics of the kin networks from which these emigrants departed can be said to have been formed within two generations. These networks at the point of origin were then characterized with respect to such features as degree of endogamy, distance of migration of people originating in such networks, and size and structure of households in the networks. Ostergren's conclusion can be cited in full:

> The experience ... studied here shows that the demographic and economic conditions for emigration were most often acted on only in certain social contexts. It was membership in the best-developed and socially central kinship networks in the community that provided the reinforcement necessary to cause families to act on the idea to emigrate. The reason for this may have been that it was this socially active and successful element of society that sought to preserve itself through resisting dispersion of its offspring. ... Faced with the possibility of dispersion of part of the younger generation in a time of crisis, the alternative of a 'closed' migration to a specific destination was particularly attractive. It offered the possibility of 'fragmenting

out' and preserving the essential social fabric of the community.
(Ostergren, 1982: 318–19)

Reconstruction in Ostergren's study was thus employed not in order to
arrive at, for example, a measure of density, but rather to characterize
networks generally so that they could be compared with the attributes of the
migrating groups which their members participated in. The question of
whether the reconstruction yielded particular kinds of kinship groups –
kindreds, descent groups, or the like – was not in this study as important as
the question of the behaviour of the individuals who emerged from them:
how often they married women from outside the kin group, how far they
eventually emigrated, what size households they formed. The fact that some
of the social networks in which emigrants were implicated had a kinship
basis is used in this study as an indicator of the degree of social embeddedness, rather than as the starting-point for the analysis of particular kinds of
kin ties. The shift in perspective is important, however, because it leads
Ostergren to be concerned not only with the connections between people
who moved, but primarily with the structural features, as expressed in
kinship networks, of the communities from which the movers originated.
Regardless of the nature of particular ties and the particular kin roles they
carried with them – both of which remain implicit – the analysis brings to
the forefront the networks as contexts of social action and decision, and
thus illustrates very well one of the directions in which the network concept
can lead.

Networks in the Community

We have observed that much of the reconstructable evidence for pre-
modern Europe exists as information about individuals. The records,
whether they are single-year enumerations or continuous registers of vital
events, do not provide all imaginable links, but only those involving people
who were present on the spot whenever a record of a vital event was made
or an inventory of the entire population taken. Though we know that a
better unit of analysis would be the community or the region, the data are
often insufficient to make the connections beyond the local boundary. Thus
if we continue to employ the network as the means for organizing data, and
concern ourselves with the attributes of networks as such, we have to
assume from the outset that the networks will be incomplete or partial.

The network concept, however, does not require complete information,
in the sense of being usable only when the points and lines employed to
reconstruct a network replicate faithfully the total numbers of actors and
relationships of some 'natural' configuration, however defined. All that is

needed is *some* set of actors and *some* evidence about relationships between them. Because of these minimal evidentiary requirements, the network concept has shown itself to be very useful for gaining control over interactional evidence, which, as will be remembered, presents a large number of closed universes of links, with links within each clearly spelt out, but links among universes difficult, if not impossible, to trace. Moreover, the concept does not require that within each universe we sort out genealogical (or kinship) links from non-genealogical (or non-kinship) ones; indeed, at this level of analysis, where the total number of links of any kind is fewer than it would be in larger units, the concept enables the analyst to examine the interaction of several different kinds of links simultaneously. The relative significance of different kinds of links thus becomes an attribute of each small interactional universe, and these attributes, when summarized for an entire collection of such universes, finally allows us to measure how, for example, kinship ties compare in significance with ties based on other criteria.

The first example of this line of investigation is the work of R. M. Smith with data from medieval England. In what has to be regarded as a pioneering essay (from the historian's viewpoint), Smith has used the network concept to deal with a central question of English (and, by extension, European) social history, namely, whether in the long pre-industrial and pre-modern era of English (and European) history kinship was an important dimension of the close-knit life of English villagers (Smith, 1979). We know very little about this matter, in England or elsewhere in Europe. The time has long since passed (at least for social historians of the European continent) when one could hypothesize a pre-industrial period during which kinship was of maximal importance in the everyday life of villagers and contrast this to a modern period when the kinship dimension had ceased to be important. But it is one thing to discard this – perhaps 'traditional' – view of the long term in European social history, and another to place something in its stead. At the moment, social historians are seeking to formulate a new general hypothesis about the importance of kinship, and Smith's efforts have to be seen in this light. He approaches the question by positing a relatively simple hypothesis, namely:

> if kinship was an important organizing principle in village society we would expect to find kin in a wide variety of relationships, ranging from informal assistance to cooperation between relatives in economic activities. ... If, on the other hand, neighbors and the wider village community were functionally more important than kin we would expect kin to figure infrequently amongst the usual village acts of aid and assistance. (Smith, 1979: 220)

Smith's data come from the manor of Redgrave, one of the properties of the abbots of the monastery of Bury St Edmonds – specifically, from the manorial court of that property in the period 1260–93 and from a general survey of the manor carried out in 1289. The court records contain information on a wide variety of village activities such as transactions about land, disputes between neighbours, debts, breaches of agreement, quarrels of all kinds, and so forth. The records have allowed Smith to consider 13,592 interactions between pairs of individuals over the period from 1259 to 1293. Among these, 8,026 interactions involved the institution of 'pledging', that is, the appearance in the court of people on behalf of the defendant or plaintiff as a guarantee that the obligations the court decision imposed on the defendant or plaintiff would be met. Smith uses the network concept in order, as he says, 'to disentangle the interplay between kinship, propinquity, and economic status in the question of an individual's social and economic relations'. The individuals mentioned in a pledging document were located, with respect to an Ego, in one of the following zones: kin, immediate neighbours, inhabitants of the same sub-area of the manor, inhabitants of the manor who were outside the Ego's sub-area or hamlet, and outsiders. Measurement of the network so constructed for a particular Ego was obtained by reference to the Ego's contacts in these five areas. Smith proceeds on the basis of the simplest kind of measurement of networks, namely, densities of zones characterized as first order, second order, and so forth, as proposed by Barnes. After a close examination of the density and content of the Ego-centred networks for different groups of people distinguished by occupation and size of property holdings, Smith concludes that the 'modal experience in this society was not one in which the peasant farm functioned as the stable center of family activities or of stable relationships within a socially homogeneous village society. . . . [The characteristics of this society were such as to] diminish sustained contact with kin and neighbors and the survival of durable networks of high density' (Smith, 1979: 248).

Smith's basic data are interactional and they generate partial networks: that is, in no instance of an Ego do we have available all of the ties that we would wish to explore. The network which is measured is therefore entirely dependent upon the ties that a record-keeper identified; it is a closed universe in which the lines that are drawn between points cannot be supplemented by the uncovering of other links, by further questioning or additional information. Even so, as Smith has clearly shown, the measurement of relationships in these clusters requires that those between non-kin be given the same standing as those with kin, with the result that the final figures draw upon two partial networks simultaneously.

Proceeding chronologically with our examples, we can consider the work of Robert Wheaton (Wheaton, 1980). Wheaton's principal source, as described in chapter 2 above, is also interactional, namely the surviving records of marriage contracts drawn up by Bordeaux notaries for a period of time in the middle of the seventeenth century. As Smith's pledging sources, Wheaton's marriage contracts also take the form of discrete documents that juxtapose the principal actors of a transaction with various kinds of kin, assistants and attendants in the contract ceremony, which came after earlier negotiations between the families of birth of the bride and the groom. A marriage contract could be a very complicated document many pages in length, because it often dealt not only with property that changed hands as a direct consequence of the marriage itself, but also laid out detailed arrangements involving the future responsibilities that principals would have toward the family members on each side. The scope for the application of the network concept in these documents is thus considerable. Wheaton's principal interest in this work is to make use of reconstructed Ego-centred networks to measure the extent to which different occupational groups in Bordeaux could be said to have exhibited solidarity. This line of inquiry requires the contract to be examined for the occupational designation of the families of the bride and the groom in relation to the occupations which the various other people present at the ceremony were involved in. Here the focus is not on whether in a particular transaction more 'strangers' than 'kin' were involved, but rather on what these small clusters of persons indicate about the larger social structure of the community. Thus the composition of networks is used as an indicator of the connections between status groups, with each group composed of a number of different occupational categories. Lines between individuals in dyad-centred networks are here scrutinized for what they reveal about connections (lines) among sub-units of the entire city population.

The larger question to which Wheaton's work is addressed concerns the appropriate conceptualization of macrostructures in the context of pre-modern European society. This question has been a troublesome one for social historians, because in these centuries an analysis of macrostructure in terms of economic classes alone obscures the fact that historical actors tended to classify themselves and others less by reference to economic criteria only, than by reference to economic criteria in combination with status criteria. Thus income derived from a particular occupation was less a reliable indicator of social standing than the position a particular occupation traditionally held in a hierarchy of occupations in the community. These classifications cut across economic criteria: for example, it was entirely possible, in pre-revolutionary Russia, for a serf to have migrated to a city, to have enjoyed considerable economic success that made him wealthier than his owner, yet to be constrained in all manner of ways by the fact that his status was still that of a serf. In order to establish how such classifications worked in terms of crucial social activities, Wheaton has focused his work on the only remaining evidence about marriage, namely, contracts. He has succeeded in showing that the network concept can be used to good effect with such sources, and how the concept forces the researcher to include non-kin as well as kin in the network analysis. As in the pledging documents analysed by Smith, network analysis of marriage contracts provides the means for viewing individuals as enactors of kin and non-kin roles simultaneously, and for subsuming networks of limited membership to more inclusive networks in which each limited network becomes a point and the analysis, by definition, pertains to a larger proportion ot the total population.

One can visualize a data file in which every person who has ever lived in a particular community figures as a point in a total network and the record of each person contains complete information on all the connections that person ever had with all other persons in the file. The utility of the network concept is that it does not prescribe the level at which its use will be most effective. As Smith and Wheaton have done, we can deal with segments of the community because interactional data provide a series of small fields of action and a limited number of ties. In this case our analysis would stay very close to the groups for which the source provides boundaries, but would at the same time seek to eliminate those boundaries by positing categorical relationships between groups. That is, we would introduce the idea that some occupational groups were 'lower' or 'higher' than others, and develop a network of ties that includes the notion of hierarchy. We could, at the same time, drop to a lower level of analysis and use individuals as the units, ignoring for a time the group boundaries specified in the source. The elements to be used as points, the relationships to be used as lines, and the meaning these lines are to carry (for example, that a relationship is reciprocal or non-reciprocal) – all these are matters of choice on the part of the researcher and, because of this, contrast sharply with the relational analysis based only on ties of descent and marriage, and on units appropriate for these ties.

The Community as a Kinship Network

All persons in a historical community can be made to appear part of the same network, if for no other reason than because they all were likely to be subject to the same political authority. So inclusive a use of the concept makes it tempting to think of past communities as having been more integrated and homogeneous than they really were. The dangers involved in this conceptualization are many, and they are particularly evident in communities with successive population listings. We can tell by looking at names and how they recur or do not recor that the denominator for any calculations is forever being altered, and therefore we can think in terms of 'closed networks' only by overlooking these continual changes. The network concept may allow us to hold steady for analysis certain elements of a system of connections in order to measure them, but, having measured them, we have to remember that we have measured the dynamics of only a part of the community at a moment in past time and the measurements that we would obtain at the next moment might very well be somewhat different. This is particularly true if we deal with such ephemeral concepts as roles, the total inventory of which was very vulnerable to being altered significantly through migration, birth and death.

Nevertheless, the network concept can be useful for certain kinds of measurement, even though we have to keep reminding ourselves that we are applying to the complex social reality of the past a concept which is of our own making. The reality itself might not have been as systematic as the network concept allows us to think it was. The larger the set of interconnected individuals becomes, and the more we rely on genealogical (or kin) connections to establish that interconnectedness, the further we are likely to be removing the networks that are finally analysed from the reality on the ground. How credible such an analysis is when an entire community is viewed as if it were a network can be judged with the help of the following experiment, which is based, once again, on the 1797 estate of Spahren, from which we have drawn earlier examples.

The theory behind network analysis has repeatedly underlined the non-prescriptive nature of the concepts involved. Such ideas as 'points', 'lines' or 'edges', 'density', 'span', 'vulnerability', etc., are all essentially empty of empirical content until the researcher selects from the evidence what these terms are to stand for in the 'real' social world. Thus a 'point' in a network can be an individual or a group; a 'line' or 'edge' connecting points can stand for rendered assistance, reception or transmission of a message, or categorical relationships such as are assumed to exist between an Ego and, for example, the Ego's mother's brother; and 'vulnerability', while referring to the extent the properties of a network will be affected by the removal of crucial elements from it, does not prescribe that the removal take place through death, migration or some other mechanism. In the application of the network concept to the real historical world, most data files – and particularly a file consisting of a maximal genealogical reconstruction – have to be simplified through a series of decisions. These decisions, of course, have to be made by reference to the objectives of the inquiry, but they do not require the discarding of the usused relationships in any permanent fashion (cf. Hackenberg, 1967).

The nature of the 1797 Spahren census forces us to consider, first, whether we can work with the entire population of the community. The most prominent social cleavage in Spahren was along what we would now call ethnic lines: the estate owner, officials and artisans were nearly always Baltic Germans, whereas the peasantry was Latvian. Intermarriage between and co-residence of these two groups was infrequent, and this is reflected in the Spahren census in the six (of 51) 1797 residential units inhabited by German-speakers who, by definition, had no local kin ties to the peasant population or to each other. Since the incorporation of these six residential units into our working file would mean rendering completeness of any kind impossible from the outset, the decision to eliminate them from the file seems a logical step. The next question is whether there is a chance of success, if individuals are used as the points of the network. Here again, the answer is in the negative, not only because genealogical information is missing (in the sense of not having been recorded) for a number of persons, but also because the census included some people who, though possessing stated genealogical links to deceased individuals, were solitaries in the year the census was taken. For the most part, these were old people, the last living representatives of their families in the population. The conjugal family unit is also a poor candidate for this purpose, because of the not-infrequent absence of genealogical information about the wife. The unit with which success is most likely, therefore, is the co-residential group – the farmstead. All of these decisions are instructive with respect to our overriding concern. If the overall make-up of the Spahren population is assumed to be typical of at least the Baltic situation, and the total amount of genealogical information not unrepresentative, then we have to conclude that complete internal genealogical linkage of the entire population at the level of the individual and conjugal family unit is an impossibility. We therefore choose to work with a subpopulation that is most likely to be interconnected, and thus the experimental file will consist of the 45 Latvian farmsteads, with the farmsteads being used as the points of the network.

Another crucial decision is concerned with the definition of kin ties. The genealogical information in the Spahren file permits us to obtain for each individual a relatives' list, the length of which is determined not so much by the social recognition accorded to various genealogical positions, but rather by the inventiveness of the computer program. It is entirely possible, for example, to extract from the file all the people who stood in the position of, say, Fa Br So Sp Fa Br So to an Ego; and, by extracting other individuals of this degree of remove, to extend the list endlessly. We therefore need a way of classifying the extractable relatives, and for this purpose we will use the general classification of dyadic ties proposed by G. P. Murdock (Murdock, 1949: 94–5). In this system, relationships are classified not according to whether they are, for example, matrilineal or patrilineal, or consanguineal or affinal, but rather in terms of genealogical space, that is, by reference to how far from an Ego a particular kin is found. Thus:

> *Primary kin* are identified by links between an Ego and the members of his or her families of birth and marriage;
> *Secondary kin* are identified as those who are primary kin of primary kin (that is, grandparents, aunts, uncles, sisters-in-law, brothers-in-law, nephews, nieces, parents-in-law, daughters-in-law, sons-in-law;
> *Tertiary kin* are identified as those who are primary kin of secondary kin.

This system can, of course, be carried out to quaternary and quinary relatives as well, but for the purpose of the experiment we have chosen to stop with the tertiary category. This category has been included in order to incorporate ties between an Ego and his or her first cousins, though we do recognize that the tertiary category does include genealogical types whose kin status (at least in the Baltic area) is problematic (for example, Br Sp Fa, Wi Fa Br, etc.).

Our choice of the farmstead as the unit of analysis means that in the case of each farmstead we shall be scrutinizing for connections with other farmsteads something like 15 or 16 relatives' lists, because the mean size of farmsteads was 15–16 persons. In each collection of lists, we shall classify the kin ties extending to other farmsteads not only in terms of the identities of these other farmsteads, but also in terms of the kinds of ties (according to our kin categories) that formed the links. Thus, for example, the residents in farmstead no. 113 (Silles farmstead) had connections with residents of farmstead no. 124 (Mazgruschniek farmstead) that included two links in the primary category, seven in the secondary category, and eight in the tertiary category. Farmstead no. 113 had such tripartite clusters of ties with a total of 25 other farmsteads. Thus another decision that has to be made concerns the amount of specific information of this kind to be used in the experiment: that is, how to conceptualize tripartite clusters of connections (or lines) between farmsteads (or points in the network). For the purpose of this experiment we shall ignore the manifold nature of these connections and consider *one* link as having existed in each kin category if, among the individuals in two given farmsteads, there existed *at least one* link in that category. Thus we shall assume that farmstead no. 113 had three connections with no 124. In doing this, we are again simplifying our evidence, but we are not eliminating the possibility of exploring the complex nature of these ties later. The result of data simplification in this step is three 45×45 matrices (there being 45 farmsteads), in which each cell contains information on the existence or non-existence (signified by 1 or by 0) of a tie between the row and column farmsteads. The first matrix identifies the connections by referring only to primary links; the second by referring only to primary and secondary links; and the third by referring to primary, secondary and tertiary links.

In order to make a discussion of these matrices easier, we shall assume that this system of ties is a communications system – that the ties were being used for something – even though we do not have an example of a 'message' passing through the system.[1] We shall assume that a message – a rumour, let us say – entered the system at a given point (a particular farmstead), was communicated by the 'receiver' (a particular individual) to all members of his or her farmstead regardless of whether or not they were relatives, left the farmstead and travelled farther *only along kin lines* to other farmsteads. In these, it was communicated by the 'receivers' to their co-residents, left these farmsteads and was communicated to still others again only along kin lines. The question (or, more precisely, the series of interrelated questions) to which an answer is needed is which of these types of kin links (or which combination of them), together with what distance from the entry points, will result in the rumour being communicated to all the other farmsteads. That is, we want to be able to specify under what conditions we can assume that an entry of a rumour into the Latvian-speaking population of this estate at any point (any farmstead) will, without fail, reach all other farmsteads and thus, in line with our assumptions, the entire Latvian-speaking population. Since we do not know the distance from the entry point which will produce the result, nor the inclusivity of the definition of kinship, we shall carry out the experiment in a stepwise fashion, using at each step a more inclusive definition of kin ties and a farther distance from the starting-point. Thus the first search will investigate positive links when only primary ties are used and the distance from the entry point is one step; the next will involve only primary ties and two steps beyond the entry point; the next only primary ties and three steps beyond the entry point. After that, we will investigate the combination of primary and secondary links, again for the three steps; and finally the combination of primary, secondary and tertiary links again for three steps.

Let us illustrate this procedure by using a single farmstead. Farmstead no. 117 was examined first to establish how many other farmsteads it had contact with when only primary links between its residents and the residents of other farmsteads are considered. The search revealed that if no. 117 were

1 This assumption is commonly made in the theoretical literature on network analysis when the discussion is of a network structure in the abstract (for example, the chapters in Boissevain and Mitchell, 1973). For historians, this is a useful position to fall back upon, since very frequently (and in the Baltic example used here) there does not exist evidence of any kind that the documented ties were being used.

the entry point for the rumour, the rumour would be communicated to 17 other farmsteads immediately after exit from no. 117, when the lines of communication were primary kin ties only. Then the search continued to establish how many *new* farmsteads (that is, excluding no. 117 and these 17) were reached by the message travelling over primary connections emanating from the 17. This search yielded 26 new farmsteads, which meant that when no. 117 served as the entry point, the rumour would have reached all but one of the 44 farmsteads in two steps. The third step produced no *new* farmsteads, which signified that the one remaining farmstead probably did not have primary kin links with any of the earlier 43. The next group of three searches concerning no. 117 would proceed in this same stepwise fashion, except that now the ties considered would be both primary and secondary simultaneously. In the third sequence of searches, the definition of kinship would include primary, secondary and tertiary links. This specific example suggests very clearly how our experiment differs from other kinds of analyses which employ the network concept. We are not here interested in the network of links which had as its centre any one particular farmstead, but rather how quickly (with 'speed' measured by the steps from a starting-point) a message diffused throughout a network-like configuration containing all farmsteads when three different definitions of kinship, each more inclusive than the last, are employed.

Table 11 contains the results of the experiment. The three main columnar divisions of the table represent the distance beyond the entry point to which the search for connections moved. The first subcolumn of each main column states the *mean* number of farmsteads contacted at that distance with a particular definition of kinship (stated in the row headings). The second and third subcolumns of each main column show, respectively, the minimum and maximum number of farmsteads reached through any single farmstead in the step, and the number of times the minimum or maximum was reached. The cell at the extreme left-hand top corner reports the results of the search which used the most restrictive definition of kinship and travelled the shortest distance from the entry point; the cell at the bottom of the first subcolumn in the third main column reports the results of the search which used the most inclusive definition of kinship and travelled the longest distance from the starting-point.

Consider, first, the results shown in the three subcolumns of the first main column. These suggest that, regardless of how inclusively we define kin (up to the 'tertiary' category), we shall not be able to reach the other 44 farmsteads from any entry point as long as we move only one step beyond the entry point. In the least productive cases of this category, no other farms would hear the rumour; in the most productive cases 34 or 37 farms would hear of it, but only if we happen to begin the search at the two starting-

Table 11 Network completeness under varying definitions of kinship and contact range for 45 farmsteads, Spahren, 1797

Category of kinship Ties	Distance from entry point								
	One step			Two steps			Three steps		
	Mean[a]	Min/freq[b]	Max/freq[c]	Mean[a]	Min/freq[b]	Max/freq[c]	Mean[a]	Min/freq[b]	Max/freq[c]
Primary	11.51	0/7	24/2	37.60	0/1	43/4	41.96	0/1	43/41
Primary and secondary	18.27	0/1	34/1	40.18	0/1	43/6	42.04	0/1	43/44
Primary, secondary and tertiary	24.84	1/1	37/1	42.67	27/1	44/25	44.00	44/45	44/45

[a] Mean of 45 sums.
[b] Minimum number of farmsteads contacted through any one entry point/frequency of the minimum.
[c] Maximum number of farmsteads contacted through any one entry point/frequency of the maximum.

points that led to these two maxima. By contrast, in the second main column in which we considered the total number of farms contacted in the first *two* steps, the mean has moved closer to the maximum of 44, and in 25 cases in this category we will have been led to all the other farmsteads when the definition of kinship is most inclusive. The third main column shows the most successful results of all. In the case of the most inclusive definition of kinship, the *mean* number of farmsteads contacted is 44, or all the farmsteads in the system beyond any of the entry points. Even in the less inclusive definitions of kinship, however, the numbers in this category have begun to show an almost completed network. With only primary ties, we are able to reach a maximum of 43 farmsteads in 41 cases; and when kinship ties include both the primary and secondary categories, we are able to reach 43 farmsteads in 44 cases. The lack of completeness in these cells was again produced by the one farmstead which had only tertiary links with other farmsteads and therefore did not register its presence until the most inclusive definition of kinship was used.

These results are still somewhat more ambiguous than we would have liked. In order to obtain a condition in which entry into the system at any point will in due course lead to all other points, we have had to make use of the tertiary category of kin ties, which, as was pointed out, includes many ties about whosem kinship status we are not at all certain. If, however, we are willing to relax our definition of completeness a little, then it does seem fair to say that the combination of primary and secondary genealogical links – all of which can be certain to have received recognition as kin ties – will give us the conclusion we want. When each of 44 out of a possible 45 entry points into a system lead us into contact with 43 out of a possible 44 other points, we can accept the definitions involved as having stated the minimal conditions in which approximate completeness can be demonstrated. This, then, is one of the ways in which, given the data at hand, we can understand in the Baltic context the statements about completeness with which this chapter began. To arrive at the point of being able to talk at all in terms of completeness, however, we have had to make a series of decisions pertaining to cleavages in the community, units of analysis, definitions of links and ties, and the basic reconceptualization of the system as a communications system. The genealogical information eliminated the need to discuss each residential group as a self-contained interactional universe, but at the same time required that we assume communication for which there is no empirical evidence.

There are at least two other directions in which further research could go. The first of these is comparative in nature. The experiment has allowed us to construct a hypothesis to be tested in other Baltic estates (and perhaps communities elsewhere) in which genealogical data are provided or can be secured, namely, that a closed communication system as we have defined it will obtain when we use the farmsteads (or residential groups) as the points of a network, primary and secondary kin ties in combination as the edges or lines between the points, and three steps beyond an entry as the maximum distance needed to produce the desired result. If in other estates, with the mean size of farmsteads and the amount of missing data remaining about the same, we cannot reach completeness in our sense under these conditions, we can infer that the density of ties in the total system has diminished. If, on the other hand, we reach completeness sooner – say, by using only primary ties as the edges or by using the combination of primary and secondary ties to only two steps beyond the entry point – then we can infer that the density of ties has become greater.

The second direction has to do with the fact that in our experiment we reduced the number of ties in each category to one if there was at least one tie of the prescribed sort. This step had the result of excluding from consideration a series of questions that are now part of network analysis and which the anthropologist G. K. Garbett has described in the following way:

> one may be interested in how some item of information is likely to be transmitted through a social network. Here one may find individuals who both receive and transmit information to a large proportion of network members directly or through very few intermediaries. These individuals may be considered 'central' to the network, at least in so far as communication is concerned. On the other hand, there may be those who receive information directly, or through few intermediaries, but who can transmit information directly to a few and only reach a high proportion of network members through long chains of inter- mediaries. Such individuals are, in a sense 'central' to the network for receiving information but 'peripheral' to it for transmitting infor- mation. Structural measures deriving from considerations of reach- ability and distance can be applied to such problems and are con- cerned with characterizing 'compactness' of a diagraph and the 'centrality' and 'peripherality' of its points. (Garbett, 1980: 201)

In continuing to probe the farmsteads of Spahren (here considered as 'individuals') for information of this kind, we would still be working in the somewhat artificial atmosphere that comes from assuming that messages in the estate flowed only along kin lines. Yet assumptions of this kind would not be abnormal in applying the network concept, as we have now seen. The more inclusive the system (network) and the less evidence we have about actual interaction, the greater the number of assumptions we have to make in order for network analysis to work at all.

Role Relations and the Network Concept

The versatility of the network concept in clarifying social relationships has had numerous demonstrations in the work of social scientists.[2] For the most part, in such work the connections between individuals (lines connecting points) have stood for exchanges involving assistance, material goods and information. The starting-point of such research is normally a set of persons observed as having effected these exchanges, and the objective of the inquiry is to describe, by means of measurements, the order or structure the exchanges have 'brought to the surface'. The order is taken as having emerged from the fact that some individuals or subgroups receive more than they give, which makes them more 'central' to the entire system; or from the fact that some individuals or subgroups are positioned closer to each other than to the rest; or from the fact that exclusion of some individuals or subgroups from the set removes it from the entire system. Many of these measures are still in the process of refinement, because the systematic application of the network concept to social data is itself a relatively recent undertaking. When completed, however, network methods should be of as much use to the analysis of historical material as they have already shown themselves to be in the case of contemporary social data.

The refinement of the network concept for use by historians will have to have cognizance of the fact that only certain kinds of historical materials – the interactional sources as used, for example, by Smith and Wheaton – are capable of being analysed readily. In these, the historian starts with recorded *activities* (pledging in a manorial court, or signing of a marriage contract), and analyses as a network the group of people that was gathered for this specific activity. Some kind of exchange is implied in the activity, and the group of people that has come together may not be connected in any other way than through their participation in the activity. But, as has now been seen, kinship sources generate other kinds of configurations which can also be conceived of as analysable networks, but in which the connections between persons are not established by documented exchanges, but by the links inherent in the definitions of categories in which such people are placed. Thus all the persons in a genealogical reconstruction may be seen as in some way 'connected' to each other and the configuration transformed into a network, but what will be missing is information about what flowed along the lines connecting the points. Still, such a group, when reconstructed, cannot be said to have been *simply* an aggregation of individuals.

2 Particularly useful introductions to this subject can be found in Barnes (1969; 1972), Foster (1978/9), Foster and Seidman (1981), Gulliver (1971), Hage (1979), Mitchell (1974) and Garbett (1980).

The question therefore is whether, at the level of individuals whose links to each other flow only from the way they are classified, there is sufficient reason to make use of the network concept, when a great many other non-network measures are available for the analysis of such groups. What advantage is there, in other words, in transforming, say, a list of 50 wholly or partially kin-based groups or an entire lineage reconstruction into network diagrams and in submitting those diagrams to analysis by using graph theory? Will the additional information about social structure gained thereby be great enough to justify the time and expense involved in such an operation?

The question is not easy to answer, but some elements of an answer can be suggested. The first of these grows out of the work of Smith and Wheaton already cited, even though their data base is of the interactional kind and connections (lines between points) stand for actual exchanges, rather than simply relationships implied in categories. Their work, however, emphasizes that investigation of historical kinship can never be considered completely until it thoroughly investigates social relationships which include not only kin, but also non-kin. Their sources are a warning that social life in the past frequently, if not always, involved dealings with non-kin, so that investigative models which help to extract kin configurations from the sources are in this sense creating artificial populations. The application of the network concept does not require such an extraction from the very start. The universe which is eventually analysed and measured can indeed be that which is created by kin ties among the individuals comprising the data set, but, if the inquiry is carried out in the context of a network in which *all* connections are shown, then the kinship analysis will have to view itself as using a partial network, in which the analysed ties are only a subset of all social ties. The network concept does not require that a separate inquiry of the kinship domain be abandoned, or that investigative models of the descent group or the lineage not be used; but it does require that the ties which are examined with the help of these models must somehow be reinserted in the original context and analysed simultaneously with other existing ties.

Let me demonstrate this point by referring to document 4, which consists of a page of a Baltic household listing (the soul revision referred to earlier), and figure 14, in which all the persons listed in the Usmeneek farmstead are represented as a network diagram or directed graph (digraph).[3] In the normal course of evaluating this group of 21 persons for 'social structure', we would make use of the well-established categories for household

3 For a discussion of the difference between 'directed' and 'undirected' graphs, see Garbett (1980: 192–4).

classification, and classify this group of persons as a multiple-family household. The reference point in this classification is the head (*Wirth*), and the structure of the group is established by evaluating each co-resident with respect to kin linkage to the head. As it turns out, the Usmeneek head was co-residing with three married male farmhands (*Knechte*), two unmarried male farmhands (*Junge*) and two unmarried female farmhands (Mägde); moreover, the wives of two of the married farmhands were sisters of the head and of the head's wife respectively, so that the 'structure' of this group, in the normal classification system, would be determined by looking at three kin-linked conjugal families. The overall classification of the group would be problematic, since, on the one hand, we could classify it as a multiple-family household with four unmarried servants; or, on the other, as a simple family household with the kin-status of some of the servants considered to be less significant than their status as subordinates (farmhands) of the household head. It does seem that in the classification process one or the other set of relational terms in the source would have to be suppressed in order for us to be able to proceed with a discussion of co-residence patterns.

If we take the position that this source provides us with information about 'social structure' that is not limited to the question of co-residence, however, it becomes clear that a different way of inventorying the human popultion of this farmstead is required. What we need at the outset is a way of representing at least all of the relationships which are given in the source, even if we do not proceed to those which the given relationships imply. With this decision we are entering the dimension of social roles, because each entry in the source in fact presents us with several different roles that somehow have to be fitted into the entire 'system'. Thus the head of the group Janne was enacting the role of 'head', a category which linked him to the farmhands as a superordinate to a group of subordinates. He was at the same time the husband of his wife, the natural father of one son, and the stepfather of two sons, all of these roles falling within the sphere of 'familial' relations, or – if kinship is defined inclusively – the sphere of kinship relations. Moreover, both the head and his wife are also in-laws to two of the farmhands through their siblings' relationships to their wives, these ties leading us into the domain of kinship in the full sense. All of these ties are 'social' and they are all, in addition, connections which provide 'structure' to this human group. The only way in which all these ties can retain their original significance and not be suppressed at the outset in favour of any particular set of them is if they are represented in a network diagram as in figure 14. In point of fact, the diagram is still incompelete, because we have differentiated only between kin ties and ties of deference or authority, and not between various kinds of kin ties (such as familial and lineal). Nor have we tried to depict relationships that existed between people because all of

Freeborn

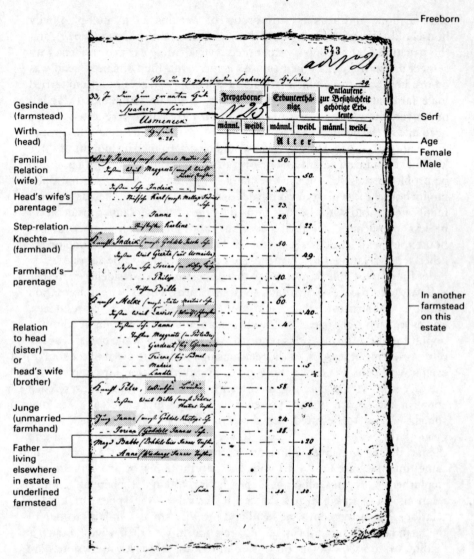

Gesinde
(farmstead)

Wirth
(head)

Familial
Relation
(wife)

Head's wife's
parentage

Step-relation

Knechte
(farmhand)

Farmhand's
parentage

Relation
to head
(sister)
or
head's wife
(brother)

Junge
(unmarried
farmhand)

Father
living
elsewhere
in estate in
underlined
farmstead

Serf

Age
Female
Male

In another
farmstead
on this
estate

Document 4 A single-year household list, Spahren, 1797
Source: J. G. Herder Institut, Marburg

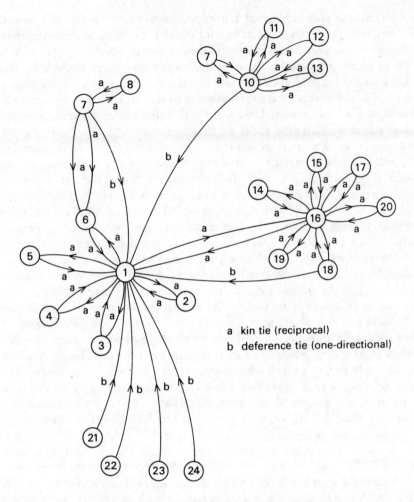

Figure 14 Multiplex ties: ideographic representation of household list in
document 4

them were related to the head. Thus the figure is only a part of one we
would have to create in order to sort out the multiplex relationships that are
involved in even so simple a social situation as a household (though
admittedly a large and complex one), in which the lines are drawn between
persons not because there is empirical proof of exchange, but because the
record-keeper placed each of these people in categories that implied mutual
linkages.

To view the co-residents of Usmeneek farmstead in terms of a social network commits us to a line of inquiry which is far more problematic than that which asks only about the social meaning of co-residence and extracts only as much information as is needed to investigate that problem. The stage we have reached in our present discussion consists of no more than a proposal of a different kind of visual aid than is normally used to study such groups, and a very simplified visual aid at that. It is useful, however, because it lays out very clearly the entire set of actors with which we have to work and could also contain, if we made it elaborate enough, the entire complex of social ties which have to be analysed. In the course of such analysis, we could very easily begin with the question of household structure, by extracting from the complex of relationships those which described the structure of the household according to whatever definition was being employed. Similarly, after the household was analysed, we could extract only those relationships which consisted of kin links, then those which consisted entirely of conjugal family links, and so forth. In the calculations that followed each of these extractive steps, however, we would have to remain cognizant of the total number of *social* ties and use that total number against which to weight the relative importance of a particular subset. Eventually, of course, we would have to evaluate the importance of each subset, by introducing evidence about the meaning of particular ties and roles which the listing evidence itself does not provide. This presumably would allow us to establish what it meant, for example, for two men to be enacting toward each other two sets of roles: those involving kinship and those involving farmstead authority. Regardless of what we extracted in a sequence of analytical steps, however, in the final description the social structure of this group of people would have to consist of all of the roles which the source indicates were being enacted, and those which were implied by the roles that were actually named.

Whether the entire range of analytical techniques which network theorists have developed to work with interactional data can actually be used for categorical relationships remains to be seen. The network concept, however, is at this time the most promising one as far as the topography of such groups is concerned. Of the various grouping concepts we have analysed for the study of kinship, it is the only one that does not require the pre-selection of the relationships to be studied, while at the same time it permits all relationships to be examined in the course of the inquiry later.

11

The History–Anthropology Nexus and the Kinship Domain

Cross-disciplinary Prospects

It would be gratifying to report, in a set of concluding remarks, that the lines of research proposed in the foregoing chapters should be thought of as self-realizing in the sense of being logically the next steps, recognized by everyone, in research directions now deeply embedded in the two disciplines with which we have been concerned. But such a report cannot be made. There is at present no consensus in either discipline in these matters, but, to contrast this somewhat negative assessment with a more optimistic one, the prospects of *some* historians and anthropologists pursuing these lines is now better than they have ever been before. For a long time historians, with their view of history as past politics, and anthropologists, with their apparent disregard of change in historical time, seemed unlikely collaborants for any task. But during the past several decades, the number of contact points between the two disciplines has grown steadily, and some anthropologists seem now as much at home with historical sources as some historians feel in using the concepts (and sometimes the specialized language) of anthropology. What has happened to bring this about can be answered, in the case of history, by reference to what by now is the well-known change of attitude among historians toward the social sciences in general, which has produced a type of historical inquiry calling itself 'social science history' or 'historical sociology'.[1] With regard to social anthropology, the question of changing attitudes requires a more complicated answer. Though occasionally social anthropologists have made statements about the congruity of the goals of the two disciplines, there can be found nothing among them to match the dimensions of the attitudinal shift among historians.[2] Even so, there are

1 For a general account of this development in English-language scholarship, see Burke (1980); similar developments in France are described in Burguière (1978), and in Germany in Leppenies (1975) and Nippedey (1973).
2 See, for example, the lecture by Evans-Pritchard (1961) and the very different viewpoint taken by Schapera (1962). Freedman (1978) provides a general context.

some anthropologists who have spent much of their research time explicating written evidence that is historical in the sense of being removed from the present by many centuries, others who have probed the antecedent conditions of the living populations they study with the help of historical documents, and still others who have been willing to serve as intermediaries between the two disciplines.[3]

These general state-of-the-art observations should not be allowed to hide the fact that the depth of interest in kinship in the two disciplines has been very uneven. The growth of our knowledge of the immense variety of social forms through which kinship ties manifest themselves is related directly to the development of social anthropology as a separate discipline, because from the time of L. H. Morgan in the nineteenth century, anthropologists have placed such ties at the very centre of their research. By contrast, historians have had, until recently, no more than a pasing interest in the systematic study of kinship in communities of the past. The explanation of the emphasis on kinship in the work of anthropologists is not hard to find: in many, if not most, of the small societies anthropologists study, kinship ties are important determinants of personal status as well as the basis of corporate social groups. It would be difficult, however, to explain historians' attitudes toward this subject entirely by reference to the greater complexity of the societies on which they have focused their work. In fact, until recent years historians did not look very carefully at any aspects of the social life of most of the people in the societies they studied, which meant that the social context of the vast majority of lives in the past remained undescribed or described superficially. Consequently, it is misleading to conclude that in historical research the kinship domain in past social life was given low priority because that domain had already been demonstrated to have been relatively unimportant.

The reason for the relative neglect of kinship in the work of historians can be found in three characteristics of the development of the historical profession in the twentieth century: the dominance until roughly the Second World War of a view of history in which social data were subordinated to other kinds; the time-lag between the acceptance of a new view of the past in which 'social structures' were seen as more important than datable 'events', and the transformation of this view into specific research projects using social-structural data; and the recalcitrance of historical social data in face of the new research questions. The first and second of these character-

---

3 Among these I would include, of course, Alan Macfarlane, and the Balkan specialists Eugene Hammel and Joel M. Halpern. In a somewhat different way, the same functions are served by the works of Robert Anderson (1971 and 1973), who has sought to write a history of the European continent from the early medieval period onward with the aid of concepts drawn from anthropological thought. See also Plakans (1981).

istics have been described in great detail elsewhere and we do not have to deal with them here, except to note the observation of Geoffrey Barraclough that the reorientation of many historians 'from the individual to the typical and from the single event (or chain of events) to the underlying structural framework within which events and personalities operate ... is probably the most distinctive single contribution of sociology and anthropology to history' (Barraclough, 1978: 54). It was one thing, however, for historians to accept in the abstract that the study of structures, including social structures, was desirable, and even to name the structures that had to be studied, and quite another to establish to what empirical historical data the notion of 'structure' should be attached. The observation of the historian Fernand Braudel that kinship was one of the 'structures of long duration' which 'impede and control the flow of history' sounded plausible, but it was not immediately obvious what the observation pointed to in the historical evidence and what had to be measured to determine whether the 'flow of history' was or was not being controlled (Braudel, 1972: 18). In kinship research, the conceptual difficulties seemed particularly great if the historian was aware of the terms in which kinship had been analysed by anthropologists working with living populations. The historical sources apparently were not going to yield structural evidence easily and the historian would have to devise ways of overcoming their recalcitrance to do so. Kinship research posed particularly hard challenges, as we have now seen, because, at the very first step, the historian encountered not the evidence anthropologists had been using in their research, but something seemingly less reliable: essentially reports by other people that historical actors stood in particular relationships to each other. Scarcely any means were available to the historian to test such statements or to extricate the historical actors from the positions in which the received evidence had permanently placed them. While anthropologists were relatively free to study the kinship involvements of individuals from many different points of view and to observe individuals separately and in the context of groups, historians apparently were fated to develop a relatively restricted view of kinship in the past because of the dearth of information about the variety of kinship ties and contexts for social action. It has seemed therefore that, in spite of the relatively optimistic statements about how the two disciplines could help each other, in this particular area of study the recalcitrance of the historical sources presents an obstacle that cannot be overcome even with the most imaginative computer programming.

The Continuing Recalcitrance of Historical Sources

The difficulties should not be minimized, notwithstanding the rapid expansion of the types of historical sources we now know can be useful in the study of historical kinship. The typology of them still has to place manuscript censuses at the head of the list, but the variety of other sources is none the less very impressive. The list would have to include all documents in which the unit of recording is small – an individual, a family, a transaction between individuals – but the number of units is very extensive, all units of the same type having entered the record whenever they made an appearance in a delineated geographical space at a point in past time, or over a long stretch of historical time, on occasion over centuries of it. These sources are more than the occasional document; they comprise entire classes of evidence which, to put the matter in crude quantitative terms, occupy many shelf-feet in archives and in many instances contain usable information about every single inhabitant of a community or region. I have in mind here primarily the now well-known 'listings of inhabitants', the structural significance of which has been demonstrated by the work of the Cambridge Group for the History of Population and Social Structure; censuses originating in the fiscal needs of governments, such as the Florentine *catasto* from which David Herlihy and Christiane Klapisch were able to derive a definitive portrait of late-medieval urban society; and parish registers, which, when transformed with genealogical techniques, prove to be as pertinent to the study of social structure as they have been demonstrated to be, when transformed with different methods, for the study of historical demography.[4] Such a typology must also include notarial documents of various kinds – marriage contracts, wills and testaments, pre– and post-mortem household inventories – and, in a word, all historical sources which record individuals as members of social groupings, describe or imply concrete relationships among them, and contain sufficient detail to permit measurement and comparison. The successful use of an exemplar of a type of record has had the effect, so to speak, of legitimizing all records of the same type, so that the rate at which the pool of potentially usable records has grown has exceeded the speed with which specific information has been extracted from them.

Certainly, one aspect of what I have termed the recalcitrance of these sources is that the recognition of their usefulness does not carry with it a solution to the difficult question of representativeness or typicality. Consider, as an example, the archival evidence that would have to figure in the study of kinship in pre-revolutionary European Russia. I use this example as much because my own empirical research has been conducted on these sources as because the Russian sources seem to me to exemplify the problem at hand in a particularly striking fashion. In the year 1800, the Empire had

---

4   Soliday (1980) is the most complete international bibliography of recent historical research using these sources.

approximately 36 million people, the vast majority of them enserfed peasants. These millions were, in one sense, anonymous, in that very few of them left a distinctive mark on the political or cultural history of the Empire. But, in principle, they were all important in the study of historical kinship structures, because they were all components of the structural units the researcher must identify and describe. Moreover, it is possible that most of these people did in fact enter the historical record in some fashion:

> Thanks to the plodding toil of numberless zealous officials there exist for eighteenth and nineteenth century Russia sources for demographic history that are multi-faceted, voluminous, and in some ways remarkable. The quality of these sources naturally varies, but some can be shown to be highly accurate and reliable. The main sources fall into three categories: soul revisions (*revizskie skazki*), enumerations of the taxable population conducted ten times between 1720 and 1858 by the central government; parish registers (*metricheskie knigi*) and parish confessional lists (*ispovednye vedomosti*), compiled continuously from the second half of the eighteen century by Orthodox ecclesiastical authorities; and household lists (*podvornye opisi*), private enumerations of agricultural serfs and household servants compiled more or less regularly by landlords beginning, as far as can be determined, in the late eighteenth century and continuing to the eve of emancipation [1861]. (Czap, 1978: 105–6)

The question of what the 'kinship structures' of this vast pre-modern population were raises all of the problems any structural inquiry faces, if it is to make any claim on representativeness. Russian peasants were not only serfs, they were also husbands and wives, sons and daughters; they were, from another perspective, consanguineal and affinal kin to each other; and, from still another, subordinates and superordinates of each other through household arrangements. But not all the inhabitants of the Empire were ethnic Russians, and the characteristics of social structures may have differed from region to region because of this fact. There were also different climatic zones in this enormous country, different regimes of cultifation, different religions and different types of ownership of the estates on which these peasants lived. In the face of a collection of usable historical data of this magnitude and variety, the question of how much and what parts of it have to be analysed to arrive at general statements about 'Russian kinship' is a daunting one (cf. Hoch, 1982).

If the documentary legacy of a society is sparse, the problem resolves itself and the researcher uses that which is available, however imperfect such fragments may be. In the societies where evidence is plentiful, on the other hand, the inescapable strategy has been to study localities. Even with this decision there are a great many obstacles that follow. The researcher must decide what evidence from a particular locality will be dealt with as relevant to kinship; what methods of reconstruction are appropriate in view of the relational terminology displayed in the sources; and which of a number of possible configurations will be reconstructed. There will also be the question of whether the configurations clearly identified in the record are the only ones present or whether there is reason to go further and speak of formations which may not have been identified because they were of no interest to the record-keepers. It has been observed that in research of this sort 'the answering of one question, however important, always leads to the raising of other questions', by which is meant a process of continuous inquiry: questions raised *ad seriatim,* with each set arising from the answers given to the previous set (Laslett, 1977: 7). Between these sources and the raw data they contain, and the 'facts' that historians might eventually use in describing kinship structures, there stands an array of intellectual operations concerned with judgements of representativeness and sampling, criteria of predominance, and interpretations of relationships when they are transformed into numbers. The difficulties are compounded by the availability of structural information not only about prominent individuals, but also about the relatively anonymous; not only about localities which were politically and culturally of the first rank, but also those which were peripheral.

A second feature of recalcitrance grows out of the fact that sources of this kind, as we have seen, permit a variety of vantage points from which they can be analysed, thus immediately raising the problem of the relationships between the individual and the group. Side by side with concrete personal information such as age, wealth and social position, there is information about the connections individuals had to each other. The problem for the historian confronting sources of this kind is how to think about them so as not to lose either the biographical information or the data about social ties, for each is equally important as historical evidence. That is, a description of the past can be developed by reference to individual actors, to how they lived out their lives and made decisions at crucial turning-points within the context of the groups in which they lived; and by reference to the groups themselves. Yet although we can have an appreciation in the abstract of the importance of kinship groups, their concrete identity remains elusive. The same sources which give us what at times is a splendid record of links between individuals may fail to specify the boundaries within which such links need to be traced, or even that the identifiable links were actually being used for social purposes. Conversely, the sources may mention groups without making clear who their members were. The interplay between the individual and the group therefore becomes very difficult to describe, precisely because the latter cannot. be made to stand out in as clear and unambiguous fashion as the former.

The third aspect of recalcitrance is that the available data frequently do not yield complete information on the structures that the researcher chooses to inquire about. This is perhaps the most serious problem facing the study of historical kinship, because no single source, nor even a collection of sources, ever permits the researcher to accumulate as complete a record as would be necessary to make generalizations certain. The interests of the record-keepers never coincided with those of the later researcher, and as a consequence there are few localities in which the documented kinship ties constitute all the ties that existed. Diary-like documents present the evidence in terms of the perceptions of a single individual, and the number of such documents available for any one locality is usually very small. Normal household listings present kinship information in terms of a large collection of self-enclosed universes (the households), in which the documented ties will be meaningful only in relation to the head of the unit. Similar self-enclosed units are present in such documents as wills and marriage contracts. Legal sources may provide a good inventory of the terms used in a region, but will not by definition contain an account of the people who enacted their kinship roles in the context of such documents. While all of these types of evidence will be 'about kinship' in some sense, they will contain evidence only about different aspects of it and, because of the difficulties presented by personal identities in historical records, will seldom make possible the kind of record linkage in which kinship information is obtained for an individual for the entirety of that individual's life. Even where such linkage is possible for all the persons in an entire community, the researcher would still need to deal with very different records to ascertain whether groups of individuals had any kind of corporate existence. The evidence that would be required to do a complete analysis will always be very short of completeness.

In the light of these general and special problems, it is not surprising that historians have sought answers in the works of social anthropologists who, presumably, have had more experience in applying the kinship concept to empirical social data. There was every reason to expect that answers would be found. As long ago as the 1940s, the anthropologist Claude Lévi-Strauss declared that history and anthropology shared 'the same subject, which is social life; the same goal, which is a better understanding of man; and in fact the same method, in which only the proportion of research technique varied' (Lévi-Strauss, 1963: 18). In the 1960s, Evans-Pritchard observed that 'social anthropology is a kind of historiography' (Evans-Pritchard, 1961); and, somewhat later in the same decade, the historian Keith Thomas explained in very precise terms the areas in which the two disciplines could be of use to each other (Thomas, 1963). Overall, however, in the field of kinship study, the borrowing by historians of kinship concepts has been hesitant and tentative, as if informed by a kind of instinct to stay as close as possible to the information the sources themselves offer and not to risk the misunderstandings cross-disciplinary borrowing of organizing concepts sometimes brings with it. There is a great deal of wisdom in this kind of methodological conservatism, because the possibilities of misunderstanding are very real. But in order to describe the conceptual borrowing that *is* possible, the problems have to be explained, even at the unavoidable risk of caricature.

The Problems of Interdisciplinary Borrowing

As far as kinship research is concerned, social anthropology as a discipline does not make borrowing very easy, because its practitioners are not agreed upon many issues on which an outsider (the historian) might very well expect consensus to exist. On kinship, methodological disputes have become sharper in recent decades, because, as one commentator puts it:

> at stake are not simply technical questions about kinship but questions about the nature of human beings and the most basic elements of human behavior and social explanation. .... It is important to know, first, that in this field of kinship and social structure the experts differ on first principles, not simply on detail; second, that these gulfs are widening, not narrowing, in the recent literature; and third, that the issues are deep and important ones, even though kinship experts may seem to phrase their debate in terms of exotic and trivial detail. (Keesing, 1975: 14)

One basic issue, as we have seen, is the role of genealogical connections in the identification of kinship ties. One position on this question is that the link between the two is non-existent or so weak as to make information about genealogical connections a very poor starting-point for inquiries about the meaning of kinship in a particular locality or society. In this view, the relational terms which anthropologists gather through fieldwork (and which come to historians in the documents) need to be understood as cultural and symbolic constructs; the total system of such constructs, oncer properly understood, will reveal that when people classify each other as 'relatives' they do so after having moved the entire system very far from the genealogical ties that obtain 'on the ground'. Another, opposing position maintains that the connection between the genealogical and symbolic (or cultural) realms is a close one and that ' "kinship" is the network of relationships created by genealogical connections, and by social ties (e.g., those based on adoption) *modelled on* the "natural" relations of genea-logical parenthood' (Keesing, 1975: 13 italics in original).[5] In order to understand kinship structures, therefore, historical researchers have to combine knowledge of the actual genealogical positions in which people stand to each other, and of how these positions are acorded social significance. If all that a historian possesses about a community in the past are data of a genealogical nature, the degree to which help can be expected from anthropological writings will therefore depend upon which of these two orientations seems more convincing. From the one, the historian is likely to learn that the genealogical sources will not produce much knowledge of kinship in such a community, and from the other, that the available data are a key to the whole phenomenon.

Another serious problem is the central role played by fieldwork data in the anthropological analysis of kinship. There is nothing in the historian's bag of tools to substitute for face-to-face encounters with the human actors whose kinship involvements the researcher is seeking to establish (Georges and Jones, 1980). Anthropologists are enabled by this method to gather enough data to explore the multidimensionality of kinship involvements: to look at these social ties, that is, in the form of the multiple roles that an individual had to enact, as well as in the form of the group in which an individual was a member. Moreover, there is the opportunity to both question an individual about the meaning such roles have and to compare this understanding with the actual enactment. This information is formid-able enough to stand out from other kinds of structural involvements and can be dealt with as an independent body of evidence in a well-rounded description of a community. By contrast, in most cass, historical data will yield relatively meagre information about kinship roles and the groups which generted them, not necessarily because kinship relations were simple, but because no contemporary record-keeper was interested enough in them to write down the information. Not being able to overcome the limitations of the historical record with respect to kinship, the historian will be tempted to shift attention to data which yield more analysable relationships, but when this analysis is concluded, he or she will still be hard put to evaluate either data set in terms of the other. There is no doubt that historical record-keepers, being functionaries of organs of authority that kept records for specific purposes, gave to historical evidence a general bias in favour of political and economic-status terms, with the use of which individuals in their charge could be allocated to such categories as taxable or untaxable

5   For a position that stands between these two poles, see Barnes (1973).

people, people in charge of a holding or servants, and so forth. Thus kinship relations not directly implicated in the spheres of life over which authorities had control or sought control would be neglected in the record and, quite possibly, in any later interpretation. For the fieldwork anthropologist, there is the likelihood of gaining direct evidence about the relative weight in a given individual's life of the roles that individual was required to enact as a kinsman, as a member of a political community, as a member of an economic unit, and so forth. The historian, however, needs to be quite inventive in order to obtain any kind of satisfactory answer to the question of whether, in a particular record, absence of kinship data signifies that kinship was unimportant in general, or simply not of interest to the recorder.

Closely associated with the strong contrast between fieldwork data about kinship and historical evidence is the synchronic mode of analysis which fieldwork data invite or, in the view of a very prominent tradition of anthropological analysis, command. Quite obviously, if kinship data are gathered only within the normally short time period anthropologists spend in the community, the structures described on an empirical basis are limited to those observed at that time, in the forms they took at that time. In criticizing the tradition in anthropology of writing the history of kinship structures on the basis of single-moment evidence, Radcliffe-Brown maintained that 'we have directly knowledge about a state of affairs existing at a certain time and place, without any adequate knowledge of the preceeding conditions and events about which we are therefore reduced to making conjectures' (Radcliffe-Brown, 1965: 50). This was, of course, quite true in relation to most of the communities in which anthropologists were doing, or were to do, fieldwork, because there was no empirical historical evidence to be had. What Radcliffe-Brown was pointing out, and what social anthropologists working in this tradition have pointed out ever since, is that processes of development that are deduced from their outcomes are not history recognizable by any historian. Regardless of how inventively presented, thse processes would still be simulations (to use a later word), not to be confused with historical evidence that is located 'on the ground' in some sort of a sequential fashion. The demand that social anthropologists not engage in 'conjectural' history could therefore be understood as an effort to bring about a division of labour by reference to the nature of the evidence, rather than as a declaration that kinship had no history. In the thinking of those who represent this tradition, there seemed to be an absolute disjunction between the labours of the historian and those of the anthropologist: the historian works with 'documents', whereas the anthropologist 'derives his knowledge, or some major parts of it, from direct observation or contact with the people about whom he writes' (Radcliffe-Brown, 1965: 2).

Actually, this viewpoint, even if stated in uncompromising language, did not become firmly established in the anthropological professions anywhere. Even in British structuralism, notes I. M. Lewis, historical investigations continued to be used widely enough in research monographs in the 1930s and 1940s to become something of a subtradition (Lewis, 1968b: xix–xv). There was also the American side of the profession, where voices such as A. L. Kroeber's and Robert Redfield's continued to speak on behalf of the historical approach to the study of communities and entire cultures.[6] None the less, the insistence that the full explication of the kinship domain has the best chance of success when all evidence is assembled within a single time-frame does pose a serious challenge to the historical researcher whose kinship evidence, as we have now seen, may be spread out over a long period of time, raising questions about continuity and discontinuity. When working in the synchronic mode, the researcher is assured that the relationships about which evidence exists were actually experienced by a set of people who were alive at the same time. The claim that these relationships were also experienced by a set of people adjacent in time to the studied set, but not observed by the researcher, would be, strictly speaking, unsupportable. But what if there is evidence, recognized as empirical by the historian, about this adjacent set, and then about another set adjacent to this: evidence, that is, which, though not observational, is none the less identifiable as being 'about kinship' in some sense? Unfortunately, there exists very little by way of theory concerning evidence of this type or, to put it another way, about what the evidence for a non-conjectural history of kinship has to be, what sources can be used to write such a history, and what conceptual problems arise when collective descriptive terms (for example, patrilineage, kindred) have to be used in reference to kinship connections disposed chronologically. Surely it cannot be an idle question to ask how a patrilineage should be expected to manifest its presence in the historical sources of a community (as in the Schwalm sources), when the founder of the lineage is identifiable, say, in the sixteenth century and his descendants are still identifiable in the community three centuries later.

Finally, there is the fact that social anthropology is a social science, concerned ultimately with producing a set of interlinked propositions about human social behaviour, each of which states 'a relationship which is expected to hold in a wide range of societies and historical epochs' (Goode, Hopkins, McClure, 1971). Although there are a number of recent historians who share this goal, others remain sceptical about the introduction of such a goal (and all that it implies for historical analysis and especially historical

6 A good introduction to the thinking of American anthropologists on the relationships between history and anthropology are Kroeber (1963) and Redfield (1963).

writing) into the historical discipline, and perhaps even about whether the goal is reachable regardless of who pursues it. These sceptics, however, may still be interested in the same phenomena that social anthropologists are concerned with, and the result may well be a continuous clash of styles of thought. Thus, for example, in the anthropological literature on kinship there is an entire sector devoted to the kinship relationships in the abstract – mathematical explorations of social space – which is likely to be of minimal interest to historians who are more concerned with theories about evidence, when they are concerned with theory at all.[7] This is essentially a conflict between researchers for whom there is a wide variety of ways to gather, modify, correct and improve evidence, and those who must work with received evidence. Historians, to use another example, are intensely interested in the correct chronological placement of particular pieces of evidence in order to avoid anachronisms, whereas anthropologists, to use Jack Goody's characterization, place their accounts of recent society 'in some overall sequence using the archeologically-based model of progression from hunting to agriculture to industrial modes of production' (Goody, 1976: 3). In this matter, historians will appear to anthropologists hopelessly pedantic in their concern with precisely where in time the generations of a patrilineage were located, and anthropologists with their vague references to 'stages of societal development' will, in turn, appear to historians as dangerously unconcerned with the time element in human affairs. More-over, anthropologists, with their wide-ranging knowledge of comparative data, will feel perfectly comfortable in drawing upon a relationship demon-strated in one locality to 'fill in' the total picture in another, where the data about that relationship may not be available. Historians, on the other hand, with their concern for the unique aspects of every historical situation, will be less prepared to use such a technique, even if it means, given the nature of historical evidence, an entire series of incomplete pictures. Along the same line, historians are likely to want a very large number of local studies, before they are ready to make the generalizations they have to make about a larger area containing these localities, whereas anthropologists may be more likely to be satisfied with a fewer number of 'case studies.'[8] These differences between practitioners of the two disciplines do not necessarily make the separate roads they travel akin to two parallel lines which, by definition, never meet. Yet the disciplinary goals creating these differences continue to be real, and they have to be remembered when the basis of successful borrowing is being sought.

7 As examples of this direction, see Ballonoff (1974) and Kay (1971).
8 This and other problems in the building of anthropological theory are discussed by Pelto and Pelto (1978: ch. 11).

The Similarity of Starting-Points

A list of such differences could be extended, but after a point it would become irrelevant to this discussion, because the evidence is clear that they are not obstacles in any absolute sense of the word. It seems to me that the nature of kinship requires of historians and social anthropologists roughly the same kind of reasoning when they set out to study it, and the use of evidence that is at least comparable. The differences of the two disciplines prevent the two types of inquiries from being identical, but they are not so great that the similarities are unrecognizable. Both the historian and the social anthropologist have to consider a series of questions concerned with the element of time in social relationships, with the relative importance of the different kinds of evidence available about kinship relations, and with what transformatory operations should be performed on that evidence for it to become useful in the testing of a hypothesis or the writing of a description. The set of questions in each problem area will not be so different as to obscure the fact that both types of inquiry are looking for understanding of the same social phenomenon.

I shall consider first the important element of time. In countering the charge that structural analysis was incapable of dealing with the factor of time in human social activities, social anthropologists working from the strict synchronist position had to re-examine their approach with this question in mind; this re-examination led to the conclusion that synchronic analysis did not in fact require neglect of the time element. Although it had to be admitted that earlier anthropologists such as Radcliffe-Brown had 'ignored the fact that the synchronic structure of a social system contains within itself a temporal extension', neglect of such an extension was not required by the synchronic approach as such (Fortes, 1969: 81). No doubt some of the confusion had to be attributed to the language used by anthropologists who performed structural analyses, since it had to be 'language suggestive of, and suitable for, static states, *as if* the positions [which people occupied] were fixed and timeless, and the relationships simply continuous' (Nadel, 1957: 128, italics in original). But the picture of a stable system that arose from such an analysis was really a 'useful "methodological fiction," required by the type of analysis we are after' (Nadel, 1957: 144). In the further development of the theory of structuralist analysis, it was not difficult to show that all the key concepts were in fact time-based concepts. So, for example, a social role, including a kinship role, had to be used with due recognition of the fact that it is 'never, strictly speaking, enacted all at once, being present so to speak in a piece. Rather [it is] enacted phase by phase, occasion by occasion, conceivably attribute by attribute, and hence in a "process" extending over time' (Nadel, 1957:

29–30). Nor were structural configurations exempt from being influenced by the passage of time; in fact, to use the concluding words of Meyer Fortes in his analysis of the time element in Ashanti domestic organization, they had to be viewed as 'an arrangement of parts brought about by an operation, through a period of time, of principles of social organization which have general validity in a particular society' (Fortes, 1970: 32). Moreover, the reinsertion of the time element in the study of social structures, exemplified in these statements, needed not to be limited to microprocesses and short-term change. The anthropologist Jack Goody has argued and demonstrated that the questions posed by nineteenth-century writers about long-term social evolution are still pertinent today, perhaps even more so, because now we are in the possession of better statistical tools to give meaningful answers to them:

> Any human institution is best understood if one can examine not only its meaning and function in a particular society but its distribution in space and time. I do not aim to substitute one approach for another, but to bring back another dimension whose elimination from our analytical repertoire impoverishes not only the total effort toward explanation but also the individual approaches themselves, since each of these has an effect upon the others. ... [In ignoring long-term change] we are not bringing our particular studies of human societies to bear upon some of man's central concerns, including the understanding of the long-term changes that have occurred in the field of interpersonal relations (and more specifically of kinship and domestic institutions). (Goody, 1976: 2, 4–5)

What consequences these reformulations have had and will have for the anthropological disciplines are best left to anthropologists to document. From the viewpoint of the outside historian, however, they have seemed to be preparing anthropologists for placing their fine-tuned synchronic analysis of structure into the medium with which historians feel most comfortable. As a consequence, it has not been very difficult for historians, on their side, to begin to review their own data and research techniques for analogies to what social anthropologists are trying to accomplish. In the realm of kinship research, such a re-examination leads to the conclusion that the major types of surviving historical evidence are similar to (though they cannot be identical with) the types which anthropological fieldworkers gather from living populations. There is therefore a greatly increased possibility that anthropological thinking on kinship matters, since the need to incorporate the element of time has now been recognized, may be even more pertinent to the historian's concerns, because of the comparable basic data.

We have already reviewed fieldwork data in anthropology as a possible source of misunderstanding between historians and anthropologists. But if the matter is examined a bit more closely, and the discussion is focused on only kinship matters, then it is clear that both the historian and the anthropologist start at the same point, that is, with no information at all. Both gain knowledge of specific kin connections only by making inquiries of others: informants in the case of the fieldworker, and record-keepers in the case of the historian. It is only after the fieldworker has been told by the actors themselves, or a third party, that A and B stand in a particular kin relationship to each other that the behaviour which has been observed can be made use of; the former cannot be deduced from the latter with the specificity that is needed. The anthropologist for whom kinship is intimately bound up with genealogy will most certainly begin fieldwork by gathering genealogies of the people he expects to observe, in a manner that has been worked out through many years of application:

> First the informant should be asked the name of his mother, the woman from whose womb he was born, then he should be asked the name of the man she married, the one who begot him. Then how he addresses each of these, or what the native word for this relationship is. Then inquiry should be made as to how each parent addresses the informant. ... Having obtained the names and sex of the other children of the informant's father and mother (his own full brothers and sisters), the next inquiry should be how the informant addresses them, and reciprocally how they address the informant. ... The names of the parents of the informant's parents should be recorded, their children other than the informant's parents, in the same way, and so on, for as many generations as the informant can remember. This will give one genealogy as far as it can be traced. The genealogy of the informant's wife may be recorded next. (*Notes and Queries*, 1951: 54–5)

Even if the anthropologist believes genealogy to be of little moment for understanding kinship, a similar inquiry will still be necessary in order to evaluate the inventory of kinship terms which the actors do employ. In either case, however, the end product will consist of notes about the population in question, arranged in a fashion that makes it easy for ties of individuals to be identified at a glance.

The point of this capsule description of the 'generalogical method', is that most of the historical sources which historians have been using in the past several decades to study social structure are, as we have now seen, replete with genealogical information, even if in most cases this information is not as precise or exhaustive as that which the fieldworker is able to gather. In the case of a few kinds of sources, however, the information can carry the research quite far beyond the primary-kin circle: I am thinking here of genealogically enhanced residential listings and of documents which local genealogists prepared from continuous registers of births, deaths and marriages. The genealogical configurations which can be obtained from these sources vary greatly in inclusiveness and their reliability can be called into question, especially when the information cannot be verified by reference to some other document. But as far as the study of kinship is concerned, the important point at the moment is the existence of this information, whatever its form or reliability. The historian who wants to use genealogy as a starting-point for the historical study of kinship relations will have to follow many of the same routines of data preparation as the anthropologist.[9] Beyond that, the historian may find that reconstructions based on historical sources pose certain analytical problems which field-work genealogies do not. The latter may be dealt with satisfactorily as a means with which living individuals located and specified their rights and obligations as members of a community, but the former may at times contain the history of an entire kin group, because the information has been pieced together from the individual life records of the members of the group. In such cases, the historical record will require as precise a treatment as the connections among living contemporaries.

In the foregoing chapters, we have made wide use of listings of inhabitants which, for historians of social structure, have been perhaps the most important source of information not only about patterns of co-residence in localities, but also about marriage, age structure and much else. Such 'household lists' also contain genealogical information, but this is usually restricted both by the lists being a record of a population at a moment in time and by the absence of information about genealogical links between persons not in co-residence. None the less, this type of evidence may be of exceptional usefulness because of the significance attached by anthropologists to residence rules. The anthropologist Ward Goodenough has presented a good summary of the position this information has had in anthropological work:

9 Consequently it becomes much easier for historians to understand what certain lines of inquiry pursued by anthropologists are trying to accomplish, even though the goals of such inquiries are not shared. I am thinking here, for example, of the fact that physical anthropologists (geneticists) use the same sources as family historians and perform the same reconstructions, but then veer off into subjects (the goals of the inquiry), concepts and statistics which are not of central interest to historians. See, for example, such studies as Harrison et al. (1970), Harrison et al. (1971), Harrison and Boyce (1972a), and Kücheman et al. (1967).

Determining a community's rule or rules of residence in marriage has long been established as a basic requirement for any satisfactory descriptive account of its social system. That residence practices are important determinants of the various forms of family and kinship organization has long been postulated by ethnologists. ... Ethnologists now take it for granted that a reliable report of residence customs is based on a house by house census of the community studied. When we read that such a census reveals a given ratio of residence types, I think most of us feel secure in what we regard as reliable information. (Goodenough, 1956: 22)

Indeed, some years earlier G. P. Murdock, in discussing the significance of the work of the anthropologist R. H. Lowie, made the point that 'the one aspect of social structure that is peculiarly vulnerable to external influences is the rule of residence', and because of this, he proceeded to theorize:

it is in respect to residence that changes in economy, technology, property, government or religion first alter the structural relationships of related individuals to one another, giving an impetus to subsequent modifications in form of the family, in consanguineal and affinal kin groups, and in kinship terminology. (Murdock, 1949: 202)

Not all anthropologists would have agreed with these statements when they were made, nor do they necessarily agree with them now. It is, however, indisputable that anthropologists have spent a great deal of time exploring the connection between residence patterns, the 'rules' that can be abstracted from them, and the general patterns of kinship prevailing in a particular community and region. On their side, historians launched an exploration of historical household censuses during the 1960s, more because of an interest in the history of family forms than for what co-residential patterns revealed about general kinship systems. Thus household lists proved to be a valuable source – perhaps the most informative source found to date – for the discussion of many questions that did not involve the link between residence rules and kinship rules. They turned out, in fact, to be a historical source with multiple uses, capable of providing precise information about the lives of vast segments of historical populations which up to that time had been described for the most part in terms of single cases assumed to have been 'typical'.

The substantial literature on co-residence which has now accumulated in both social anthropology and social history has not succeeded, however, in producing a consensus on the question in which we are interested, namely, how the patterns of co-residence observable in residential censuses allow us to generalize about more general kinship patterns. Simply put, the question is whether household lists are a way of entering the kinship domain. While it is certainly possible to characterize residential patterns as 'neolocal', 'patrilocal', 'bilocal', etc., it is by no means a foregone conclusion that, for example, a 'patrilocal' rule of residence always and everywhere 'goes with' patrilineal rules of descent, a patrilocal extended form of the family, or a particular type of kinship terminology with which cousins are described (Murdock, 1949: 153–4). Though historians do not make such correlations the principal aim of their work, preferring instead to use information about co-residence to discuss the context of the lives of past individuals, they are concerned with the question of variability in their sources. At times, historical communities that could be expected to have similar dominant structural patterns, because of geographical proximity, in fact do not. Whether it is 'normal' for a region with an identifiably uniform kinship ideology to have, at the level of the locality, many different kinds of residential rules is thus a question which has yet to receive a satisfactory answer. This question is but one of many that historical research must cope with, all of them being subquestions of the general problem of how facts about kinship should be expected to emerge in the various types of historical sources which a community will have generated over a long period of historical existence. For both anthropologists and historians, therefore, the residential listing is a major concern, and the techniques devised for its analysis in one discipline are of great interest to researchers in the other.

As we have seen, a third type of source which has loomed large in recent investigations of historical kinship is the interactional document. The term 'interactional' should not be interpreted too narrowly in this connection. The document is a record of a particular social activity – such as the signing of a marriage contract, the drawing up of a will, the record of a trial – in which the historical actors vary from occasion to occasion, while the form of activity remains the same. In historical societies where such activities required the imprimatur of a representative of the law, these records have proved to be numerous, but their exploitation for the study of kinship has just now barely begun. What is significant for the present discussion is that each record of this type resembles the notations a fieldworker will have made about the participants in important social activities which he is allowed to be a witness to or is told about by others. Fortes characterized these activities in the following manner:

> Structure is not immediately visible in the 'concrete reality.' It is discovered by comparison, induction, and analysis based on a sample of actual social happenings in which the institution, organization, usage, etc., with which we are concerned appears in a variety of contexts. (Fortes, 1970: 3)

The principal difficulty with historical sources of the interactional type is that the selection of the social occasions that were documented was entirely in the hand of the record-keeper. While the fieldworker will seek to have notes about as many such occasions as possible, from those that are seemingly trivial to others such as marriages and funerals which are of extreme significance, the historian has to be satisfied with what has been passed down. The total collection of these sources may already be only a fragment, and this fact makes the drawing of the 'sample' referred to by Fortes about doubly difficult. There is some comfort in knowing that the range of historical documents under this heading has not yet been fully inventoried for all the historical societies which are likely to have produced them. Sometimes authorities created records of activities concerning which official interest could not have been predictd. Thus, for example, the Statistical Committee of the government of the Russian Baltic province of Livland in 1884 carried out a wide-ranging survey of the social relationships of peasant landowners and farmhands through questions about whether they lived together and whether they ate at the same table (Plakans, 1983: 188–90). Systematic information about the eating habits of several hundred thousand people in the past is not typical of the information historians would expect to have at their disposal, though fieldwork anthropologists would most certainly make notes of these habits for the several dozens of families coming under their scrutiny.

As with the other evidence, the important point about transactional sources is that the information they contain has parallels in the anthropological experience (Kapferer, 1976). Both the historical and anthropological researcher is called upon to understand the structural information 'wrapped up' in seemingly everyday occurrences: whether and how the people involved in them were related, whether on the occasion in question they arranged themselves in a hierarchy, what actual or symbolic goods were transmitted from one party to another, and so forth. The fieldworkers may have only a handful of such occasions to interpret, all of them having occurred during a short period of time; the historian, by contrast, may have to make sense of hundreds of such occasions, which will have occurred over a long period of time. The fieldworker will be able to establish direct links between the actors in such occasions; the historian may have no opportunity to make any links at all. Whereas the fieldworker will be able to question the participants about their understanding of the occasion, the historian will not have this opportunity, and may have to deal with the document reporting the event as if it were, to repeat Claude Lévi-Strauss's term, 'the testimony of an amateur ethnographer' in need of very careful reinterpretation. The assumption in both cases, however, will be the same: that the activity is more than simply a chance occurrence with no significance beyond the moment, that it in fact contains important data about structural relationships.

Non-conjectural Kinship History

This discussion of genealogical, residential and interactional historical sources – the three most important types of documents which historians have made use of in recent decades for the study of kinship – was meant to underline that all three have direct analogues to types of information used by kinship analysts of fieldwork evidence, and that the kinds of questions that are likely to be asked about them will be similar up to a point. Whether individual historians were guided to these sources by a knowledge of what anthropologists do, or whether they began to look at anthropology after establishing the utility of these sources is not a question we need to answer here; it would require a careful examination of the work of many individual scholars to understand the progress of thought in each case. All we need to observe is that the use of these sources is now accepted among historical analysts of social structure and that their potential has proved to be sufficiently great to overcome whatever hesitations historians might have had about borrowing anthropological concepts to help in understanding them.

There is one more parallel that needs mention, and that is concerned with the fact that both the fieldworker and the historian have to make use of the discrete empirical information, regardless of its original form, by submitting it to various kinds of reconstruction procedures. That is, general statements about structure are abstracted not from each individual piece of infor-mation, but from a configuration which is pieced together, using as a mechanism whatever internal linkages are provided in the entire available data set. Understandably, such reconstructions are far easier to carry out reliably in the fieldwork situation than in historical communities. In the former, an individual can be observed and questioned as a participant in different transactions, as the member of a co-residential group and as the source of a genealogy; the individual records can be reassembled by reference to the known fact that an identifiable individual has been part of all of them. As we have seen, historical sources offer such an opportunity only infrequently, and the historian may have to proceed with analyses without having anything like a complete record of the structural involve-ments of individuals. But even an incomplete set of records is better than a single record because, as Alan Macfarlane puts it: 'the effect of bringing in further records is not merely additive; each extra record illuminates all the previously assembled ones' (Macfarlane, 1977a: 36). My own experience with the truth of this statement, ironically, came not from the linkage of different documents, but from a single document – the genealogically enhanced Baltic revision referred to earlier. There, it was obvious that the genealogical information provided for each member of a particular household permitted the reconstruction of kin-based configurations which not only created a new unit for interpretation, but also 'illuminated' the relationships within the household that was the starting-point. The guiding principle is that additional information about individuals not only creates new contexts in which the individual can be understood, but also requires the explanation of the embeddedness of groups within each other. And this is, of course, precisely what the fieldwork anthropologist is seeking to establish through the questioning of individuals about their simultaneous involvement in kin-based structures such as families and descent groups.

Among social historians in the last several decades, evidence that required reconstruction of some kind has loomed very large, with its use being encouraged by a widespread desire to write history 'from the bottom up' about large numbers of people, as well as by the presence in the computer of the technological capabilities of doing so. The consequence of the need to reconstruct has been to bring historians face-to-face, in particular localities, with very large numbers of social microstructures ranging from families and households to descent groups, and not only with 'perfect' exemplars of these groups, but also with fragments of them. Historians have had to learn that the availability of individual-level data about an entire population of a past community does not make the job of generalization easier, even while it does make the generalizations arrived at more satisfying. This trend has parallels in the anthropological study of kinship where, as noted by a recent commentator:

> reanalyses [of societies studied by earlier anthropologists] together with work done in societies with cognatic descent groups or kin groups which cannot be unambiguously described as unilineal, indicate the growing dissatisfaction with existing anthropological classifications. ... But [this dissatisfaction] does not derive solely from this new data; more significantly, it is generated by asking new questions and by redefining what is treated as problematic. A distinct trend in a substantial corpus of contemporary anthropological writings on kin groups is a growing preoccupation with *what people actually do and with whom they do it* rather than with the formulation of jural norms and formal structures. (Holy, 1976: 128, my italics)

What people actually do and with whom they do it – this question was cited earlier and is repeated now because, when placed in the context of historical evidence, it describes very pointedly what is at stake in working toward a non-conjectural history of European kinship. Both parts of the question are significant, but in this book more stress has been placed on the second part. What people actually did in the past is a question which has preoccupied all historians, and the documentation of activities as such has been and continues to be in plentiful supply. With whom they did what they did, however, is a very different question, because it brings to the forefront the problem of precise identities and precise linkages. When we ask what the precise kinship ties were between a historical actor and those with whom that actor participated in various social actions, reconstruction becomes inevitable. We cannot deduce precise ties from the nature of the activity, nor can we carry over into explanations of this activity the lists of participants from other activities. Moreover, we cannot ascribe to the participants of an activity only those kinship roles which the participation required: we have to be able to surround the activity with a more inclusive context in order to be able to evaluate the enacted roles. And only through the recreation of such more inclusive contexts can we ultimately make precise statements about the presence of kinship groups.

There is a price to be paid for seeking access to the kinship domain in this way, and that is that information gained in this manner calls into question (though it does not immediately invalidate) generalizations that have a different base. In the historical study of kinship, it is no longer possible to be entirely satisfied with 'typical cases', unless they can be clearly demonstrated to have been typical. This, of course, requires the reconstruction of many more structures than the ones to be isolated for their typicality. Sources which mention statements by contemporaries about kin groups and kin behaviour seem now less credible until a described group can be examined with respect to actual composition and a described behaviour scrutinized in terms of the people involved in actual examples of it. Nor is it possible to rest the examination of kinship in the past on statements that the kin behaviour of well-documented elite sectors of any society can 'stand for' or be understood as having 'diffused downward' without some demonstration, through reconstruction procedures, of the kin structures and behaviour of the common people. Whether this scepticism toward evidence not based on reconstructions is warranted or not will eventually come out, but not until reconstructions are used to the limits set by historical data.

Bibliography

Anderson, Michael. 1971. *Family structure in nineteenth-century Lancashire.* Cambridge.

Anderson, Michael. 1980. *Approaches to the history of the western family 1500–1914.* London.

Anderson, Robert T. 1963. 'Changing kinship in Europe', *Kroeber Anthropological Society Papers,* no. 28: 1–48.

Anderson, Robert T. 1971. *Traditional Europe: a study in anthropology and history.* Belmont, California.

Anderson, Robert T. 1973. *Modern Europe: an anthropological perspective.* Pacific Palisades, California.

Baker, Paul T. and William T. Sanders. 1972. 'Demographic studies in anthropology', *Annual Review of Anthropology,* 1: 151–73.

Ballonoff, Paul A. (ed.). 1974. *Mathematical models of social and cognitive structures: contributions to the mathematical development of anthropology.* Urbana, Illinois.

Banton, Michael (ed.). 1965. *Roles: an introduction to the study of social relations.* London.

Banton, Michael (ed.). 1966. *The social anthropology of complex societies.* London.

Banton, Michael (ed.). 1968. *The relevance of models for social anthropology.* London.

Barnes, J. A. 1961. 'Physical and social kinship', *Philosophy of Science,* 28: 296–9.

Barnes, J. A. 1969. 'Networks and political processes', in J. C. Mitchell (ed.) (1969).

Barnes, J. A. 1971. *Three styles in the study of kinship.* Berkeley and Los Angeles.

Barnes, J. A. 1972. *Social networks.* Reading, Massachusetts.

Barnes, J. A. 1973. 'Genetrix: Genitor: : Nature: Culture', in J. Goody (ed.) (1973).

Barnes, J. A. 1979. 'Genealogies', in A. L. Epstein (ed.) (1979).

Barnes, J. A. 1980. 'Kinship studies: some impressions of the current state of play', *Man,* 15: 293–303.

Barraclough, Geoffrey. 1978. *Main trends in history.* New York.

Berkner, Lutz K. 1972. 'The stem family and the developmental cycle of a peasant household: an eighteenth-century Austrian example', *American Historical Review* 77: 398–418.

Blum, Jerome. 1978. *The end of the old order in rural Europe.* Princeton.

Boissevain, Jeremy and J. Clyde Mitchell (eds). 1973. *Network analysis: studies in human interaction*. The Hague and Paris.

Braudel, Fernand. 1972. 'History and the social sciences', in P. Burke (ed.) (1972).

Buchler, Ira R. and Henry A. Selby. 1968. *Kinship and social organization: an introduction to theory and method*. New York.

Burguière, Andre. 1978. 'L'anthropologie historique', in J. LeGoff (ed.) (1978).

Burke, Peter (ed.). 1972. *Economy and society in early modern Europe: essays from Annales*. New York.

Burke, Peter. 1980. *Sociology and history*. London.

Burt, R. S. 1980. 'Models of network structure', *Annual Review of Sociology*, 6: 79–141.

Burt, R. S. 1982. *Towards a structural theory of action: network models and social structure, perception, and action*. New York.

Conze, Werner (ed.). 1976. *Sozialgeschichte der Familie in der Neuzeit Europas*. Stuttgart.

Cordell, Linda S. and Stephen Beckermann (eds). 1980. *The versatility of kinship: essays presented to Harry W. Basehart*. New York.

Crump, Thomas. 1980. 'Trees and stars; graph theory in southern Mexico', in J. C. Mitchell (ed.) (1980).

Cuisenier, Jean (ed.). 1979. *Europe as a cultural area*. The Hague.

Czap, Peter. 1978. 'Marriage and the peasant joint family in the era of serfdom', in D. Ransel (ed.) (1978).

Czap, Peter. 1982. 'The perennial multiple family household: Mishino, Russia, 1782–1858'. *Journal of Family History*, 7: 5–26.

Czap, Peter. 1983. '"A large family: the peasant's greatest wealth": serf households in Mishino, Russia, 1814–1858', in R. Wall, J. Robin and P. Laslett (eds) (1983).

D'Andrade, Roy G. 1971. 'Procedures for predicting kinship terminologies from features of social organization', in Kay (ed.) (1971).

Davis, Natalie Z. 1982. 'The possibilities of the past', in T. K. Rabb and R. I. Rotberg (eds) (1982).

Debus, Friedhelm. 1958. 'Die deutschen Bezeichnungen fur die Heiratsvervand-schaft', in L. E. Schmitt (ed.) (1958).

Duby, Georges. 1978. *Medieval marriage: two models from twelfth century France*. Baltimore.

Duby, Georges and Jacques LeGoff. 1977. *Famille et parente dans d'occident medieval*. Rome.

Dyke, Bennet and Jean Walters MacCluer (eds). 1973. *Computer simulation in human population studies*. New York.

Dyke, Bennet and Warren T. Morrill (eds). 1980. *Genealogical demography*. New York.

Epstein, A. L. (ed.). 1979. *The craft of social anthropology*. London and New York.

Evans-Pritchard, E. E. 1951. *Kinship and marriage among the Nuer*. Oxford.

Evans-Pritchard, E. E. 1961. *Anthropology and history: A lecture*. Manchester.

Evans-Pritchard, E. E. 1980. *The Nuer*. Oxford.

Farber, Bernard. 1981. *Conceptions of kinship*. New York.

Fei, John C. H. and Ts'ui-jung Liu, 1982. 'The growth and decline of Chinese family clans', *Journal of Interdisciplinary History*, 12: 375–408.

Firth, Raymond (ed.). 1956. *Two studies of kinship in London*. London.

Firth, Raymond. 1957. *We, the Tikopia: kinship in primitive Polynesia*. New York.

Fischer, Claude S. 1982. 'The dispersion of kinship ties in modern society: contemporary data and historical speculation', *Journal of Family History*, 7: 353–75.

Flandrin, Jean Louis. 1979. *Families in former times: kinship, household, and sexuality*, trans. Richard Southern. Cambridge.

Floud, Roderick. 1979. *An introduction to quantitative methods for historians*. 2nd edn. London.

Fortes, Meyer. 1945. *The dynamics of clanship among the Tallensi*. Oxford.

Fortes, Meyer. 1969. *Kinship and the social order*. Chicago.

Fortes, Meyer. 1970. *Time and social structure*. London.

Foster, Brian L. 1978/9. 'Formal network studies and the anthropological perspective', *Social Networks*, 1: 241–55.

Foster, Brian L. and Stephen B. Seidman. 1981. 'Network structure and the kinship perspective', *American Ethnologist*, 8: 329–55.

Foster, George M., Thayer Scudder, Elizabeth Colson, Robert V. Kemper (eds). 1979. *Long-term field research in social anthropology*. New York.

Fox, Robin. 1967. *Kinship and marriage: an anthropological perspective*. London.

Fox, Robin. 1975a. 'Primate kin and human kinship', in R. Fox (ed.) (1975b).

Fox, Robin (ed.). 1975b. *Biosocial anthropology*. London.

Freedman, Maurice. 1978. *Main trends in social and cultural anthropology*. New York.

Freeman, J. D. 1961. 'On the concept of the kindred', *Journal of the Royal Anthropological Institute*, 91: 192–220.

Friedrich, Paul. 1964. 'Semantic structure and social structure: an instance from Russian', in W. H. Goodenough (ed.) (1964).

Garbett, G. K. 1980. 'Graph theory and the analysis of multiplex and manifold relationships', in J. C. Mitchell (ed.) (1980).

Gaunt, David. 1982. *Memoir on history and anthropology*. Stockholm.

Georges, Robert A. and Michael O. Jones. 1980. *People studying people: the human element in fieldwork*. Berkeley and Los Angeles.

Gellner, Ernest. 1960. 'The concept of kinship', *Philosophy of Science*, 27: 187–204.

Goode, William J., Elizabeth Hopkins and Helen M. McClure (eds). 1971. *Social systems and family patterns: a propositional inventory*. Indianapolis and New York.

Goodenough, Ward H. 1956. 'Residence rules', *Southwestern Journal of Anthropology*, 12: 22–37.

Goodenough, Ward H. (ed.). 1964. *Explorations in cultural anthropology: essays in honor of George Peter Murdock*. New York.

Goodenough, Ward H. 1970. *Description and comparison in cultural anthropology*. Cambridge.

Goody, Jack (ed.). 1958. *The development cycle in domestic groups*. Cambridge.

Goody, Jack (ed.). 1973. *The character of kinship*. Cambridge.

Goody, Jack. 1976. *Production and reproduction: a comparative study of the domestic domain*. Cambridge.

Goody, Jack. 1983. *The development of the family and marriage in Europe*. Cambridge.

Goody, Jack, J. Thirsk, E. P. Thompson (eds). 1976. *Family and inheritance: rural society in Western Europe 1200–1800*. New York.

Gulliver, P. H. 1971. *Neighbors and networks: the idiom of kinship in social action among the Ndendeuli of Tanzania*. Berkeley and Los Angeles.

Hackenberg, Robert A. 1967. 'The parameters of an ethnic group: a method for studying the total tribe', *American Anthropologist*, 69: 478–92.

Hackenberg, Robert A. 1974. 'Genealogical method in social anthropology: the foundations of structural demography', in J. J. Honigman (ed.) (1974).

Hage, Per. 1979. 'Graph theory as a structural model in cultural anthropology', *Annual Review of Anthropology*, 8: 115–36.

Hajnal, John. 1973. 'Two kinds of preindustrial household formation system', in Wall 1983, 65–104.

Hajnal, John. 1982. 'Two kinds of preindustrial household formation systems', *Population and Development Review*, 8: 449–94.

Halpern, B. K. 1977. 'Genealogy as genre', in B. K. Halpern and J. M. Halpern (eds) (1977).

Halpern, B. K. and J. M. Halpern (eds). 1977. *Selected papers on a Serbian village*. Amherst, Massachusetts.

Halpern, J. M. and B. K. Halpern. 1972. *A Serbian village in historial perspective*. New York.

Halpern, J. M. and Richard Wagner. 1982. 'Demographic and social change in the village of Orasac: a perspective over two centuries', *Serbian Studies*, I (1): 51–70; II (1): 65–91; III (2): 33–60.

Hammel, E. A. 1968. *Alternative social structures and ritual relations in the Balkans*. Englewood Cliffs, New Jersey.

Hammel, E. A. and Peter Laslett, 1974. 'Comparing household structure over time and between cultures', *Comparative Studies in Society and History*, 16: 73–103.

Hammel, E. A. and Charles Yarborough. 1974. 'Preference and recall in Serbian cousinship: power and kinship ideology', *Journal of Anthropological Research*, 30: 95–115.

Harrison, G. A., R. W. Hiorns, C. F. Küchemann. 1970. 'Social class relatedness in some Oxfordshire parishes', *Journal of Biosocial Science*, 2: 71–80.

Harrison, G. A., R. W. Hiorns, C. F. Küchemann. 'Social class and marriage patterns in some Oxfordshire populations', *Journal of Biosocial Science*, 3: 1–12.

Harrison, G. A. and A. J. Boyce. 1972a. 'Migration, exchange, and the genetic structure of populations', in G. A. Harrison and A. J. Boyce (eds) (1972b).

Harrison, G. A. and A. J. Boyce (eds). 1972b. *The structure of human populations*. Oxford.

Heers, Jacques. 1977. *Family clans in the middle ages: a study of political and social structures in urban areas*, trans. Barry Herbert. Amsterdam, New York and Oxford.

Hoch, Steven L. 1982. 'Serfs in imperial Russia: demographic insights', *Journal of Interdisciplinary History*, 13: 221–46.

Hodgen, Margaret T. 1974. *Anthropology, history and cultural change*. Tucson, Arizona.

Holy, Ladislav. 1976. 'Kin groups: structural analysis and the study of behavior', *Annual Review of Anthropology*, 5: 107–31.

Honigman, John J. (ed.). 1974. *Handbook of social and cultural anthropology*. New York.

Hudson, Charles. 1974. 'The historical approach in anthropology', in J. J. Honigman (ed.) (1974).

Hughes, Diane. 1975. 'Domestic ideals and social behavior: evidence from medieval Genoa', in C. Rosenberg (ed.) (1975).

Imhof, Arthur E. 1977. *Einführung in die historische demographie*. München.

Johnson, Allen W. 1978. *Quantification in cultural anthropology*. Stanford.

Kapferer, Bruce (ed.). 1976. *Transaction and meaning: directions in the anthropology of exchange and symbolic behavior*. Philadelphia.

Karnoouh, Claude. 1979. 'Kinship and politics in a village of Lorraine: the impossible democracy', in J. Cuisenier (ed.) (1979).

Kay, Paul (ed.). 1971. *Explorations in mathematical anthropology*. Cambridge, Massachusetts.

Keesing, Roger M. 1975. *Kin groups and social structure*. New York.

Kent, F. W. 1977. *Household and lineage in Renaissance Florence*. Princeton.

Knodel, John and Edward Shorter. 1976. 'The reliability of family reconstitution data in German village genealogies (Ortssippenbücher)', *Annales de demographie historique*, pp. 77–113.

Kroeber, A. L. 1963. *An anthropologist looks at history*. Berkeley and Los Angeles.

Küchemann, C. F.., A. J. Boyce, G. A. Harrison. 'A demographic and genetic study of a group of Oxfordshire villages', *Human Biology*, 39: 251–75.

Kuper, Adam. 1973. *Anthropology and anthropologists: the British school 1922–1972*. New York.

Kuper, Adam. 1982. 'Lineage theory: critical retrospect', *Annual Review of Anthropology*, 11: 71–95.

Laslett, Peter. 1977. *Family life and illicit love in earlier generations*. Cambridge.

Laslett, Peter. 1983. 'Family and household as work group and kin group: areas of traditional Europe compared', in R. Wall, J. Robin, P. Laslett (1983).

Laslett, Peter and Richard Wall (eds). 1972. *Household and family in past time*. Cambridge.

LeGoff, Jacques (ed.). 1978. *La nouvelle histoire*. Paris.

Leppenies, Wolf. 1975. 'Geschichte und Anthropologie', *Geschichte und Gesellschaft*, 1: 325–43.

Lévi-Strauss, Claude. 1963. *Structural anthropology*, vol. I, New York.

Lévi-Strauss, Claude. 1976. *Structural anthropology*, vol. II, New York.

Lewis, I. M. 1968a. 'Problems in the comparative study of unilineal descent', in M. Banton (ed.) (1968).

Lewis, I. M. (ed.). 1968b. *History and social anthropology*. London.

Macfarlane, Alan. 1970. *The family life of Ralph Josselin: a seventeenth century clergyman: an essay in historical anthropology.* Cambridge.

Macfarlane, Alan. 1977a. (In collaboration with Sarah Harrison and Charles Jardine), *Reconstructing historical communities.* Cambridge.

Macfarlane, Alan. 1977b. 'History, anthropology, and the study of communities', *Social History*, 5: 631–52.

Mair, Lucy. 1972. *An introduction to social anthropology.* 2nd edn. Oxford.

Mitchell, J. C. (ed.). 1969. *Social networks in urban situations.* Manchester.

Mitchell, J. C. 1974. 'Social networks', *Annual Review of Anthropology*, 3: 279–99.

Mitchell, J. C. (ed.). 1980. *Numerical techniques in social anthropology.* Philadelphia.

Mitterauer, Michael and Reinhard Sieder. 1982. *The European family,* trans. Karla Osterveen and Manfred Hörzinger. Oxford.

Morgan, Kenneth. 1973. 'Computer simulation of incest prohibition and clan proscription rules in closed finite populations', in B. Dyke and J. W. MacCluer (eds) (1973).

Murdock, G. P. 1949. *Social structure.* New York.

Murdock, G. P. 1967. *Ethnographic atlas.* Pittsburgh.

Murphy, Robert. 1967. 'Tuareg kinship', *American Anthropologist*, 69: 163–70.

Murphy, Robert F. 1971. *Dialects of social life.* New York.

Nadel, S. H. 1957. *The theory of social structure.* London.

Needham, Rodney. 1960. 'Descent systems and ideal language', *Philosophy of Science*, 27: 96–101.

Netting, Robert McC. 1981. *Balancing on an Alp: ecological change and continuity in a Swiss mountain community.* Cambridge.

Nipperdey, Thomas. 1973. 'Die anthropologische Dimension der Geschichtswissenshaft', in G. Schulz (ed.) (1973).

Notes and Queries on Anthropology. 1951. 6th edn. London.

Ostergren, Robert C. 1982. 'Kinship networks and migration: a nineteenth century Swedish example', *Social Science History*, 6: 293–320.

Palli, H. 1983. 'Estonian households in the seventeenth and eighteenth centuries', in Wall 1983, 207–16.

Pasternak, Burton. 1976. *Introduction to kinship and social organization.* New York.

Pedlow, Gregory. 1982. 'Marriage, family size, and inheritance among Hessian nobles 1650–1900', *Journal of Family History*, 7: 333–52.

Pehrson, Robert N. 1957. *The bilateral network of social relations in Könkämä Lapp district.* Bloomington, Indiana.

Pelto, Pertti J. and Gretel H. Pelto. 1978. *Anthropological research: the structure of inquiry.* 2nd edn. Cambridge.

Peristiany, J. G. (ed.). 1976. *Mediterranean family structures.* Cambridge.

Phillpotts, Bertha. 1913. *Kindred and clan in the middle ages and after.* Cambridge.

Pitt-Rivers, Julian. 1976. 'Ritual kinship in the Mediterranean: Spain and the Balkans', in J. G. Peristiany (ed.) (1976).

Plakans, Andrejs. 1975. 'Peasant farmsteads and households in the Baltic littoral, 1797', *Comparative Studies in Society and History*, 17: 2–35.

Plakans, Andrejs. 1977. 'Identifying kinfolk beyond the household', *Journal of Family History*, 2: 2–37.

Plakans, Andrejs. 1978. 'Parentless children in the soul revision: a study of methodology and social fact', in D. Ransel (ed.) (1978).

Plakans, Andrejs. 1981. 'Anthropology, history, and the European joint family: reflections on modes of research', *Ethnologia Europaea*, 12: 117–32.

Plakans, Andrejs. 1982. 'Ties of kinship and kinship roles in an historical Eastern European peasant community: a synchronic analysis', *Journal of Family History*, 7: 52–75.

Plakans, Andrejs. 1983. 'The familial contexts of early childhood in Baltic serf society', in R. Wall, J. Robin and P. Laslett (eds) (1983).

Pouyez, Christian, Raymond Roy, François Martin. 1983. 'The linkeage of census name data: problems and procedures', *Journal of Interdisciplinary History*, 14: 129–52.

Rabb, T. K. and R. I. Rotberg. 1982. *The new history: The 1980s and beyond.* Princeton.

Radcliffe-Brown, A. R. 1965. *Structure and function in primitive society.* New York.

Radcliffe-Brown, A. R. and Daryll Forde (eds). 1950. *African systems of kinship and marriage.* London.

Ransel, David (ed.). 1978. *The family in imperial Russia.* Urbana, Illinois.

Rebel, Hermann. 1983. *Peasant classes: the bureaucratization of property and family relations under early Habsburg absolutism 1511–1636.* Princeton.

Redfield, Robert. 1963. *The little community.* Chicago.

Rosenberg, Charles (ed.). 1975. *The family in history.* Philadelphia.

Rutman, Darrett B. 1980. 'Community study', *Historical Methods*, 13: 29–41.

Sabean, DAvid. 1976a. 'Vervandschaft und Familie in einem württenbergischen Dorf', in W. Conze (ed.) (1976).

Sabean, David. 1976b. 'Aspects of kinship behavior and property in rural western Europe before 1800', in J. Goody et al. (eds) (1976).

Schapera, I. 1962. 'Should anthropologists be historians?' *Journal of the Royal Anthropological Institute*, 92: 143–56.

Schmitt, L. E. 1958. *Deutsche Wortforschung in europäischen Bezügen*, vol. I. Giessen.

Schoof, Wilhelm. 1977. 'Alte schwälmer Familiennamen', *Schwälmer Jahrbücher*, 41–3.

Schulz, Gerhard. 1973. *Geschichte Heute: Positionen, Tendenzen, und Probleme.* Göttingen.

Schusky, Ernest L. 1972. *Manual for kinship analysis.* 2nd edn. New York.

Segalen, Martine. 1972. *Nuptialité et alliance: le choix du conjoint dans une commune de l'Eure.* Paris.

Segalen, Martine. 1979. 'Mating in French preindustrial rural areas', in J. Cuisenier (ed.) (1979).

Segalen, Martine. 1983. *Love and power in the peasant family: Rural France in the nineteenth century.* Trans. Sarah Matthews. Oxford.

Skolnick, M., L. L. Cavalli-Sforza, A. Morini, E. Siri. 1976. 'A preliminary analysis of the genealogy of Parma Valley, Italy', in R. H. Ward and K. M. Weiss (eds) (1976).

Smith, J. F. 1983. 'The computer simulation of kinship sets and kinship counts', paper presented to conference on methods of family demography sponsored by the International Union for the Scientific Study of Population, New York.

Smith, R. M. 1979. 'Kin and neighbors in a thirteenth-century Suffolk community', *Journal of Family History*, 4: 219–56.

Soliday, Gerald L. 1977. 'Marburg in Upper Hesse: a research report', *Journal of Family History*, 2: 164–8.

Soliday, Gerald L. (ed.). 1980. *History of the family and kinship: a select international bibliography*. Millwood, New York.

Stone, Lawrence. 1977. *The family, sex, and marriage in England 1500–1800*. New York.

Swedlund, Alan and George J. Armelagos. 1976. *Demographic anthropology*. Dubuque, Iowa.

Thomas, Keith. 1963. 'History and anthropology', *Past and Present*, 24: 3–24.

Wachter, Kenneth, Eugene Hammel and Peter Laslett. 1978. *Statistical studies of historical social structure*. New York.

Wall, Richard (in collaboration with Jean Robin and Peter Laslett). 1983. *Family forms in historic Europe*. Cambridge.

Ward, R. H. and K. M. Weiss (eds). 1976. *Demographic evolution of human populations*. New York.

Warner, W. Lloyd. 1958. *A black civilization: a study of an Australian tribe*. New York.

Wheaton, Robert B. 1973. 'Bordeaux before the Fronde', 2 vols. Dissertation, Harvard University, Cambridge, Massachusetts.

Wheaton, Robert B. 1980. 'Affinity and descent in seventeenth-century Bordeaux', in R. B. Wheaton and T. Hareven (eds) (1980).

Wheaton, Robert B. and Tamara Hareven (eds). 1980. *Family and sexuality in French history*. Philadelphia.

Whitaker, Ian. 1968. 'Tribal structure and national politics in Albania 1910–1950', in I. M. Lewis (ed.) (1968b).

White, Leslie A. 1957. 'How Morgan came to write "Systems of consanguinity and affinity"', *Papers of the Michigan Academy of Science, Arts, and Letters*, 42: 257–68.

Wolf, Eric R. 1966. 'Kinship, friendship, and patron–client relations in complex societies', in M. Banton (ed.) (1966).

Wrightson, Keith and David Levine. 1979. *Poverty and piety in an English Village: Terling 1525–1700*. New York.

Wrigley, E. A. 1966a. 'Family reconstitution', in E. A. Wrigley (ed.) (1966b).

Wrigley, E. A. (ed.) 1966b. *An introduction to English historical demography*. New York.

Wrigley, E. A. (ed.) 1973. *Identifying people in the past*. London.

Yanagisako, Sylvia J. 1979. 'Family and household: the analysis of domestic groups', *Annual Review of Anthropology*, 8: 161–205.

Zubrow, E. B. W. (ed.), 1976. *Demographic anthropology: quantitative approaches*. Albuquerque, New Mexico.

Index

Abbreviations: *Doc.* = Document
Fig. = Figure
n = note